About the Front Cover Design

The antique Bible in the cover photo is an heirloom belonging to my husband's family. It was in the Craggs family and was passed down to us from his mother, Freda Jean Craggs Roeger (1909 - 2007). The Bible contains records of family marriages, births and deaths back to the early 1800's. Pressed between its yellowed pages is the original 1857 marriage certificate of Francis Craggs and Anna Longstaff — my husband's great grandparents who immigrated to America from Durham County, England. The antique pocket watch was also in the Craggs family and is believed to have belonged to Freda's father, Francis Arthur Craggs (1868-1954).

Books by Deborah Roeger

God Still Speaks (paperback [978-1-63199-795-2]
and e-book [978-1-63199-796-9])

Other Titles in *Lost in Translation* Series

The Power of Obedience: Reading Scripture Through The Lens Of Obedient Discipleship (Released July, 2022)

My Dwelling Place: Reading Scripture Through The Lens of God's Desire To Dwell Among Us (Expected Release Date: 4th quarter, 2023)

PASTOR AND MINISTRY LEADER INTRODUCTIONS

Debbie and Derf Roeger are not new to their calling to teach, however they are newcomers in their assignment to publish studies Debbie has written. Allow them to introduce themselves to you through the words and experiences of some of the Pastors and Ministry Leaders who know them.

Few couples have dedicated themselves to personal discipleship, to listening for Divine direction, and to preparation for Kingdom service as have Derf and Debbie Roeger. Their partnership for many years in the family of Worthington Christian Church was a great encouragement and blessing to the whole congregation. Debbie is a careful thinker, a diligent student of the Bible, and a skillful teacher with well-prepared and delivered lessons. She and her husband share a devotional life and a commitment to prayer, as the primary equipment for their service.

Dr. Marshall Hayden
Retired Sr. Minister, Worthington Christian Church
Worthington, Ohio

I have known Debbie and Derf Roeger for nearly 20 years. Over the years our friendship and ministry relationship grew into several prison ministry assignments, numerous prayer walks, and various worship assignments both in Ohio and Washington, D.C. Debbie is a devoted disciple of Christ, an effective leader, and mentor, filled with a passionate love for Christ and others. She is a bright, innovative, prolific teacher of God's Word and she reaches a multicultural audience. Her classes are informative and challenging creating a hunger for more. Her teachings are solid and sound! They set a foundation on which one cannot only stand but build greater understanding to facilitate greater participation and a greater expression of God's desire on the earth as it is in heaven. Her consistency in her commitment to the

Lord, her husband, her family, and the expansion of God's Kingdom is unchanging. All would benefit from her insightful teachings, which I highly recommend.

Carolyn A. Quinichett, M.A., Prayer Life Ministry/Ministry Leader, Rhema Christian Church, Columbus, Ohio

Debbie is very gifted in organizing and creating a complete Bible-based study on many subjects. She and her husband both have the gift of presenting Bible studies in an interactive way that engages the participants to grow in their knowledge, understanding, and faith. They are both deep prayer warriors!

Pastor Tom Sharron, Chumuckla Community Church, Pace, Florida

I am one blessed ministry leader to have Debbie Roeger on my teaching team at Calvary and in my life personally! Her knowledge of God's Word is deep and is reflected in her writing, and her teaching. She is diligent to record her sources and takes no credit for her ministry. As iron sharpens iron, her sensitivity to Holy Spirit, encourages me, excites me, teaches me, and loves me. Debbie strives to seek God's face every day, and it shows!

Carol DeBlasis, Senior Director of Women's Ministry, Calvary Chapel, Melbourne, Florida

Debbie and Derf Roeger love the Lord and love His Word! They both have been gifted by God to teach His Word. As you study with them, expect fresh insights and a deeper understanding and desire to follow the One who first loved us!

David Roberson, Retired Sr. Pastor, Worthington Christian Church, Worthington, Ohio

Debbie and Derf are not only our dear friends, but they are also amazing leaders and mentors who are filled with a passionate love for the Lord and others. They are devoted disciples of Christ and are intent on leading others to be disciples as well. They teach from the core

of Christianity in a manner that is not only relatable, but is also life changing. They live their lives as beautiful examples of ones who know true intimacy with God. And their international ministry, "Hope of the Nations" is to draw others into that same close relationship with our Lord and Savior. Truly it is men and women like Derf and Debbie who personify the 'Hope of the Nations'!

Diane Daniels, Women's Ministry Leadership, Worthington Christian Church, Worthington, Ohio

As a successful lawyer, now retired, Debbie Roeger has developed and mastered key transferable skills such as organization, research, analysis, critical thinking, and the like, which she utilizes as she studies God's Word from a historical, socio-economic, cultural, and spiritual perspective. She articulates profound biblical principles in a way that is simple for readers and students to comprehend. Throughout the years I have witnessed the humility she and Derf embody, their love for people, and their passion to make disciples for God's Kingdom. As prayer warriors, they have developed a keen ability to "hear" God's voice, producing a lifestyle of obedience and worship unto the Lord. I recommend their teachings and classes without reservation as they offer a roadmap for discipleship and the development of a deeper relationship with the Lord.

Dorcas Hernandez, MS, Hannah Ministries, Inc./Overseer

I know Debbie Roeger to be a woman of integrity. Our church is blessed that she is using her teaching gifts in our Small Group Ministry. I know her to be sensitive to the voice of the Holy Spirit and having a passion for intercessory prayer. Her walk with the Lord is an encouragement to the church body as well as myself. She allows God to move through her in every gifting. It is a blessing to know her.

Pastor Bob Russell, Calvary Chapel, Melbourne, Florida

THE POWER OF HOPE

READING SCRIPTURE THROUGH THE LENS OF HOPE

Lost in Translation
Bible Study Series
#2

Energion Publications
Gonzalez, Florida
2023

Copyright © 2021, edited 2022, Deborah L. Roeger. All rights reserved worldwide. No part of this book may be reproduced or used in any manner without the written permission of the copyright owner except for the use of quotations in a book review.

Unless otherwise noted, Scripture throughout this study is quoted from *New American Standard Bible* (NASB 1995), copyright © 1960, 1962, 1963, 1968, 1971, 1972, 1973, 1975, 1977, 1995 by The Lockman Foundation. Used by permission. All rights reserved. www.lockman.org.

Scripture quotations marked HCSB are from the *Holman Christian Standard Bible*®. Used by Permission. HCSB copyright ©1999, 2000, 2002, 2003, 2009 Holman Bible Publishers. Holman Christian Standard Bible®, Holman CSB®, and HCSB® are federally registered trademarks of Holman Bible Publishers.

Scripture quotations marked NJPS *Tanakh* are from *The Jewish Study Bible*, Jewish Publication Society TANAKH Translation, copyright ©1985, 1999 by the Jewish Publication Society. Published by Oxford University Press, Inc. copyright© 2004. www.oup.com.

Scripture quotations marked NIV are from *The Holy Bible*, New International Version® NIV®, copyright © 1973 1978 1984 2011 by Biblica, Inc.™ Used by permission. All rights reserved worldwide.

Scripture quotations marked MSG or "The Message" are from *THE MESSAGE*, copyright © 1993, 2002, 2018 by Eugene H. Peterson. Used by permission of NavPress, represented by Tyndale House Publishers. All rights reserved.

Scripture quotations marked AMP are from the *Amplified® Bible* (AMP), copyright © 2015 by The Lockman Foundation. Used by permission. www.lockman.org.

Scripture quotations marked NLT are from the *Holy Bible*, New Living Translation, copyright ©1996, 2004, 2015 by Tyndale House Foundation. Used by permission of Tyndale House Publishers, Carol Stream, Illinois 60188. All rights reserved.

Scripture quotations marked CJB are from the *Complete Jewish Bible*, Copyright © 1998 and 2016 by David H. Stern. Used by permission. All rights reserved worldwide.

Scripture quotations marked ESV are from ESV® Bible (*The Holy Bible*, English Standard Version®), copyright © 2001 by Crossway, a publishing ministry of Good News Publishers. Used by permission. All rights reserved.

Scripture quotations marked PHILLIPS are from *The New Testament in Modern English* by J.B Phillips copyright © 1960, 1972 J. B. Phillips. Administered by The Archbishops' Council of the Church of England. Used by permission.

Scripture quotations marked NKJV are from *New King James Version*®, copyright © 1982 by Thomas Nelson. Used by permission. All rights reserved.

ISBN: 978-1-63199-820-1
eISBN:978-1-63199-821-8
Library of Congress Control Number: 2023933477
Lost in Translation – P.O. Box 841 – Gonzalez, FL 32560 – pubs@energion.com
An Imprint of Energion Publications

The *Lost in Translation* series of Bible Studies is dedicated to Henri Louis Goulet and Messianic Studies Institute located in Gahanna, Ohio. You taught us that an inherently Jewish perspective of the Messianic worldview and way of life is the principle that all learning is for living. Through your teaching and encouragement my husband and I became lifelong learners!

DISCLAIMER: In this Bible Study I will cite a wide variety of references. While I am comfortable citing the identified source for the specific point referenced, that does not mean that I have read, understand, or necessarily agree or disagree with that source on other points of theology or doctrine. Therefore, referencing various authors or Study Bibles is not intended to be a blanket endorsement of either.

NOTE: The presentation of Hebrew and Greek words I have used is designed to make those words easier to read and pronounce. As a result, some letters are not precisely represented.

TABLE OF CONTENTS

Acknowledgements vii
Introduction To *Lost In Translation* Series ix
Preface xiii

1	Abraham Believed	1
2	Abraham's "Beyond Hope" Hope	19
3	The Promise and the Promise Keeper	35
4	The Promise Keeper's Appointed Time	59
5	Patient, Confident, Expectant Waiting	75
6	The Strength Gained Through Hope Filled Waiting	97
7	The Hope of Every Christ-Follower	117
8	What's Love Got To Do With It?	139
9	Adversity Strengthens Hope	159
10	Overflowing With Hope	179
11	Lose Your Identity ~ Lose Your Hope!	199
12	The Powerful Hope of God's New Creation	221

How to do basic WORD STUDIES
when you don't read Hebrew or Greek 245
Index to the Word Studies 259
Meet the Author: Deborah L. Roeger 261

Acknowledgements

My thanks must first be expressed to my sisters in Christ at Calvary Chapel Melbourne who participated in *The Power of Hope* Bible study, 2021 Fall Semester. The text for that 12-week study was a pre-publication copy of this manuscript. The insightful in-class comments and deeply thoughtful questions led to extremely beneficial changes in the study. I am uniquely grateful to Donna LaPrade who prepared for class by meticulously reading that week's lesson and supplying me with keenly detailed changes many other readers would have missed.   God's plans are always perfect. I'm confident one reason He led me to teach the study was to improve it. Thank you, ladies! I loved studying with you.

Once again, this study has benefitted from the careful proofread of Joan Winchell. I had expected Joan to "take the summer off" for a well-deserved break from her multitude of responsibilities and caregiving. Instead she encouraged me to provide her with the manuscript for this study which she powered through with ease and grace. The end result is definitely an improvement over the original manuscript.

I am also tremendously grateful to my son, Jeremy Roeger, for taking time to read through the final manuscript. His keen eye for details caught a lot of little things I would have missed! Thank you so much Jeremy.

Diane Daniels continues to deserve my most heartfelt thanks for her seemingly inexhaustible supply of encouragement. She has stayed the course month after month, year after year as I have written draft upon draft of this study and many others. She never fails to inspire with her words, her love and her prayers! What a gift God has given me through your friendship.

I am also grateful for the faithful prayers of so many of our prayer partners through all of the writing stages and the teaching of this study. I remain standing because you are on your knees praying!

My continued respect and gratitude also belong to Henry Neufeld and Energion Publications. Because this study deals with the vitally important biblical concept of faith, Henry's knowledge of original Hebrew and Greek was my safety net that what I wrote accurately presented the true biblical understanding of faith. I would not have the confidence to publish these studies without that safety net! Thank you, Henry for graciously sharing your gifts for the benefit of our readers.

This is the second study Energion Publications has released in the *Lost in Translation* series. Publishing that first study became a marathon as we experienced nothing short of an all-out spiritual battle. Henry and Jody stayed the course with patience and grace. Your persistence in addressing every detail in that study set the course for this second study. For that I am humbled and thankful.

And lastly to my husband, Derf, my best friend and the love of my life. You know how much I mean it when I say, "Thank you!"

To God be the glory, great things He has done!

Introduction To
Lost In Translation Series

God instilled in me a love for digging deep into His Word. He added to that a passion for "getting it right" and the ability to assimilate a wealth of diverse material into an understandable lesson. Those gifts have enabled me to write well-researched meaningful studies. Each one incorporates numerous "Word Studies" along the way to ensure that original word meanings which have been largely lost in translation are brought to life again. The end result is a series of Bible Studies that have a scholarly emphasis on rightly dividing God's Word while highlighting personal application for spiritual growth and transformation. When asked, I succinctly describe *Lost in Translation* as connecting biblical scholars with the rest of us who sit in the church pews. However, I have come to understand that these studies also move toward providing a bridge between conservative evangelicals and pentecostal/charismatics. An explanation of that last statement will be helpful.

Through my research mentor I am able to reach into the best and most current scholarship of the subject matter of the study. With diligent research I become equipped to culturally and historically contextualize Bible passages. Doing so provides relevant background to aid the reader in their understanding of original language word meanings and concepts. My goal is never about increasing intellectual knowledge. My orientation is always a right understanding of God's Word with a focus on personal application and discipleship.

At times God adds to my research with revelation and understanding that does not come directly from the pages of the

Commentaries, Bible Dictionaries or other sound scholarly materials I customarily reference. At those times, He simply speaks His heart to me on the matter. Often what He says answers a question I had been pondering but had been unable to draw to a satisfactory conclusion.[1] It wasn't until I started fine-tuning the manuscripts to begin the publication process that I caught a glimpse of what God had been doing through this combination of research and revelation. Here I'll need to insert a bit of background information.

In 2014 R. T. Kendall released, *Holy Fire: A Balanced, Biblical Look At The Holy Spirit's Work In Our Lives.* In it, Kendall wrote about an unplanned "divorce" that had silently taken place in the church between God's Spirit and God's Word.[2] Using broad brushed descriptive strokes he defined two separate and distinct categories of churches.

- Denominations majoring on the written Word of God. Their focus is on the inerrancy of the written Word, expository preaching and sound doctrine. They may be virtually silent about the Holy Spirit. Generally, these congregations are labeled: *conservative evangelical* – strong in Word, much less emphasis on Holy Spirit.
- Other congregations seeking to experience the power that was present in the book of Acts. Their desire to see the gifts of the Spirit operating in the church today leads to an active pursuit of signs, wonders and miracles. General-

---

1   In our international teaching/discipling ministry I have been asked to deliver sermons during a Sunday morning worship service. I imagine my preparation for those messages most likely happens in a way that is similar to those who are called to be Preacher/Pastors. The end result from sound prayerful preparation is a combination of searching out the Word through other resources and the divine guidance of Holy Spirit to bring greater understanding. It's a good example of the way in which God has led me to write Bible Studies.
2   I had already come to recognize an invisible but distinct separating line between groups of Christ-followers. Thankfully Kendall's book equipped me with a way to articulate what I had observed.

ly, these congregations are labeled: *charismatic/pentecostal* – major emphasis on power manifestations of the Spirit, often much less emphasis on God's written Word.

There is nothing in what Kendall says that intends to indict either evangelicals or charismatics for their respective passionate pursuits. Kendall's point is that Scripture presents a clear and compelling picture of the early church as being *simultaneously strong in both Word and Power*. He credits some congregations with having found that proper balance between Word and Spirit which existed in the early church. Kendall stresses the need for that to be the goal of *every* church.

In his first epistle to the Corinthians, Paul identifies two groups of people but the distinction he makes is *not within* the body of Christ it is between those who are *in Christ* and those who are *outside of Christ*. To all of those *in Christ* Paul urged unity in the midst of their diversity.[3] The encouraging conclusion of Kendall's book is that he envisions a day when God will sovereignly *remarry* His Word and His Spirit. As that happens, proper first-century balance will be restored to the body of Christ.

It occurs to me that the *Lost in Translation* Bible Study series works towards that coming remarriage. To that end, the reader may find the series somewhat unique in its orientation – a well-researched Bible Study inseparably joined with Holy Spirit inspired counsel and revelation.

To God be the glory for what He has done, is doing and will yet do!

---

3 "For even as the body is one and *yet* has many members, and all the members of the body, though they are many, are one body, so also is Christ. For by one Spirit we were all baptized into one body ... God has placed the members ... just as He desired.... now there are many members, but one body. And the eye cannot say to the hand, 'I have no need of you'; or again the head to the feet, 'I have no need of you.'... But God has *so* composed the body, giving more abundant honor to that *member* which lacked, so that there may be no division in the body, but *that* the members may have the same care for one another." 1 Corinthians 12:12-25, italics in original

[B]ut just as it is written, "Things which eye has not seen and ear has not heard, And which have not entered the heart of man, All that God has prepared for those who love Him." For to us God revealed them through the Spirit; for the Spirit searches all things, even the depths of God. 1 Corinthians 2:9-10

In His Service by His Grace,

Deborah L. Roeger

Preface

A Word from the Author: My goal for this study is to enable participants to have a life-transforming encounter with God. Our Western culture values *knowledge* for the sake of knowledge, but the culture of the Bible valued knowledge for the sake of guiding righteous behavior. J. I. Packer who is considered to be among the most influential evangelicals in North America has asserted that attempts to interpret God's Word without personal application do not deserve the title "Interpretation."[4] In the world of the ancient Hebrew, the goal of *every* student of *every* rabbi was to go well beyond learning what the rabbi knew and to be like the rabbi – to walk the way the rabbi walked through life. The purpose of education was not to gain head knowledge and become more intelligent but to inform perspective which would transform behavior. May the cry of your heart with every page of this study be, "O God, change me from the inside out, let me be more like you!" As your cry ascends and joins with my prayers for you, I am trusting God will hear and answer in unimaginable ways! Let the change begin!

Use of Yahweh: In the study I may use "Yahweh"– the most frequent Name for God in the Hebrew Bible. It is composed of four Hebrew letters: Yud (Y), Hey (H), Vav (V) and Hey (H) which combine as *Yahweh* or *YHVH*.

---

[4] "…. Exegesis without application should not be called interpretation at all." J.I. Packer quoted by Dr. Grant C. Richison, Website Homepage *Verse-By-Verse Commentary by Dr. Grant C. Richison.* Retrieved from https://versebyversecommentary.com/ (last accessed September 15, 2021)

Yahweh is the personal covenant Name by which the ancient Hebrews knew God. The first biblical reference is found in the exodus story.

> Moshe said to God, "Look, when I appear before the people of Isra'el and say to them, 'The God of your ancestors has sent me to you'; and they ask me, 'What is his name?' what am I to tell them?" God said to Moshe, "*Ehyeh Asher Ehyeh* [I am/will be what I am/will be]," and added, "Here is what to say to the people of Isra'el: '*Ehyeh* [I Am *or* I Will Be] has sent me to you.'" God said further to Moshe, "Say this to the people of Isra'el: '*Yud-Heh-Vav-Heh* [Adonai], the God of your fathers, the God of Avraham, the God of Yitz'chak and the God of Ya'akov, has sent me to you.' This is my name forever; this is how I am to be remembered generation after generation. Exodus 3:13-15 CJB, italics in original

With this answer, God announced His eternal Name to Moses. As noted in the *Complete Jewish Bible* translation quoted above, the Hebrew verb *'ehyeh* can be translated as "I Am" *or* "I Will Be." Notice in this more Jewish rendering of Exodus 3:13-15 how the four Hebrew letters mentioned above are used in this translation, "Say this to the people of Isra'el: '*Yud-Heh-Vav-Heh* [Adonai], the God of your fathers, the God of Avraham [Abraham], the God of Yitz'chak [Isaac] and the God of Ya'akov [Jacob], has sent me to you.'"

In context, the primary focus of God's answer to Moses is His promise *to be with* Moses and with the people Moses is sent to lead out of Egypt.[5] In the setting of the Old Testament, a name served a much greater function than simply an identification marker. A name communicated that which was essentially true of the one it

---

5   *ESV Study Bible* (Crossway Books 2008) study note Exodus 3:14, p. 149

identified.⁶ Yahweh equates His Name with His character as being "absolute and unchanging. This immutability provides inflexible reliability that the [promises He makes] will be realized."⁷ To the Hebrew mind, Yahweh above all else meant the God who faithfully keeps covenant with His people.⁸

Yahweh (often translated as Jehovah or L<small>ORD</small> in most modern Bible translations) is the most intensely sacred Name to the Jewish people and many will not even pronounce it. In its place, they may say the four-letters Yud-Hey-Vav-Hey (YHVH) or will often simply use *Hashem* (literally "the Name"). Because of this sacredness, "God" is often written "G-d" in Jewish writings to avoid writing/saying the Name.⁹

Use of "the" Holy Spirit and Use of Holy Spirit: Throughout this study I will interchangeably refer to "the Holy Spirit" (His title) and "Holy Spirit" (His name). Because some might find that objectionable an explanation will be helpful. It is noteworthy

---

6   Motyer, J. Alec, *The Prophecy of Isaiah: An Introduction & Commentary* (InterVarsity Press 1993) Isaiah 65:15-16d, p. 528

7   Sarna, Nahum M., *Exploring Exodus: The Origins Of Biblical Israel* (Schocken Books 1986, 1996) p. 52

8   "The verb form used here is אֶהְיֶה (*'ehyeh*) the Qal imperfect, first person common singular, of the verb הָיָה (*haya* 'to be')…. [W]hen God used the verb to express his name, he used this form saying, 'I AM.' When his people refer to him as Yahweh, which is the third person masculine singular form of the same verb, they say 'he is.'… The idea of the verb would certainly indicate that God is not bound by time, and while he is present ('I AM') he will always be present, even in the future …." *NET Bible Notes*, translator's note 47, Exodus 3:14. The source for this information is "Net Notes" however it will be descriptively cited as "Net Bible Notes" throughout the study."

9   The Jewish people understand Deuteronomy 12:4 as a prohibition against "erasing, destroying or desecrating the name of G-d." Jewish Community Center, *Writing G-d*. Retrieved from https://www.jccmb.com/templates/articlecco_cdo/aid/1333937/jewish/Writing-G-d.htm (last accessed August 9, 2021). As a result, many special precautions are taken both when writing the Name and when eliminating any documented format on which the Name has been written.

that in the original Greek of John 20:22, for example, the phrase *"pneuma hagion"* (translated Holy Spirit) could properly be a name or a title, depending on how one reads the Greek. Similarly, we find in Scripture references to "Jesus" as His name, while "Christ" (Messiah) is His title. We alternate between name and title often in the English language. For example, we say, "When Lincoln was the president" or "President Lincoln." If we are thinking of Holy Spirit as a name, it is already definite without the use of "the" because a name does not need to be preceded by a definite article. I suggest discomfort with a reference to "Holy Spirit" may be due to lack of familiarity with using His name. However, using His name rather than His title emphasizes the personal nature of the Holy Spirit. And that's my point.

Use of Hebrew word *Talmid* (singular) or *Talmidim* (plural): By the time of Jesus, discipleship was well-established within the Jewish culture. All the great sages, rabbis and teachers of Torah had *talmidim* (disciples). A *talmid* (a disciple) was on a pilgrimage that was far more than an intellectual pursuit. The *talmid's* goal was to be *like* the rabbi – he wanted to assimilate the essence of who the rabbi was into his own life. This was radical discipleship – it was a complete re-making of the one who was being discipled so as to become like his rabbi in knowledge, wisdom and ethical behavior.

In other words, a *talmid's* deepest desire was to follow his rabbi so closely that he would start to think and act just like his rabbi. Jesus summed up the goal of discipleship this way: *"[A]fter [each disciple] has been fully trained, [he] will be like his teacher."*[10] A *talmid's* behavior would be a reflection on their teacher's reputation – either positively or negatively.[11] That means perseverance was

---

10 Luke 6:40
11 Keener, Craig S., *The Gospel Of John: A Commentary*, Volume Two (Hendrickson Publishers 2003) John 13:34-35, citing e.g., Aeschines Timarchus 171-173 among others, pp. 926-927

a standard requirement for every *talmid*.[12] Once a *talmid* was fully trained, he would become a teacher and he would disciple *talmidim* of his own. What Jesus had begun by making *talmidim* of His first followers, the body of Christ now does as they make new *talmidim* of Jesus. We see the apostle Paul following this established rabbinic pattern when he says, *"Imitate me, as I also imitate Christ. Now I praise you because you always remember me and keep the traditions just as I delivered them to you."*[13]

When we understand disciple-making in its first-century context, most of us would have to admit that Jesus' (and likewise Paul's) idea of making disciples is vastly different than many self-designated "Christians" or what we often call a "follower," a "believer" or even a "disciple" today.

Throughout the study when I use the phrase "Christ-follower" or the word "Believer" I intend those word choices to be synonymous with the definition and culturally relevant understanding of a *talmid*.

About Word Studies: Hebrew scholar Tremper Longman refers to Bible translations as "commentaries with no notes."[14] I think he is spot on! Because no language easily and accurately translates word-for-word one to another, every translator makes judgment calls as to which word best fits the context as he sees it. Longman calls these "interpretive decisions" and that's why he suggests that any translation amounts to that translator's commentary on the text.[15] Even so, by the very nature of translation, the person trans-

---

12 Keener, Craig S., *The Gospel Of John: A Commentary*, Volume Two (Hendrickson Publishers 2003) John 13:34-35, p. 926
13 1 Corinthians 11:1-2
14 Longman, Tremper III, *How To Read Proverbs* (InterVarsity Press 2002) p. 18
15 Longman, Tremper III, *How To Read Proverbs* (InterVarsity Press 2002) p. 18

lating typically leaves no notes behind for future readers to follow his line of reasoning.[16]

"Our sacred literature does not use obscure language, but describes most things in words clearly indicating their meaning. Therefore, it is necessary at all times to delve into the literal meaning of words to achieve complete understanding of what is actually meant."[17] To that end, from time to time in our lessons it will be advantageous to stop and do a "Word Study" which will allow us to consider the contextual meaning of that word from its original Hebrew or Greek language.

A diligent assessment of original word meanings relies on several factors. Both the authors and the original audience of the Scriptures lived in a different world than today's modern world. Politics, culture(s), ethics, worldview, theology as well as the realities of daily life were all radically different from what we know and experience. Those factors shaped the thoughts and expectations of the biblical writers which in turn shaped their words. An important task in biblical understanding is to discern, as much as possible, what any given word meant to the *original* audience. Therefore, the more we are able to appreciate the ancient mindset of the Bible the better equipped we are to understand what God was trying to communicate in a given text.

When we work to understand the Greek language of the New Testament, it is critical to realize just how much Hebrew thought impacted the New Testament authors. Most recent scholarship suggests *all* of those authors were Hebrew men who grew up in Jewish homes and were educated in the Old Testament writings.[18] As a result, the Hebrew thought-world of the Old Testament is

---

16 In my research experience, the *New English Translation* (NET) seems to be the exception to this rule in that according to netbible.com it contains 60,932 translator notes.
17 Rabbi Samson Raphael Hirsch (1808-1888). Retrieved from https://www.thiss.org/ (last accessed August 8, 2021)
18 According to Henri Goulet, my research mentor, recent research suggests that absent evidence otherwise even Luke must be held to be Jewish.

the beginning source for proper understanding of New Testament Greek words. Although those men wrote in Greek, the thinking behind their writings was informed by their Hebrew heritage making the Old Testament the best starter dictionary we have for the New Testament.

To understand Greek words in the New Testament we may also need to consider ordinary everyday word usage in the first-century Greco-Roman world. Paul authored approximately 50% of the books in the New Testament. As an apostle to Greek-speaking Gentiles, he desired to shape those who had begun to follow Christ into new social communities. He understood that God's way is a whole new way to live, not a simple re-ordering of the *world's* way. Therefore, Paul was intent on providing direction to new Christ-followers about how they should re-orient their lives to walk out life according to their new identity *in* Christ.[19] To quote scholar Teresa Morgan, "New communities forming themselves within an existing culture do *not* typically take language in common use in the world around them and immediately assign to it radical new meanings.… This is all the more likely to be the case where the new community is a missionary one [as it was in Paul's case]. One does not communicate effectively with potential converts by using language in a way which they will not understand."[20] Paul "writes with what he assumes will be shared cultural assumptions regarding language and concepts that he uses without detailed explanation."[21] In other words, Paul, along with the other New Testament authors, would have chosen Greek words which already had common meaning to their audience. That cultural consideration may also supply important interpretive guidance which will aid in our proper un-

---

Henri Louis Goulet, Email to Deborah Roeger March 27, 2022, citing the work of Isaac Oliver on Luke

19 Tucker, J. Brian, *Reading 1 Corinthians* (Cascade Books 2017) p. 4
20 Morgan, Teresa, *Roman Faith and Christian Faith: Pistis and Fides in the Early Roman Empire and Early Churches* (Oxford 2015) p. 4
21 Keener, Craig S., *Romans*, New Covenant Commentary (Cascade Books 2009) Introduction, p. 2

derstanding of New Testament word meanings. When we fail to put biblical words in their proper historical, cultural context they end up getting lost in translation.

No matter what language we are discussing, it is common for words to have more than one meaning. The semantic range of a word is observed by its usage in various contexts. The more times a word is used in different ways, the broader its semantic range. As a result, scholars often advise that words do not mean anything outside of a context. My friend and research mentor Henri Goulet, shares this example he uses at the Messianic Studies Institute in Gahanna, Ohio. Take the English word "trunk: It could mean a host of things from an elephant's [nose], a suitcase, an ornamental chest, the rear compartment of a car, the main stem of a tree, the main part of a human body to which the head and appendages are connected, the principal channel of a tributary, or a circuit between two telephone exchanges."[22]

In the lessons in this study, Word Studies are not intended to explore the entire semantic range of a given word. Every author determines the meaning of a word by how he uses it within a context. The focus of each word studied will be narrowed by the specific context in which the author originally used that word in the particular passage we are studying. To that end, I will always seek to place Word Studies in original literary context as well as to add relevant cultural context where possible.

Refer to the supplement at the end of this study for helpful guidance on how to complete your own research of Hebrew and Greek words using free internet resources.

The Bible's Use of Ancient Near East Background: Because our lessons, where applicable, will seek to point out the histori-

---

22   Henri Louis Goulet, Academic Dean, Executive Director, & Faculty Messianic Studies Institute; Ph.D. Studies (Unfinished), University of Cape Town, Biblical Studies, 2007–2010; S.T.M., Capital University, Biblical Studies, 2007; M.A., Ashland University, Biblical Studies, 2003; B.S., The Ohio State University, Pharmaceutical Sciences, 1984

cal context for Scripture, I will include references to ancient Near Eastern[23] beliefs as appropriate. As Jewish scholar Nahum Sarna points out: "modern scholarship has shown that the Torah made use of very ancient traditions which it adapted to its own special purposes."[24] For example, there are poems in Proverbs that clearly depict creation in imagery and expressions drawn from ancient pagan myths.[25] When a biblical author used ideas and concepts from the ancient culture around him the purpose was to borrow from the imagery to make his communication clear. That does not mean that the author endorsed the original pagan theology.[26] As Sarna noted, "the [pagan] materials used have been transformed so as to become the vehicle for the transmission of completely new ideas" which are entirely consistent with the nature and character of Yahweh.[27] In fact, some scholars believe that the very purpose of "borrowing" from ancient Near Eastern concepts was to demonstrate the absolute superiority of Yahweh over every false god.[28] According to Jewish scholar Joshua Berman, "For weak and oppressed peoples, one form of cultural and spiritual resistance is to

---

23 The ancient Near East is the region which includes modern Turkey, Syria, Lebanon, Israel, Palestine, Jordan, Egypt, Iraq and Iran. Important ancient civilizations in this region were the Egyptians, Arameans, Babylonians, Assyrians and Persians. Power, Cain, *Kingship in the Hebrew Bible*. Retrieved from https://www.sbl-site.org/assets/pdfs/TBv3i3_PowerKingship.pdf (last accessed August 8, 2021)

24 Sarna, Nahum M., *Understanding Genesis Through Rabbinic Tradition and Modern Scholarship* (The Jewish Theological Seminary 2015) p. 39

25 See for example: Proverbs 3:20; 8:29; 30:4; Waltke, Bruce K., *The Book of Proverbs: Chapters 1-15*, The New International Commentary on the Old Testament (Eerdmans 2004) Theology, p. 68

26 Waltke, Bruce K., *The Book of Proverbs Chapters 1-15,* The New International Commentary on the Old Testament (Eerdmans 2004) Theology, p. 68

27 Sarna, Nahum M., *Understanding Genesis Through Rabbinic Tradition and Modern Scholarship* (The Jewish Theological Seminary 2015) p. 4

28 See for example: Longman III and Garland, general editors, *The Expositor's Bible Commentary: Psalms*, Vol. 5, Revised Edition (Zondervan 2008) *Reflections: Yahweh Is The Divine Warrior*, p. 734

appropriate the symbols of the oppressor and put them to competitive ideological purposes."[29]

It is worth noting that not all scholars embrace the use of ancient literature outside the Bible itself to assist in biblical interpretation. Some argue that it is a dangerous practice. I am inclined to agree with Professor Jon D. Levenson, Harvard Divinity School, who rightly warns on the one hand that historical criticism should never replace "the more traditional modes of study within religious communities." On the other hand, he advises that neither should modern research of the Bible's historical context be "disregarded or neutralized." Instead, he advocates: "[T]he worthiest course ... is one that combines the modern and the traditional modes of study in an intellectually honest and theologically sophisticated way."[30]

---

29 Berman, Joshua, *Ani Maamin: Biblical Criticism, Historical Truth, and the Thirteen Principles of Faith* (Maggid Book 2020) p. 55. Berman points out during much of its early history "ancient Israel was in Egypt's shadow." Ibid., p. 55

30 Levenson, Jon D., *The Shema and the Commandment to Love God In Its Ancient Contexts*, TheTorah.com, August 14, 2016, last updated June 20, 2021. Retrieved from https://www.thetorah.com/article/the-shema-and-the-commandment-to-love-god-in-its-ancient-contexts (last accessed June 29, 2021)

LESSON 1:

ABRAHAM BELIEVED

 "[Abraham] believed the LORD; and [Yahweh] credited it to him as righteousness." Genesis 15:6 HCSB

THIS IS A STUDY on hope and the supernatural power released to a follower of Christ every time hope is chosen in the face of what appears to be hopeless circumstances. In 7 we will consider the hope that should fill the heart of every Christ-follower. However, it will be helpful to have a foundational understanding of biblical hope before we get there.

Right at the start, we are going to see that the line between *faith* and *hope* can become so blurred that in the natural it becomes difficult to distinguish one from the other.[1] To that end, we will use our first two lessons to become well acquainted with biblical words related to faith and hope. We will follow that up with a close look at the three inter-related elements of biblical hope. Then we will be ready to delve into the hope we have as disciples of Christ.

To avoid confusion, I want to make clear that throughout the study we are going to encounter the word "faith" to denote *active believing or trusting that results in personal action* as well as "faith" in its *noun* form. In this lesson we will be using the word "faith" to refer to the act of believing. That usage is consistent with a common way the word "faith" (a verb) is used in the English language. In Lesson 3 we will learn that when the Bible uses "faith"

---

[1] Schreiner, Thomas R., *Romans*, 2nd edition, Baker Exegetical Commentary on the NT (Baker Academic 1998, 2018) Romans 4:18, p. 245

as a noun it refers to the content of faith – the promise God has revealed. In that case, faith can be defined *as revelation that finds its home in a heart.*[2] These differences in usage will become clearer as the study proceeds.

So, let's get started! Our Key Scripture for this lesson is from the book of Genesis and refers to the most prominent case of hope recorded in the Bible – the hope of Abraham for a son. The word "Genesis" actually translates the Greek word *Geneseos* meaning "Of Birth."[3] In other words, Genesis refers to "the origin or coming into being of something."[4] That explains why Genesis is sometimes called the "Book of Beginnings." True to its purpose, Genesis introduces us to the very first biblical examples of both faith and hope. Some background to Abraham's story will be helpful.

Until Genesis chapter 17 Abraham is referred to as "Abram." God renamed him "Abraham" to reflect his status as the father of a multitude.[5] He descended from Shem, one of Noah's sons. Shem, as you may recall, received a blessing from his father Noah for his righteous action (Genesis 9:23-27). That blessing may well have included God-honoring descendants who would know and obey the voice of Yahweh[6] just as their ancestor Noah did! If the question is, how did Abraham know the "god" who first spoke to him was Yahweh, the fact that he descended from Shem might provide the answer.

---

2 Personal Journal February 7, 2019 recording the working definition God gave me in response to my prayerful requests to understand "faith"
3 *Holman Christian Standard Bible*, Study Bible edition (Holman Bible Publishers 2010) Genesis Introduction, p. 1
4 *Merriam-Webster.com Dictionary*, entry for *Genesis*. Retrieved from https://www.merriam-webster.com/dictionary/genesis (last accessed July 2, 2022)
5 Yahweh said to Abraham, "No longer shall your name be called Abram, But your name shall be Abraham; For I have made you the father of a multitude of nations…. (Genesis 17:5)." Abraham means "father of a multitude" or "father of many nations."
6 See Preface for use of Yahweh in this study

The first time we know of Abraham hearing Yahweh's voice is when he lived in Mesopotamia.[7] There Yahweh gave him a commandment to leave that country and go to the place he would be shown.[8] The original Hebrew text makes clear that the author intends to communicate the idea of Abraham being separated, detaching himself from what he had known for the first 75 years of his life.[9] For Abraham to leave the country of his birth would have been less than admirable, perhaps even disgraceful in the culture of his day.[10] Moreover, since a person's identity was closely connected to his place of origin, to ask Abraham to leave that place meant Yahweh was asking him to change his identity.[11] Even so, the immediacy

---

7   The Bible is silent on Abraham's life up until the time he was 75 years old. Jewish tradition identifies Cutha, in Mesopotamia, as his birthplace. Mindel, Nissan, *Abraham's Early Life* (Kehot Publication Society 2004) Chabad.org, Jewish History. Retrieved from https://www.chabad.org/library/article_cdo/aid/112063/jewish/Abrahams-Early-Life.htm (last accessed July 13, 2021). Ur began to be excavated in 1854 when it was first discovered. We might be inclined to think Abraham didn't have to leave much behind; however, from excavations it has been determined that Ur was a great metropolis with a highly developed culture. The excavations reveal wealth, the work of skilled craftsmen and advanced technology. Deffinbaugh, Bob, *12. The Call of Abram (Genesis 11:31-12:9)*, from the Series: Genesis: From Paradise to Patriarchs, Bible.org. Retrieved from https://bible.org/seriespage/12-call-abram-genesis-1131-129 (last accessed February 22, 2022)

8   Acts 7:2

9   When used following the verb, the preposition *l* gives the verb *h-l-k*, "to walk, go" the sense of "separating, taking leave of." Sarna, Nahum M., *The JPS Torah Commentary: Genesis,* The Traditional Hebrew Text with the New JPS Translation Commentary (The Jewish Publication Society 1989) Genesis 12:1, p. 88

10 "In the ancient world [of Abraham] loyalty to one's place of birth and citizenship was a cardinal virtue." Cockerill, Gareth Lee, *The Epistle to the Hebrews*, New International Commentary on the New Testament (Eerdmans 2012) Hebrews 11:14-16a, p. 552, references in footnote 55 omitted

11 Strauss, Mark, "Luke," in *Zondervan Illustrated Bible Backgrounds Commentary*, Vol. 1, edited by Clinton E. Arnold (Zondervan 2002) Luke 13:25 under *Where you come from*, pp. 437-438

of Abraham's response is highlighted by the author of Hebrews who tells us that he did not hesitate nor did he procrastinate. As soon as Abraham was called, he obeyed Yahweh by leaving Mesopotamia even though he did not know where he was going.[12]

In response to his remarkable obedience, Yahweh gave Abraham an incredible seven-fold promise: 1) Yahweh would make him a great nation; 2) he would be blessed with material prosperity; 3) Yahweh would make his name great, he would be highly esteemed; 4) Abraham would be a blessing to others; 5) Yahweh would bless all those who blessed Abraham; 6) whoever disparaged, abused, or caused harm to Abraham would be cursed by Yahweh and 7) all the people of the earth would be blessed through (because of) Abraham.[13]

Years passed during which time Abraham experienced famine, family strife and war. Then Scripture introduces us to the first recorded time Abraham spoke to Yahweh.

> After these things the word of the LORD came to [Abraham] in a vision, saying, "Do not fear, [Abraham], I am a shield to you; Your reward shall be very great." [Abraham] said, "O Lord God, what will You give me, since I am childless, and the heir of my house is Eliezer of Damascus?" And [Abraham] said, "Since You have given no offspring to me, one born in my house is my heir." Genesis 15:1-3

By the time of this vision, Abraham had become extremely wealthy. He was very rich in livestock, silver and gold (Genesis 13:2). We are told that his concern was the fact that he did not have

---

12 Hebrews 11:8. Commentator Gareth Lee Cockerill notes that in the original Greek text of Hebrews 11:8 the initial phrase "by faith" is immediately followed by the present participle "being called" and the aorist verb "he obeyed." As a result, the original text can be properly translated: "as soon as Abraham was called he obeyed." Cockerill, Gareth Lee, *The Epistle to the Hebrews*, New International Commentary on the New Testament (Eerdmans 2012) Hebrews 11:8, p. 538

13 Genesis 12:2-3

an heir. Ancient documents reveal the practice of a man without biological children of his own adopting one of his male servants to be the heir of his estate.[14] In modern western society, adoption is typically done for purposes of making sure a child is provided for. However, in ancient society, an adult could be "adopted" to provide for a childless couple. Such an adoption kept property and possessions together, but it also ensured there would be someone to care for the adoptive parents in their old age and provide them with a proper burial.[15] God graciously assured Abraham that adopting his servant Eliezer would not be necessary.

> Then behold, the word of the LORD came to him, saying, "This man will not be your heir; but one who will come forth from your own body shall be your heir." And He took him outside and said, "Now look toward the heavens and count the stars, if you are able to count them." And He said to him, "So shall your descendants be." Genesis 15:4-5

God's astonishing promise to Abraham, who is now about 85 years old, was that *God* would provide a son born to Abraham as his heir. At this point in their marriage Sarai, Abraham's wife, was 75 years old and barren. It is clear that on their own they were not going to be able to bring this promise to fulfillment. Only God could do it!

---

14 Stern, David H., *The Complete Jewish Study Bible* (Hendrickson Publishers Marketing 2016) study note Genesis 15:3-6 under *"This man will not be your heir."* p. 19

15 Walton, John H., "Genesis," in *Zondervan Illustrated Bible Backgrounds Commentary*, Vol. 1, edited by John H. Walton (Zondervan 2009) Genesis 15:2 under *Inherit my estate*, p. 84; Harrison and Hagner, "Romans," in *The Expositor's Bible Commentary: Romans ~ Galatians*, Vol. 11, Revised Edition, edited by Longman III and Garland (Zondervan Academic 2008) Romans 4:3, p. 78

Although Abraham had demonstrated obedience based on God's assurance of land inheritance before this (see Genesis 12),[16] the belief God is prompting at this moment transcends anything Abraham can *do*. He cannot turn God's promise of offspring as numerous as the stars into reality. Yet God summons Abraham's trust, his belief, his faith to go beyond what is humanly possible. Amid his doubt, Abraham had to decide to replace his own "I can't" with God's "I can!" That's faith!

Our Key Scripture for this lesson records Abraham's response to God's promise which is nothing short of amazing!

> [Abraham] **believed** the LORD; and [Yahweh] credited it to him as righteousness. Genesis 15:6 HCSB, bold added

For the purposes of our study, it is the word "believed" that we want to consider in that it is the evidence of Abraham's faith and the basis for his hope. "Believed" is a translation of the Hebrew word *'aman* {aw-man'}. According to BibleWorks 9.0 software, it is used 108 times in the KJV translation, but we find the first instance of its use here in Genesis 15:6. The initial use of a key word in the Bible is often very important. It generally establishes the primary or most significant meaning of that word for the remainder of its biblical uses. This general principle holds true in the use of the Hebrew word *'aman* in Genesis 15:6.[17]

In contrast to its ancient biblical meaning, our modern western culture has often watered down the word "faith" to mean a simple mental assent to something – what can rightly be referred to as "easy believism." On the other end of the extreme, faith is used to refer to the idea that if you want something bad enough

---

16 God had previously asked Abraham to depart from his homeland on the promise that he would be blessed. Abraham obediently did so. Genesis 12:1-5

17 *Hebrew Definitions*, entry for *Believe Hebrew = 'Aman,* Precept Austin. Retrieved from https://www.preceptaustin.org/hebrew_definitions (last accessed August 8, 2021)

and believe hard enough for it, then God will give it to you. In yet another modern misuse of the word Mark Twain famously said, "Faith is believing what you know ain't so."[18] As we are going to see, none of these popular uses of the word *faith* line up rightly with the biblical use of the word. If we are going to understand how Abraham becomes the premier biblical example of *faith* (in the active sense of believing, a personal action) we need to park here for a moment so we can develop a solid working definition of the ancient Hebrew meaning of belief/believing/faith.[19]

This is a Bible Study in the Series called, *Lost in Translation*. The series title was intentionally chosen. There are many factors which have led to gaps in our modern-day understanding of various key biblical terms. The word "faith" is one of those key words that has been truncated along the way from ancient use to modern use. Our aim is not directed towards figuring out how or why various words are lacking full-bodied biblical meaning today. Rather our goal is to focus on re-orienting ourselves to proper meaning of key terms as they were originally used in the Bible. As we do, I believe our investment will provide huge dividends for our biblical understanding.

One of the primary ways we will unpack biblical word meanings is through a Word Study. To that end our focus on the word "believed" (commonly referred to as *faith*) will begin there. Because this is our first Word Study in *The Power of Hope* I think it is important to remind you of something I pointed out in the Preface. In this series, Word Studies are *not* intended to explore the entire semantic range of a given word. The focus of each word we study will be narrowed by the specific context in which the author originally used that word. "If we are seeking the meaning intended by the author to the original recipients, that meaning *must* be the meaning they could understand at the time, not the meaning

---

18 Quoted from *Following the Equator,* Pudd'nhead Wilson's Calendar. Retrieved from http://www.twainquotes.com/Faith.html (last accessed August 8, 2021)
19 In Lesson 3 we will see that the premier biblical example of faith in its noun form also involves Abraham.

we would determine based on our position of advanced historical developments."[20] As we will see, the ancient Hebrew understanding of faith is radically different than any of those modern concepts I have noted.

> ### WORD STUDY
>
> *As we have noted, in Genesis 15:6 the word **believed**, is the Hebrew verb 'aman {aw-man'}. The basic root idea of 'aman is firmness and certainty.*[21] *In the Hebrew verb form used in Genesis 15:6 'aman means "to cause to be certain, sure or to be certain about, to be assured."*[22]
>
> *"Biblical faith is an assurance, a certainty, in contrast with modern concepts of faith as something possible, hopefully true, but not certain."*[23]

"In the *Tanakh* [the Hebrew Bible often referred to as the Old Testament], faith does not mean believing in spite of the evidence. It means trusting profoundly in a person."[24] In the case of Abraham, faith means he trusted profoundly in Yahweh, the personal God,

---

20 Firth and Wegner, "Introduction," in *Presence Power And Promise The Role of the Spirit of God in the Old Testament*, edited by Firth and Wegner (IVP Academic 2011) p. 18, quoting Klein, Blomberg and Hubbard, *Introduction to Biblical Interpretation*, 2nd edition (Word 2004) p. 11, italics in original
21 Harris, Archer, and Waltke, editors, *Theological Wordbook of the Old Testament* (Moody Press 1999) word #116, p. 51
22 Harris, Archer, and Waltke, editors, *Theological Wordbook of the Old Testament* (Moody Press 1999) word #116, p. 51
23 Harris, Archer, and Waltke, editors, *Theological Wordbook of the Old Testament* (Moody Press 1999) word #116, p. 51
24 Berlin and Brettler, editors, *The Jewish Study Bible: Featuring The Jewish Publication Society Tanakh Translation* (Oxford University Press 2004) study note Genesis 15:6, p. 35

on the basis of the promise He had given.²⁵ We can readily see this ancient biblical understanding of faith properly reflected in the 1999 Jewish Publication Society translation of our Key Scripture:

> And because [Abraham] put his trust [*'aman*] in [Yahweh], He reckoned it to his merit. Genesis 15:6 NJPS *Tanakh*

Abraham understood God's promise required his response. That act of wholehearted commitment to what God promised him is described by the verb *'aman*. Now, let's continue with our study of this important word. The King James Version of the Bible most often translates *'aman* as believe (44 times) and among other translations also renders it as: faithful (20 times), sure (11 times), or established (7 times).²⁶ It is instructive, however, to consider that *'aman* "is radically [by the root] connected with the words"²⁷ doorposts, guardian and nurse. Those connections with a word primarily referring to the act of "believing" may seem quite odd to us. In reality, these concrete word pictures help us better capture the idea of what is generally a more abstract concept in the English language. As we will see, the idea of firmness is a consistent thread that runs through the biblical concept of the Hebrew word *'aman*.

By way of introduction, the *Theological Wordbook of the Old Testament* (*TWOT*) points out, "[s]ince Hebrew does not lend itself to the abstract," the Bible often uses earthly-oriented picturesque ways and parallel words to express otherwise abstract concepts.²⁸ The example used in *TWOT* points to the fact that the Bible enables the abstract word "strength" to be more clearly understood

---

25 Berlin and Brettler, editors, *The Jewish Study Bible: Featuring The Jewish Publication Society Tanakh Translation* (Oxford University Press 2004) study note Genesis 15:6, p. 35
26 *BibleWorks 9.0* software, entry for *0539 אמן 'aman {aw-man'}*
27 Hill, Gary, *The Discovery Bible*, HELPS Ministries, Inc., [H]3b (SN 539) *'āman* under *Key quotes* citing Edwin Abbott. Abbott was an Anglican priest and theologian.
28 Harris, Archer, and Waltke, editors, *Theological Wordbook of the Old Testament* (Moody Press 1999) word#1596b, p. 660

by depicting strength in many different picturesque ways. For example, in Psalm 30:7 strength is portrayed as a mountain, in Psalm 61:3 it is a strong tower and in Psalm 62:7 it is a rock. Sometimes the same Hebrew word can be used to describe both abstract and concrete ideas. For example, *'ap* {af} is one of the Old Testament words for "anger."[29] Even though it is most often translated as *anger*,[30] it can also be properly rendered as *nose, nostrils,* or *face*.[31] That may sound strange to us. However, Hebrew thought notices that anger sometimes results in "an evident physical disturbance in one's facial expression [flaring of the nostrils]."[32] That fact permits the same Hebrew word to be used for a physical face, nose or nostrils and also for the abstract concept of anger. *TWOT* concludes, "The main use of *'ap* is to refer to the anger of men and of God.... '[A]p gives specific emphasis to the emotional aspect of anger and wrath ...."[33]

As we have pointed out, the Hebrew language can rely on concrete depictions of physical realities in order to communicate

---

29 Longman III and Garland, general editors, *The Expositor's Bible Commentary: Psalms*, Vol. 5, Revised Edition (Zondervan 2008) *Reflections: Anger In The Psalms* under *Synonyms for Anger*, p. 643

30 *'Ap* refers to Yahweh's anger 177 times in the Old Testament. Durham, John I., *Word Biblical Commentary: Exodus*, Volume 3 (Word Books 1987) Exodus 15:1-21 under *Notes 8.a.*, p. 201, citing *BDB* (60)

31 See for example: "By the sweat of your **face** [*'ap*] You will eat bread, Till you return to the ground .... (Genesis 3:19, bold added);" "Then [the servant of Abraham] asked her, 'Whose daughter are you?' And she said, 'The daughter of Bethuel ...' and I put the ring on her **nose** [*'ap*], and the bracelets on her wrists (Genesis 24:47, bold added);" "At the blast of [Yahweh's] **nostrils** [*'ap*] the waters were piled up .... (Exodus 15:8, bold added)." The word *'ap* is a derivative of a verb which is "used exclusively in the OT of the 'snorting anger, violent rage' of God." Durham, John I., *Word Biblical Commentary: Exodus*, Volume 3 (Word Books 1987) Exodus 15:1-21 under *Notes 8.a.*, p. 201

32 Longman III and Garland, general editors, *The Expositor's Bible Commentary: Psalms*, Vol. 5, Revised Edition (Zondervan 2008) *Reflections: Anger In The Psalms* under *The word 'ap*, p. 643

33 Harris, Archer, and Waltke, editors, *Theological Wordbook of the Old Testament* (Moody Press 1999) word #133a under *'ap. Nostril, face, anger,* p. 58

concepts and ideas in ways the people could see and therefore understand. Now with that background, let's return to our goal to better understand the Hebrew word *'aman*. Our first example of a concrete concept of *'aman* is found in 2 Samuel 4 where it refers to Mephibosheth's nurse.

> Now Jonathan, Saul's son, had a son crippled in his feet. He was five years old when the report of Saul and Jonathan came from Jezreel, and his nurse [*'aman*] took him up and fled. And it happened that in her hurry to flee, he fell and became lame. And his name was Mephibosheth. 2 Samuel 4:4

In ancient times the position of the nurse was one of honor and importance. For example, Naomi took charge of Ruth's child "and became his nurse."[34] A "nurse" was a guardian or governess – a person who had charge of infants or young children. The essence of Old Testament nursing is supportive nurture and care. As a result, strong connections were formed between a child and his nurse. Because of this bond, a child's nurse could retain a significant place in the family long after the child had grown into adulthood.[35] The ancient role of the nurse conveys the idea of firm support in the sense that strong attachments naturally flow from their guard-

---

34 Ruth 4:16
35 See for example: "And [Rebekah's brother and mother] said, 'We will call [Rebekah] and consult her wishes.' Then they called Rebekah and said to her, 'Will you go with this man?' And she said, 'I will go.' Thus they sent away their sister Rebekah **and her nurse** with Abraham's servant and his men (Genesis 24:57-59, bold added)." Notice that even as Rebekah agrees to go with Abraham's servant to become Isaac's wife, her family sends her nurse with her. Ryken, Wilhoit and Longman III, editors, *Dictionary of Biblical Imagery* (Intervarsity Press 1998) entry for *Nurse*, p. 600; Unger, Merrill F., *The New Unger's Bible Dictionary* (Moody Press 1988) entry for *Nurse, Nursing*, p. 929; Orr, James, general editor, *International Standard Bible Encyclopedia* (Eerdmans 1915) entry for *Nurse; Nursing*. Retrieved from https://www.studylight.org/encyclopedias/eng/isb/n/nurse-nursing.html (last accessed January 25, 2022)

ian-type relationship. In Hebrew thought, this idea of firm reliable support connects "nurse" with the word *'aman*.³⁶

In an even more concrete sense of reliability and support, the author of 2 Kings uses a noun directly related to *'aman* to refer to doorposts in the Temple.

> At that time Hezekiah cut off *the gold from* the doors of the temple of the LORD, and *from* the doorposts [*'omenah*] which Hezekiah king of Judah had overlaid, and gave it to the king of Assyria. 2 Kings 18:16, italics in original

In this verse, the word "doorposts" is a translation of the Hebrew noun *'omenah* {om-me-naw'}, which is a derivative of *'aman*. In an ancient house, a door had two main sections: a fixed frame and a moving board or slab.³⁷ The frame had two vertical sides known as its two doorposts. They provided stability to the physical structure of the building as well as firmness and support for the door. *TWOT* points out that the basic idea of support contained in the word *'aman* is seen here in reference to these physical pillars of support.³⁸

Our last example of *'aman* is found in Isaiah 22.

---

36 *NET Bible Notes*, translator's note 20, Genesis 15:6. As noted in Preface, FN 8, the source for this information is "*Net Notes*" however it will be descriptively cited as "*Net Bible Notes*" throughout the study. *TWOT* connects the idea of strong arms supporting an infant who is helpless with the basic root idea of firmness or certainty. Harris, Archer, and Waltke, editors, *Theological Wordbook of the Old Testament* (Moody Press 1999) word #116, p. 51

37 *Encyclopaedia Judaica*, Jewish Virtual Library, entry for *Door and Doorpost*, citing Pritchard, *Pictures*, 219, pl. 675; Y. Kaplan, *Ha-Arkhe'ologyah ve-ha-Historyah shel Tel Aviv-Yafo* (1959), 60, fig. 20, pls. 9–11; Y. Yadin et al., *Hazor*, 2 (1960), pl. 16:1. Retrieved from https://www.jewishvirtuallibrary.org/door-and-doorpost?msclkid=b4314cbfb4ef-11ec8320302003adfe9f (last accessed April 05, 2022)

38 Harris, Archer, and Waltke, editors, *Theological Wordbook of the Old Testament* (Moody Press 1999) word #116, p. 51

> I will drive [Eliakim] *like* a peg [*yathed*] in a firm ['*aman*] place, And he will become a throne of glory to his father's house. Isaiah 22:23, italics in original

The Hebrew word *yathed* {yaw-thade'} which is translated as "peg" in Isaiah 22:23 is used for a fastener like a nail or a spike. It commonly refers to the large spikes driven into the ground to fasten tent cords as well as the spikes that were placed in soft mortar while the walls were going up in a new house. The fact that the spike was anchored into the mortar made it a firm place to hang clothing and other family items. In Isaiah 22:23 '*aman* describes Eliakim as a leader in Israel.[39] "Eliakim is given the key, [in other words he is given] the authority to legislate and make binding decisions; his purpose is to be a peg, to hold the kingdom firm … The picture is of a tent peg driven into a firm place, holding the tent secure in the wind"[40] or a secure nail driven into a solid place like a wall.[41] The metaphor provides an image that relates to the security (firmness) of Eliakim's leadership position. He is secure in his position with a tenure that is stable and will not change.[42]

Each of our examples, 2 Samuel 4:4, 2 Kings 18:16 and Isaiah 22:23, provides concreteness to an otherwise abstract notion of believing. We can learn from these more physical uses that to *believe* is beyond intellectual agreement to something. It undeniably denotes a sense of firmness, certainty and reliability. To *believe* is to firmly entrust yourself to reliable God.[43] This entrustment serves to

---

39 Barnes, Albert, *Barnes' Notes On The Old And New Testaments*, Isaiah 22:23. Retrieved from Hill, Gary, *The Discovery Bible*, HELPS Ministries, Inc.

40 Motyer, J. Alec, *The Prophecy of Isaiah: An Introduction & Commentary* (InterVarsity Press 1993) Isaiah 22:22-23a, p. 188

41 Baker and Carpenter, *The Complete WordStudy Dictionary of the Old Testament* (AMG Publishers 2003) word #539, p. 69

42 *NET Bible Notes*, study note 54, Isaiah 22:23; Spence-Jones & Exell, general editors, *Pulpit Commentary*, Isaiah 22:23. Retrieved from Hill, Gary, *The Discovery Bible*, HELPS Ministries, Inc.

43 Keck, Leander E., *Romans*, Abingdon New Testament Commentaries (Abingdon Press 2005) Abraham's Rectitude, Earned or Unearned? ([Ro-

motivate a person's action based on their reliance on God's faithfulness and His promise(s). As one source concluded, "In summary, when aman means to believe it pictures the firm, wholehearted committal of one's self to the truth which is revealed and which calls for a response ...."[44]

Let's conclude this lesson by looking at the Greek word which was first chosen to translate the verb *'aman* in Genesis 15:6. We'll begin with a little background allowing us to see how we can speak of a *Greek* word in a *Hebrew* Old Testament. Greek had become the dominant language in the world by the fourth century B.C. largely as a result of the successful conquests of Alexander the Great.[45] Therefore, not surprisingly, the first major translation of the Old Testament from its Hebrew origin was into the Greek language. This is the translation that is commonly referred to as the LXX or The Septuagint.[46] That team of translators chose the Greek verb *pisteuo*[47] to translate the Hebrew verb *'aman* in Genesis 15:6.

---

mans] 4:1-8), p. 124

44 *Hebrew Definitions*, entry for *Believe Hebrew = 'Aman*, Precept Austin. Retrieved from https://www.preceptaustin.org/hebrew_definitions (last accessed August 8, 2021)

45 Alexander the Great was "a Macedonian king, [who] conquered the eastern Mediterranean, Egypt, the Middle East, and parts of Asia in a remarkably short period of time. His empire ushered in significant cultural changes in the lands he conquered and changed the course of the region's history." *National Geographic*, Resource Library, nationalgeographic.org, Encyclopedic, entry for *Alexander the Great*. Retrieved from https://www.nationalgeographic.org/encyclopedia/alexander-great/?msclkid=b-c0a18f4b4f211ecbe87660188440d80 (last accessed April 05, 2022)

46 The fact that many Jews could no longer read Hebrew was of great concern to the Jewish leaders. About 300 B.C. the Old Testament began to be translated from Hebrew into Greek. That translation was completed around 200 B.C. Over time this Greek translation of the Old Testament was widely accepted and used in many synagogues. The International Bible Society, *In what language was the Bible first written?* Retrieved from www.biblica.com/en-us/bible/bible-faqs/in-what-language-was-the-bible-first-written (last accessed August 8, 2021)

47 *Hebrew Definitions*, entry for *Believe Hebrew = 'Aman*, Precept Austin. Retrieved from https://www.preceptaustin.org/hebrew_definitions (last

Pisteuo is one of the most frequent and important verbs in the New Testament being employed 241 times.[48] As a result, it is worth our time to do a Word Study here.

> ## Word Study
>
> *As noted, the word **believed** in the Greek translation of Genesis 15:6 is the verb pisteuo {pist-yoo'-o}. According to the leading Greek-English Lexicon of the New Testament, the semantic range of pisteuo includes: 1) to consider something to be true and therefore worthy of one's trust: [translated as] believe, 2) to entrust oneself to someone or something in complete confidence: [translated as] believe (in), trust, with the implication of total commitment to the one who is trusted, 3) to entrust something to someone, 4) to be convinced or confident about and 5) to think or consider possible.* [49]

As we can see from our Word Study, *pisteuo* far exceeds the common range and scope of the English verb "to believe." In ordinary English usage our concept of *believing* is probably most akin to the fifth definition in our Word Study – thinking something is possible. On the other hand, *pisteuo* can intertwine definitions 1 – 4 as equally important elements of faith meaning: 1) confidence that a promise is true and trustworthy *and as a result* 2) trust in

---

accessed August 8, 2021)

48 *1 Thessalonians 2:13 Commentary*, Precept Austin. Retrieved from https://www.preceptaustin.org/1thessalonians_213 (last accessed August 8, 2021)

49 Goulet, Henri Louis, *What Is Biblical Faith Beyond Easy Believism and Cheap Grace Part 2*, Messianic Studies Institute, December, 2020, citing Bauer, Danker, Arndt, and Gingrich, *Greek-English Lexicon of the New Testament and Other Early Christian Literature*, 3rd edition (*BDAG*) (University of Chicago 2000) revised by Frederick Danker

the promisor which rises to the level of committed entrustment. To quote my research mentor and friend, Henri Louis Goulet, "'faith' as it is typically used is best understood as '[our] trust leading to [our] trustworthiness' or '[our] faith leading to [our] faithfulness.'"[50] Consistent with that definition is the use of "faith" in Jewish contexts where it "implies not just belief in something but also fidelity, commitment, and truth."[51]

In other words, "… the full biblical concept of believing in both the OT and NT is not merely acknowledging something to be true, nor is it the popular notion of belief that implies little more than having a deep emotional resonance with something. The biblical concept of believing involves action."[52] "Faith is a conscious choice to act on what God says is true …. Faith … is released through acts of obedience."[53] To summarize what we are learning the biblical concept of believing can refer to our faith *in* something/someone *and* it can also refer to our *faithfulness*.

Let's finish up our discussion of the Greek translation of Genesis 15:6. As noted in our Word Study, the use of the word *pisteuo* informs us that Abraham believed God's promise. Then he entrusted himself to God in such complete confidence that he willingly undertook action based on that confidence. His *belief* implied total commitment to the One he trusted.[54] Abraham's initial trust led him to become a faithful servant of Yahweh.

In our next lesson we will look at the biblical meaning of the word *hope* which overlaps with biblical faith. As we will learn, both

---

50 Goulet, Henri Louis, *What is Biblical 'Faith'? Beyond Easy Believism and Cheap Grace*, Messianic Studies Institute Online Course, December, 2020
51 McCartney, Dan G., *James*, Baker Exegetical Commentary on the New Testament (Baker Academic 2009) James 1:3, p. 86
52 Mounce, William D., editor, *Complete Expository Dictionary of Old & New Testament Words* (Zondervan 2006) entry for *Believe*, p. 61
53 *Spirit Filled Life Bible* (Thomas Nelson 1991) Truth-In-Action through Psalms (Book Two: Psalms 42-72) under *Truth Psalms Teaches #4*, p. 815
54 *1 Thessalonians 2:13 Commentary*, Precept Austin. Retrieved from https://www.preceptaustin.org/1thessalonians_213 (last accessed August 8, 2021)

hope and faith have to do with something you cannot yet see or possess in the natural.

Hear What The Spirit is Saying to the Church: *Now that you rightly understand what I mean when I ask you to believe Me, the question is: "How willing are you to believe what I say is true?"*

Lesson 2:

Abraham's "Beyond Hope" Hope

 "Against all hope, Abraham in hope believed and so became the father of many nations, just as it had been said to him, 'So shall your offspring be.'" Romans 4:18 NIV

A GOOD PLACE to begin Lesson 2 is by placing our Key Scripture in context. In his letter to Christ-followers in Rome Paul was arguing that no person is put into a right relationship with God except by faith. In Chapter 4 he points to Abraham as the consummate proof for his "by-faith-alone" argument. Paul quotes Genesis 15:6 (the Key Scripture from Lesson 1) to drive home the point that Abraham's trust in God's promise was the exclusive means by which God initially granted Abraham the status of right standing. In other words, the starting place for Abraham's righteousness was hearing God's promise and trusting God by entrusting himself and his future to Him.

The Bible uses the word "righteous" to refer to the condition of the human heart that is acceptable to God. The core of biblical righteousness is expectation.[1] A righteous person is one who behaves in the way expected in that relationship.[2] In his letter to the

---

1 Meier, Sam, *Misunderstood Terms in the Bible 2020*, Lesson 1, Messianic Studies Institute, Term 4 2020. Dr. Meier is a Professor in the Department of Near Eastern Languages and Cultures, The Ohio State University. He holds a Ph.D. from Harvard University (1987) in Hebrew and Semitic Languages and Literatures.
2 Meier, Sam, *Misunderstood Terms in the Bible 2020*, Lesson 1, Messianic Studies Institute, Term 4 2020

Romans Paul remains steadfast in his argument that it was Abraham's belief that met God's expectation for righteousness. Critical to Paul's understanding is the Hebrew word translated as "credited" in Genesis 15:6 which Paul quotes in Romans 4:3.

> For what does the Scripture say? "ABRAHAM BELIEVED GOD, AND IT WAS **CREDITED** TO HIM AS RIGHTEOUSNESS."
> Romans 4:3, uppercase text in original, bold added

Since Paul is quoting the Old Testament (as reflected in the uppercase text) let's go back to the actual verse in Genesis 15 so we can look at the word "credited" in the Hebrew language.[3]

> [Abraham] believed the LORD; and [Yahweh] **credited** [*chashab* {khaw-shab'}] it to him as righteousness. Genesis 15:6 HCSB, bold added

The *Theological Wordbook of the Old Testament* points out that on several occasions, such as in Genesis 15:6, the Hebrew word *chashab* is used in a specialized sense of making a judgment with the meaning "to impute."[4] The ordinary meaning of impute is "to credit or ascribe (something) to a person; regard a quality as belonging to."[5] God imputed righteousness to Abraham when he chose to trust God and believe His promise that a son born to him and Sarah would be his heir. The construction of the original Hebrew

---

3   The Greek word Paul used in Romans 4:3 which is translated as "credited" is *logizomai* {log-id'-zom-ahee}. It essentially means "to consider something true." Harrison and Hagner, "Romans," in *The Expositor's Bible Commentary: Romans ~ Galatians*, Vol. 11, Revised Edition, edited by Longman III and Garland (Zondervan Academic 2008) Romans 4:3, p. 78

4   Harris, Archer, and Waltke, editors, *Theological Wordbook of the Old Testament* (Moody Press 1999) word #767, p. 330

5   *Merriam-Webster.com Dictionary*, entry for *impute*. Retrieved from https://www.merriam-webster.com/dictionary/impute (last accessed August 8, 2021)

text in Genesis 15:6 clarifies that his faith alone was "the *means* by which God graciously gave Abraham the status of righteousness."[6]

Chashab places the focus on God's actions – by *His* grace *He* "considered" and *He* "counted" Abraham's trust in Him as that which met His expectation. Imagine Abraham had a spiritual bank account and his right relationship with God depends on what is *in* that account. *Chashab* says that God looked at Abraham's heart (in the way only God can) and saw the trust (confident expectation) that was there. Then God made a judgment to credit Abraham's spiritual bank account with righteousness.

As we continue looking at the context of our Key Scripture, notice Paul says *that* understanding of the text makes clear that this ascribing or reckoning was not on the basis of anything Abraham *did* (Romans 4:4-5).[7] It was the pure grace of God that He chose to consider Abraham's initial rudimentary trust in the promise of an heir as righteousness. The point of Paul's argument is that both Jews and Gentiles[8] meet God's expectations and are put right with Him by the very same means. Regardless of ethnic ancestry, it is trust (even initial, elementary trust is sufficient) not individual merit that graciously establishes a right relationship with God.

---

6   Moo, Douglas J., "Romans," in *Zondervan Illustrated Bible Backgrounds Commentary*, Vol. 3, edited by Clinton E. Arnold (Zondervan 2002) Romans 4:3 under *Abraham believed God, and it was credited to him for righteousness*, p. 26, italics added

7   Schreiner, Thomas R., *Romans*, Baker Exegetical Commentary on the New Testament, 2nd edition (Baker Academic 1998, 2018) Romans 4:4-5, pp. 223-224; Keck, Leander E., *Romans*, Abingdon New Testament Commentaries (Abingdon Press 2005) Abraham's Rectitude, Earned or Unearned ([Romans] 4:1-8), pp. 123-124

8   God divided all of humanity into two groups. A "Jew" is anyone who belongs to one of the twelve tribes of Israel and a "Gentile" refers to everyone else. The word "Gentile" is of Latin origin and means "belonging to a people." As typically used in the Gospels, "Gentile" simply means "non-Jewish." Niles, Randall, *Jews and Gentiles in the Gospels*, DriveThruHistory, October 3, 2016. Retrieved from https://drivethruhistory.com/jews-and-gentiles-in-the-gospels/ (last accessed August 8, 2021)

Paul then continues in verses 17-22 to explain to his readers the kind of belief/trust God saw in Abraham. Before Paul concludes Chapter 4 he will apply these lessons from Abraham to his readers. "The necessity of faith for righteousness is ... indispensable for all who want to be right with God [both Jew and Gentile]."[9] Notably, scholar Leander Keck rightly points out:[10]

> In short, for Paul, neither affirming right ideas about God nor believing in God generally is enough for a right relation to God ... what *is* enough for a right relation to God is **entrusting oneself to God**.

With this in mind, let's zoom in on verse 18 in Romans 4, our Key Scripture for this lesson, to see what we can learn about the biblical concept of hope.

> In hope [*elpis*] against hope [*elpis*] [Abraham] **believed**, so that he might become a father of many nations according to that which had been spoken, "SO SHALL YOUR DESCENDANTS BE." Romans 4:18, uppercase text in original, bold added

In Romans 4:18 the word "believed" (highlighted in bold) is the Greek verb *pisteuo*. You'll recall that in our last lesson we concluded *pisteuo* communicates that Abraham affirmed what God said is true and he entrusted himself to God in complete confidence. His "belief" carried with it the implication of total trust and commitment to God. In fact, only a heart that has confidence in God will be submissive to Him.[11] Recognition of God's

---

9   Schreiner, Thomas R., *Romans*, 2nd edition, Baker Exegetical Commentary on the New Testament (Baker Academic 1998, 2018) C. Abraham as the Father of Jews and Gentiles ([Romans] 4:1-25), pp. 219
10 Keck, Leander E., *Romans*, Abingdon New Testament Commentaries (Abingdon Press 2005) Abraham's Rectitude, Earned or Unearned ([Romans] 4:1-8), pp. 124-125, italics in original, bold added
11 Longman III and Garland, general editors, *The Expositor's Bible Commentary: Psalms*, Vol. 5, Revised Edition (Zondervan 2008) Psalm 25:4-7, p. 265

sovereignty produces a heart attitude that willingly "*waits* in *active submission.*"[12] God personally acts as the guarantor to fulfill every promise He encourages us to hope for through faith. His guarantee enables us to be secure in hope. We will return to these critical truths in a later lesson.

Paul highlights the remarkable nature of Abraham's complete confidence and commitment by explaining that Abraham "hoped against hope." The Message translation renders that enlightening phrase this way:

> … When everything was hopeless, Abraham believed anyway, deciding to live not on the basis of what he saw he *couldn't* do but on what God said he *would* do…. Romans 4:17-18 MSG, italics in original

Even though there appeared in the natural absolutely no objective grounds for hope, Abraham chose to hope.[13] In other words, Abraham anchored himself in hope. So, what is hope? We will begin by looking at the Greek word Paul used in our Key Scripture.

> ### Word Study
>
> *In Romans 4:18 the word* **hope** *is a translation of the Greek noun elpis {el-pece'} which means sure confidence, a favorable and confident expectation based on solid certainty.*[14]

---

12 Hill, Gary, *The Discovery Bible*, HELPS Ministries, Inc., [G]1680 *elpis*, under *In Brief,* italics in original
13 Ellicott, Charles John, *Ellicott's Commentary for English Readers*, Romans 4:18. Retrieved from Hill, Gary, *The Discovery Bible*, HELPS Ministries, Inc.
14 Schreiner, Thomas R., *Romans*, 2nd edition, Baker Exegetical Commentary on the New Testament (Baker Academic 1998, 2018) Romans 5:2, p. 262; *Vine's Expository Dictionary of NT Words*, entry for *hope*. Retrieved from https://www.studylight.org/ /dictionaries/eng/ved/h/hope-hope.html (last accessed August 8, 2021); *Spirit Filled Life Bible*

> *Elpis refers to absolute assurance of future good. In the Bible, it is used objectively to refer to confidence or trust in the character and nature of God rather than upon ourselves or our circumstances.*[15] *Biblically hope has certainty because it rests on a promise made by God.*[16]

Paul was a "Hebrew of Hebrews." He acted, spoke and thought like a Hebrew. However, when he wrote his letters to the early groups of Christ-followers who were Greek-speaking he wrote in the Greek language. That meant important concepts like belief, faith and hope had to be translated from the ancient Hebrew language into the Greek language. Paul would have been greatly aided in his arduous translation task by the LXX.[17] We briefly mentioned this Hebrew-to-Greek translation in our last lesson. It was completed about 300 years before Paul's ministry to the Gentiles in the Roman Empire.[18]

Because the Greek language in which Paul wrote was informed by the Hebrew thought-world of the Old Testament, the Old Testament is the best starter dictionary we have for the New Testament. The LXX already expressed those Hebrew words and concepts in

---

(Thomas Nelson 1991) *Word Wealth [1 Thessalonians] 1:3, hope, elpis*, p. 1826

15   Wenstrom, William E., Jr., *Greek Word Studies* (Wenstrom.org 2016) entry for *Elpis*. Retrieved from https://www.wenstrom.org/downloads/written/word_studies /greek/elpis.pdf (last accessed August 8, 2021)

16   *Spirit Filled Life Bible* (Thomas Nelson 1991) *Word Wealth [1 Thessalonians] 1:3, hope, elpis*, p. 1826

17   This early translation is called the *Septuagint* (from the Latin word for "seventy"). According to the traditional account of its origin, seventy-two translators worked on this translation.

18   The Septuagint translation of the Hebrew Bible into Greek is traditionally dated during the reign of Ptolemy II Philadelphus of Egypt (285-246 B.C.).

The Power of Hope

Greek. It provided the authors of the New Testament with a ready-made Hebrew-Greek dictionary.

In the Old Testament, there is no such thing as a *neutral* concept of expectation; however, there is no one Hebrew word that has the exact meaning and force of "expectation of some good thing."[19] According to *Easton International Standard Bible Encyclopedia*, in the King James Version of the Old Testament, the English word "hope" translates 15 different Hebrew words.[20] When the LXX uses the Greek noun *elpis* and the related verb *elpizo* they always translate various Hebrew words in the Old Testament which denote confidence and trust.[21] Most notable is the LXX use of *elpis* (and the related word *elpizein*) for *batah*; but *elpis* (or one of the Greek words related to *elpis*)[22] also translates close synonyms for *batah* like *yahal*, *qavah* and *tiqvah*.[23] The *Theological Dictionary of the New Testament* points to the Hebrew verb *batah* as being the word that most influenced the way in which the early church

---

19 Scott, Burton, *Easton International Standard Bible Encyclopedia*, entry for *hope, hop. 1.* under *In The Old Testament*. Retrieved from https://www.studylight.org/encyclopedias/eng/isb/h/hope.html (last accessed August 8, 2021)

20 Scott, Burton, *Easton International Standard Bible Encyclopedia*, entry for *hope, hop. 1.* under *In The Old Testament*. Retrieved from https://www.studylight.org/encyclopedias/eng/isb/h/hope.html (last accessed August 8, 2021)

21 Wenstrom, William E., Jr., *Greek Word Studies* (Wenstrom.org 2016) entry for *Elpis*. Retrieved from https://www.wenstrom.org/downloads/written/word_studies/Greek /elpis.pdf (last accessed August 8, 2021)

22 The noun *elpis* belongs to the following word group. 1) *elpis* (noun) "confidence, confident expectation," 2) *elpizo* (verb) "to have confidence in, to trust in, to expect," 3) *apelpizo* (verb) "to despair" and 4) *proelpizo* (verb) "to have confidence in before the promise or expectation is fulfilled." Wenstrom, William E., Jr., *Greek Word Studies* (Wenstrom.org 2016) entry for *Elpis*. Retrieved from https://www.wenstrom.org/downloads/written/word_studies/greek/elpis.pdf (last accessed August 8, 2021)

23 Bromiley, Geoffrey W., *Theological Dictionary of the New Testament*, Abridged in One Volume (Eerdmans 1985) entry for *elpis* under *B. The OT View of Hope*, p. 230

used the Greek word *elpis*.[24] We will begin our study with that important Hebrew verb.

> ### WORD STUDY
>
> *The Hebrew verb **batah** {baw-takh'} (also transliterated as batach) refers to reliance that is based on "a sense of security."*[25] *Batah is commonly translated as "trust" and is usually employed to denote that type of secure trust in the face of danger.*[26]

Batah is about "committing to something already known or received, like the decision to have confidence with an attitude of expectation."[27] Our Word Study helps us see that biblical hope inherently envisions a sense of well-being and security which results from placing confidence in God. *Batah* stresses the feeling of well-being, safety and security that naturally results when you are able to trust something or someone reliable especially when facing danger.[28]

As we continue in our quest to understand biblical hope, the three close synonyms of *batah* that we have already identified – *yahal, qavah* and *tiqvah* – will provide additional insight into a

---

24 Bromiley, Geoffrey W., *Theological Dictionary of the New Testament*, Abridged in One Volume (Eerdmans 1985) entry for *elpis* under *E. The Early Christian Concept of Hope*, p. 231
25 Waltke, Bruce K., *The Book of Proverbs: Chapters 1-15*, The New International Commentary on the Old Testament (Eerdmans 2004) Proverbs 3:5-6, p. 243
26 Waltke, Bruce K., *The Book of Proverbs: Chapters 1-15*, The New International Commentary on the Old Testament (Eerdmans 2004) Proverbs 3:5-6, p. 243
27 Hill, Gary, *The Discovery Bible*, HELPS Ministries, Inc., [H]3d (SN 982) bāṭaḥ
28 Harris, Archer, and Waltke, editors, *Theological Wordbook of the Old Testament* (Moody Press 1999) word #233, p. 101

richer understanding of what it means to hope. We will consider each of these synonyms one by one beginning with *yahal*.

> **WORD STUDY**
>
> The Hebrew verb **yachal** *{yaw-chal'}* (also transliterated as *yahal*) is a primitive root meaning "to wait, to hope, to tarry" with confident expectation of some future action.[29] It denotes a waiting attitude or waiting in anticipation.[30]

Yachal is used in the Bible for the simple concept of waiting for a short time as in Noah waited expectantly [*yachal*] seven more days for the water to recede before sending the dove out again (Genesis 8:12). However, *yachal* can also describe patiently trusting in God and waiting on His future action during great hardship. See for example: Job 13:15a "Though [Yahweh] slay me, I will hope [*yahal*] in Him."

This type of hope "is not a pacifying wish of the imagination which drowns out troubles, nor is it uncertain, but rather *yahal* 'hope' is the solid ground expectation for the righteous. As such it is directed towards God" and results in patient waiting.[31] This confidence and encouragement to remain in patient expectancy as you wait on God to act can be clearly seen in Psalm 130:

---

29 Baker and Carpenter, *The Complete WordStudy Dictionary of the Old Testament* (AMG Publishers 2003) word #3176, p. 443; Harris, Archer, and Waltke, editors, *Theological Wordbook of the Old Testament* (Moody Press 1999) word #859, pp. 373-374

30 *Brown-Driver-Briggs Hebrew and English Lexicon,* Unabridged, Electronic Database. Copyright © 2002, 2003, 2006 by Biblesoft, Inc. All rights reserved. Retrieved from https://biblehub.com/bdb/3176.htm (last accessed August 8, 2021)

31 Harris, Archer, and Waltke, editors, *Theological Wordbook of the Old Testament* (Moody Press 1999) word #859, p. 373

O Israel, **wait** [*yachal*] for the LORD; for with the LORD there is steadfast love and great power to redeem. Psalm 130:7 NJPS *Tanakh*, bold added

Israel, put your **hope** [*yachal*] in the LORD. For there is faithful love with the LORD, and with Him is redemption in abundance. Psalm 130:7 HCSB, bold added

Now let's move on to the Hebrew synonym *qavah*.

WORD STUDY

*The Hebrew verb **qavah** {kaw-vaw'} is related to the word qaw which means "tense string."[32] Concretely qavah can refer to "twisting or winding a strand of cord or rope."[33]*

When it is used figuratively the basic idea is to wait for or look for with eager expectation.[34] Qavah depicts "expectation and hope as a tense attitude with reference to a specific goal."[35] Its biblical use includes the elements of certainty, patient waiting and trustful resting on God.[36]

Brown-Driver-Briggs Hebrew and English Lexicon (*BDB*) outlines the progression of the *qavah* from its concrete to its figu-

---

32 Waltke, Bruce K., *The Book of Proverbs: Chapters 15-31,* The New International Commentary on the Old Testament (Eerdmans 2004) Proverbs 20:22, p. 153

33 Baker and Carpenter, *The Complete WordStudy Dictionary of the Old Testament* (AMG Publishers 2003) word #6960, p. 986

34 Harris, Archer, and Waltke, editors, *Theological Wordbook of the Old Testament* (Moody Press 1999) word #1994, p. 791

35 Waltke, Bruce K., *The Book of Proverbs: Chapters 15-31,* The New International Commentary on the Old Testament (Eerdmans 2004) Proverbs 20:22, p. 153

36 Motyer, J. Alec, *Isaiah,* Tyndale Old Testament Commentaries (IVP Academic 1999) Isaiah 40:29-31, p. 283

rative meaning. *BDB* notes that originally *qavah* probably referred to something being *twisted* or *stretched*. Over time it came to refer to the *tension* involved in enduring and waiting.[37] In other words, when used in the sense of waiting it pictures someone who is being stretched in a tense waiting season. We see this type of "tense attitude" for example in Proverbs 20:22.

> Do not say, "I will repay evil"; Wait [*qavah*] for the Lord, and He will save you. Proverbs 20:22

Here the person in covenant relationship with Yahweh is counseled to *look expectantly* to Yahweh to right wrongs no matter how long it takes for His divine intervention to manifest. The specific goal for which he is waiting in tense expectation is for Yahweh to execute vengeance on his enemies rather than taking matters into his own hands.

The last of the close synonyms for *batah* we want to consider is the word *tiqvah*. It is one of the most interesting and picturesque words translated as "hope" in the LXX.

Word Study

*The Hebrew noun **tiqvah** {tik-vaw'} is a derivative of qavah (which we just discussed). It refers to a collection of fibers that are twisted together to make a strong firm cord. The original meaning of tiqvah was "to stretch like a rope."*[38] *Its first use in the Old Testament is found in Joshua 2:18,21 where it is usually translated as "cord" or "rope."*

---

37 *Brown-Driver-Briggs Hebrew and English Lexicon,* Unabridged, Electronic Database. Copyright © 2002, 2003, 2006 by Biblesoft, Inc. All rights reserved. Retrieved from https://biblehub.com/bdb/6960.htm (last accessed August 8, 2021)

38 *Spirit Filled Life Bible* (Thomas Nelson 1991) *Word Wealth [Hosea] 2:15 hope, tiqvah*, p. 1260

> *Figuratively it denotes expectancy – in the sense of "to wait for" or "to look hopefully" in a particular direction.*[39]

We have already noticed in our study that the Hebrew language will connect a word which has an abstract meaning with a word that defines something very concrete. In doing so, an abstract concept becomes more understandable through the concrete nature of the connected word. *Tiqvah* provides us with another good illustration of how this works in Hebrew. Our Word Study pointed out that the first occurrence of the word *tiqvah* in the Bible is in the second chapter of Joshua. We find the word used in the account of the two Israelite spies and their Jericho encounter with the woman Rahab.

> "... Now therefore, please swear to me by the LORD, since I have dealt kindly with you, that you also will deal kindly with my father's household, and give me a pledge of truth, and spare my father and my mother ... with all who belong to them, and deliver our lives from death." So the men said to her, "Our life for yours if you do not tell this business of ours; and it shall come about when the LORD gives us the land that we will deal kindly and faithfully with you." Then she let them down by a rope through the window .... The men said to her, "We *shall be* free from this oath to you which you have made us swear, unless, when we come into the land, you tie this cord of scarlet **thread** [*tiqvah*] in the window through which you let us down, and gather to yourself into the house your father and your mother and your brothers and all your father's household...." Joshua 2:12-18, italics in original, bold added

---

39 *Spirit Filled Life Bible* (Thomas Nelson 1991) *Word Wealth [Hosea] 2:15 hope, tiqvah*, p. 1260

[Rahab] said, "According to your words, so be it." So she sent them away, and they departed; and she tied the scarlet **cord** [*tiqvah*] in the window. Joshua 2:21, bold added

Rahab was instructed to tie a scarlet *tiqvah* (thread, cord, or rope) in her window. That stretched-out cord was not merely a marker, it was the tangible means of her hope that she and her family would be saved. Here hope is figuratively pictured as an *extended rope*. The concrete image is that the rope (signifying hope) attaches Rahab safely to her rescuers. It was like Rahab was standing still in expectation at one end of the rope and in hope she could imagine the Hebrew rescuers were at the other end of that rope.

However, hope is invariably rooted in expectantly waiting on some *future* action. Rahab had a present promise of future good; however, she still had to wait for the realization of the forthcoming safety the spies had promised. Because she maintained her expectation that the promise of the spies would be fulfilled she did what they instructed her to do. She placed that scarlet cord out her window and left it there. Her actions demonstrated that she was confidently anticipating the rescue she was expecting. As a result, she and her family were spared the destruction of Jericho according to the commitment the spies had made. The word *tikvah* is used in its literal sense in Joshua 2 as a stretched-out "cord" or "thread." However, its use also reveals the figurative picture of hope. That scarlet cord was Rahab's hope. It was her only guarantee that her household would be spared by the Israelites in the future; a picture of a rope – a cord of safety – linking her present circumstances with her expected future deliverance.

As we have seen, the concrete use of *tiqvah* in Joshua 2 pictures the hope of a person connected to the future promise by a rope. *Tiqvah* becomes a more generalized picture of hope when we expand it to picture a lifeline God extends to those who know and trust Him. In this case, *tiqvah* depicts a person who is standing firm as they confidently grasp a rope God has offered. That extended rope provides the means of connecting their present with the future God has planned. Because they are attached safely to God, their secure grasp on the rope leads them to action which is consistent with the hope they have.

In fact, the very next use of *tiqvah* in the Old Testament explicitly extends the meaning of *tiqvah* to the abstract idea of hope.

> And Naomi said to her two daughters-in-law, "Go, return each of you to her mother's house. May the LORD deal kindly with you as you have dealt with the dead and with me. May the LORD grant that you may find rest, each in the house of her husband." Then she kissed them, and they lifted up their voices and wept. And they said to her, "*No*, but we will surely return with you to your people." But Naomi said, "Return, my daughters. Why should you go with me? Have I yet sons in my womb, that they may be your husbands? Return, my daughters! Go, for I am too old to have a husband. If I said I have **hope** [*tiqvah*], if I should even have a husband tonight and also bear sons, would you therefore wait until they were grown? Would you therefore refrain from marrying? No, my daughters; for it is harder for me than for you, for the hand of the LORD has gone forth against me." Ruth 1:8-13, italics in original, italics in original, bold added

Tiqvah is not used here as a reference to an actual cord or rope. *Tiqvah* works to create a word picture of Naomi being connected to her future by a rope God has extended to her. It pictures her having a firm conviction about her future. In other words, Naomi was essentially saying to her daughters-in-law, "Even if God were to extend a rope [*tiqvah*] to me that pulled me into my future with a new husband. And even if I had a firm conviction of that promise becoming a reality, you wouldn't be able to wait long enough for me to be married again and have two sons who would grow up and become your new husbands."

As we have seen, the concept of hope in the New Testament is built on the Old Testament and has "the elements of expectation, a trust in God, and the patient waiting for God's working of His plan."[40] The word definitions in this lesson contain several recurring themes that jump out at us allowing us to conclude that biblical hope is like a strong rope composed of three essential interwoven strands: 1) hearing the promise made by the Promise Keeper, 2) the Promise Keeper's appointed time and 3) patient, confident, expectant waiting. When these three components harmoniously work together, the outcome is a manifestation of what was promised. We will use the next three lessons in our study to look at each element one at a time.

Hear What The Spirit is Saying to the Church: *Because I am who I am everyone who hopes in me can hope against hope for the fulfillment of that which I have promised.*

---

40 Hoehner, Harold W., "Romans," in *The Bible Knowledge Word Study, Acts-Ephesians*, edited by Darrell L. Bock (Victor 2006) Romans 4:18 under *Hope*, pp. 150-151, citing *TDNT* 2:530-31

Lesson 3:

The Promise and the Promise Keeper

"'I don't think the way you think. The way you work isn't the way I work.'… Just as rain and snow descend from the skies and don't go back until they've watered the earth, Doing their work of making things grow and blossom, producing seed for farmers and food for the hungry, So will **the words that come out of my mouth** not come back empty-handed. They'll do the work I sent them to do, **they'll complete the assignment I gave them**…." Isaiah 55:8-11 MSG, bold added

IN OUR QUEST to understand biblical hope, it will be beneficial to carefully study each of the interwoven strands of hope that we identified at the end of our last lesson. To that end, this lesson looks at the first of these three elements: the promise and the Promise Keeper. We'll begin by looking at the promise and conclude our lesson by thinking about the character of the Promisor.

In the Greek language the two words most commonly related to faith are the verb *pisteuo*, almost always translated as "believe" and *pistis*, which is a noun almost always translated as "faith." We have already considered the verb *pisteuo* in Lesson 1. As a short refresher, we concluded that *pisteuo* refers to two intertwining (equally important) elements of what we commonly call "faith." Those two elements are: 1) belief that a promise is true and trustworthy and 2) trust in the promisor that rises to the level of committed entrustment. At this point, it will be helpful to add to our understanding with a Word Study of *pistis*.

> ### WORD STUDY
>
> *As noted, the noun pistis {pis'-tis} is frequently translated as* **faith**. *The semantic range of pistis includes: 1) That which evokes trust and faith: a) the state of being someone in whom confidence can be placed - faithfulness, reliability, fidelity, commitment, allegiance,[1] b) a solemn promise to be faithful and loyal: assurance, oath and c) token offered as a guarantee of something promised: proof, pledge. 2) The state of believing on the basis of the reliability of the one trusted - meaning trust, confidence, faith in the active sense: a) pistis is found mostly without an object - faith, firm commitment, b) authentic piety or devotion.[2]*

Let's look at some very familiar verses that use the Greek noun *pistis* and routinely translate it with the word "faith." These verses are a very small sampling of the 243 occurrences of *pistis* in the New Testament.[3]

> So **faith** [*pistis*, noun] *comes* from hearing, and hearing by the word of Christ. Romans 10:17, italics in original, bold added

---

1 Goulet, Henri Louis, *What Is Biblical Faith Part 2*, Messianic Studies Institute, December, 2020, citing *BDAG* and noting that he added the word "allegiance" to his course slide

2 Goulet, Henri Louis, *What Is Biblical Faith Part 2*, Messianic Studies Institute, December, 2020, citing *BDAG*, the numbering here has been revised slightly from original course slide

3 *Bible Hub*, entry for *4102. pistis* reporting 243 occurrences for Strong's Greek 4102. Retrieved from https://biblehub.com/greek/4102.htm (last accessed July 28, 2022)

[F]or we walk by **faith** [*pistis*, noun], not by sight— 2 Corinthians 5:7, bold added

For we through the Spirit, by **faith** [*pistis*, noun], are waiting for the hope of righteousness. Galatians 5:5, bold added

For by grace you have been saved through **faith** [*pistis*, noun]; and that not of yourselves, *it is* the gift of God. Ephesians 2:8, italics in original, bold added

Now **faith** [*pistis*, noun] is the assurance of *things* hoped for, the conviction of things not seen. Hebrews 11:1, italics in original, bold added

I'm intentionally repeating the point that the Greek word *pistis* is a *noun*. My purpose is to make clear that in every case its use in these quoted verses actually refers to "faith" as the content of what is believed. It is what I referred to in Lesson 1 as the *revelation from God that finds its home in a heart*. In fact, just to stress the point to make it even more understandable, let's paraphrase each of those verses by substituting that definition of *pistis* for the word faith.

So **revelation from God that finds its home in a heart** *comes* from hearing, and hearing by the word of Christ. Romans 10:17, italics in original, bold added

[F]or we walk by **revelation from God that finds its home in our heart**, not by sight— 2 Corinthians 5:7, bold added

For we through the Spirit, by **revelation from God that finds its home in our heart**, are waiting for the hope of righteousness. Galatians 5:5, bold added

For by grace you have been saved through **revelation from God that finds its home in your heart**; and that not of yourselves, *it is* the gift of God. Ephesians 2:8, italics in original, bold added

Now **revelation from God that finds its home in a heart** is the assurance of *things* hoped for, the conviction of things not seen. Hebrews 11:1, italics in original, bold added

Many people read these New Testament verses as if the author used the **verb** *pisteuo* – referring to the personal action we take when we trust what God said. That's not only a misunderstanding of the original text which has been lost in translation, it is getting the cart before the horse so-to-speak. These verses make abundantly clear that "faith" revelation (often in the form of a promise) from God always precedes "faith" (as the action of believing). Until we have heard that revelation, there is nothing to believe. Both concepts of faith (revelation and belief/trust) are vital to our relationship with God. Both inform our hope. The two are intimately related to each other – but they are definitely different. One requires *God's action* (faith or promise that can only be initiated by Him), the other requires *our action* (faith or trust that can only be initiated by us in response to God's promise). We saw how those two aspects of faith worked in Abraham's life. Faith as a noun (*pistis*) refers to *what* Abraham believed. Faith as an action (*pisteuo*) refers to his *act* of believing.

As we have been learning, faith (and therefore hope) does not operate in a vacuum; it is "never general or abstract, but *always* the response to a concrete word of promise."[4] As the Bible understands it, faith (as action we must initiate) and hope (which flows

---

4   Beale and Carson, editors, *Commentary on the New Testament Use of the Old Testament* (Baker Academic 2007) Romans 4:1-8, p. 624, italics added; Keener, Craig S., *The Gospel Of John: A Commentary*, Volume One (Hendrickson Publishers 2003) Introduction, p. 327, citing Painter, *John*, p. 77, italics added

from faith) are *always* man's reactions to God's primary action.⁵ Properly understood, "[t]rue faith leads to an inner recognition of and complete surrender to God that expresses itself in humble obedience."⁶ When we are initially persuaded or convinced God is trustworthy, I'll call that *positional faith*.⁷ Belief begins then hope looks ahead to the supernatural fulfillment of that revelation from God. "*Hope believes the faith God imparts* and leaves the fulfillment to Him (as He sees fit)!"⁸ The result is a life walked out in *obedient faithfulness*. For purposes of our study, I'll point out that there is a place on that continuum of obedient lifestyle where initial positional faith transitions, by choice, into solid hope. Humanly speaking that line between faith and hope blurs such that they are virtually indistinguishable.⁹ Only God is able to see when that faith to hope transition occurs.

Of critical importance to our understanding of faith is the fact that both *pistis* and *pisteuo* are directly related to the word *peitho* (pi'-tho).¹⁰ The meaning of *peitho* helps orient us toward a proper understanding of faith and belief as those words are used biblically. In most cases, *peitho* means to "persuade, particularly to move or affect by kind words or motives.... Generally, to persuade

---

5   Kittel, Bromiley, and Friedrich, editors (1964–) *Theological Dictionary of the New Testament* (Eerdmans) (electronic ed.) p. 18. Exported from Logos Bible Software, 12/27/18
6   Cockerill, Gareth Lee, *The Epistle to the Hebrews*, New International Commentary on the New Testament (Eerdmans 2012) Hebrews 11:7, p. 532
7   The phrase "positional *pistis*" is not used in the Bible. I use the term here simply to aid our understanding of how faith operates.
8   Hill, Gary, *The Discovery Bible*, HELPS Ministries, Inc., [G]1680 *elpís* under Observations, 2, *Reflection*, italics in original
9   Schreiner, Thomas R., *Romans*, 2nd edition, Baker Exegetical Commentary on the New Testament (Baker Academic 1998, 2018) Romans 4:18, p. 245
10 Hill, Gary, *The Discovery Bible*, HELPS Ministries, Inc., [G]4102 *pistis*; [G]4100 *pisteúō*

another to receive a belief, meaning to convince."[11] Accordingly, *peitho* refers to being *"swayed from one opinion to the opinion held by another."*[12] It fundamentally refers to inner persuasion of trustworthiness.[13] Someone who is said to have acted *in faith* acts on the basis of having been divinely persuaded. In other words, *peitho* flows into obedience as the result of persuasion.[14] Obedience *always* stems from faith (the result of being persuaded by God) and true biblical faith *always* leads to obedience.[15] When God's revelation finds a home in our heart and we act on what we have come to believe "divine approval is the primary consequence of [that] faith."[16]

"Faith requires a singleness of commitment that draws us from doubt and wavering."[17] On the other hand, disobedience indicates a refusal to be persuaded which results in withholding belief. Unbelief begins in the heart but is revealed in concrete action which evidences a refusal to trust God.[18] God's word must be met with a heart condition of belief (*pisteuo*) to produce the intended result.[19]

---

11 Zodhiates, Spiros, *The Complete Word Study Dictionary: New Testament* (AMG Publishers 1992) word #3982, p. 1134
12 Renner, Rick, *Sparkling Gems from the Greek* (Harrison House Publishers 2003) November 14, p. 867
13 Hill, Gary, *The Discovery Bible*, HELPS Ministries, Inc., [G]3982 *peithō*
14 *Hebrews 3:18-19 Commentary*, Precept Austin, citing Vincent, M. R., *Word Studies in the New Testament*, Vol. 2, pp. 1-109. Retrieved from https://www.preceptaustin.org/hebrews_318-19 (last accessed August 8, 2021)
15 Cockerill, Gareth Lee, *The Epistle to the Hebrews*, New International Commentary on the New Testament (Eerdmans 2012) Hebrews 3:12, p. 183
16 *Holman Christian Standard Bible*, Study Bible edition (Holman Bible Publishers 2010) study note Hebrews 11:1-40, p. 2126
17 *Spirit Filled Life Bible* (Thomas Nelson 1991) Truth-In-Action through Psalms (Book Two: Psalms 42-72) under *4 Key Lessons in Faith*, p. 815
18 Hebrews 3:18, Cockerill, Gareth Lee, *The Epistle to the Hebrews*, New International Commentary on the New Testament (Eerdmans 2012) Hebrews 3:12, p. 183
19 The author of Hebrews warns that even when the Good News of the gospel has been proclaimed it will have no effect if "those who heard it did not combine it with trust (Hebrews 4:2 CJB)."

The fact that the root of *pistis* (faith) is a word that means to persuade or be persuaded signals the core meaning of faith in the Bible. At its very core faith (*pistis*) refers to "the Lord's inworked (inbirthed) persuasion."[20] Because it is always our choice to initiate belief and then continue to believe God, it is possible for a Christ-follower to have faith without hope. However, because faith is the starting place for hope, he can never choose biblical hope without first having faith. That truth leads us to dig deeper into this idea that underlying both faith and hope is the concept of persuasion. I'll begin with a very natural question: "Why do we need to be persuaded?" The answer is simple: persuasion is necessary because God's revelation is always of things we can't yet *see*. As a matter of fact, the very definition of biblical revelation is associated with the idea of revealing, uncovering, or disclosing something. Revelation denotes bringing to light that which had been previously hidden.[21] Even so, that which is brought to light in the form of a promise remains unseen by our natural senses.[22] If we could *see* it we wouldn't need to be persuaded, nor would we need faith or hope, because we could immediately experience the revelation with one or more of our five senses.

"The goal of revelation is the *internalization* of God's word in our hearts so as to [presently] transform our way of life."[23] God is highly motivated for us to share in what He sees, but the fact remains that the fulfillment of His promise is completely invisible when He first speaks of it. The process that He uses to help us *see* is to give us His revelation. As we line up with that revelation by taking it into our heart, incubating it and nurturing it we begin

---

20 Hill, Gary, *The Discovery Bible*, HELPS Ministries, Inc., [G]4102 *pístis*, quoting Gleason Archer
21 Hebrew word *galah* {gaw-law'} means to reveal, to uncover, remove. The Greek word *apokalupsis* {ap-ok-al'-oop-sis} refers to disclosing truth which was unknown.
22 By natural senses I mean: taste, smell, touch, hearing, sight
23 Longman III and Garland, general editors, *The Expositor's Bible Commentary: Psalms*, Vol. 5, Revised Edition (Zondervan 2008) *Reflections on the Word of God* under *"Law,"* p. 220, italics in original

to see what God sees. When we are persuaded, our trust in God's promise *sets before our eyes things that are invisible.*[24] We'll perceptively see that which has been promised with spiritual eyes even though it is still invisible to our natural senses. Our continuing act of forward-facing belief is called *hope* – the confident expectation of ultimately obtaining that which God has promised.

The revelation that contains persuasion and invites faith can be sudden and dramatic as a one-time event or a slowly dawning realization like softly falling snow which builds up over time. Let's return to our example of Abraham. As we've seen, Scripture records that God spoke the promise of a son directly to Abraham. Since faith in its noun form (*pistis*) refers to *what* is believed and what Abraham believed was the revelation from God in the form of a promise, then it was the *revelation* itself that contained the persuasion. But how can revelation contain persuasion?

The fact that God's word is living and powerful is an undeniable biblical truth. We first see this truth in the Genesis creation narrative. Remember all God had to do was speak and the world was shaped by the creative power of His word. In a very familiar New Testament verse, the author of Hebrews calls God's word "living and active and full of energizing power."

> For the word of God is living and active *and* full of power [making it operative, energizing, and effective]. It is sharper than any two-edged sword, penetrating as far as the division of the soul and spirit [the completeness of a person], and of both joints and marrow [the deepest parts of our nature], exposing *and* judging the very thoughts and intentions of the heart. Hebrews 4:12 AMP, italics in original

---

[24] *Geneva Bible* (Tolle Lege Press 1599) Hebrews 11:1, Footnote a., italics added. Retrieved from BibleGateway, 1599 Geneva Bible (GNV) (last accessed April 12, 2022)

God's word, just like God Himself, is both "living" and "active" therefore His word is effective in all it does.[25] God's living word has a penetrating quality and this penetrating power discerns or judges all that goes on in the human heart. It is at the same time an energizing and effective power for persuasion and even creation to accomplish God's purpose. Let's continue with the author of Hebrews to see how he understands the persuasive power of God's word.

> Now **faith** [*pistis*] is the **reality** [*hupostasis*] of what is hoped for, the **proof** [*elegchos*] of what is not seen. Hebrews 11:1 HCSB, bold added

Here we learn that faith, as a noun, is both the reality *and* the proof of things we cannot see. At first blush, it seems inconsistent to say that something we trust, *but cannot yet see*, can be described as "proof." Our Word Study will help clear up the confusion.

Word Study

The Greek word translated as **proof** *in Hebrews 11:1 is elegchos {el'-eng-khos}. Other common translations are conviction or evidence. The root verb is elegcho which can refer to exposing something or bringing it to the light.*[26]

BDAG, a leading Greek Lexicon, identifies the primary definition of elegchos as "the act of presenting evidence for the truth of someth[ing], proof, proving."[27] *Thayer's, another*

---

25 Cockerill, Gareth Lee, *The Epistle to the Hebrews*, New International Commentary on the New Testament (Eerdmans 2012) Hebrews 4:12, p. 215
26 Hill, Gary, *The Discovery Bible*, HELPS Ministries, Inc., [G]1651 *elégxō*
27 Bauer-Danker, *Greek-English Lexicon of the NT (BDAG)*, entry for 2482 ἔλεγχος. Retrieved from BibleWorks 9.0 software

> *well-known Greek Lexicon, lists the primary definition as "1. a proof, that by which a thing is proved or tested."*[28]

In Hebrews 11:1 *elegchos* indicates "an inner conviction that is not based on visible matters."[29] It is "the inward conviction from God that what He has promised, He will perform."[30] The author of Hebrews is using *elegchos* to refer to something that happens supernaturally. The *Holman New Testament Commentary* compares the convicting faith that is spiritually feasible with the conviction possible because of our natural eyesight.[31]

> Eyesight produces a conviction about objects in the physical world. Faith produces the same convictions for the invisible order.

In other words, whereas our physical eyes can provide proof or evidence of what is visible in the natural, faith supernaturally empowers us to see what is invisible.

> Faith does not do the convincing, but God, for the whole point in Hebrews is that faith stands on the revelation, word, promise of God. Faith is the divinely given

---

28 Thayer, *Greek-English Lexicon of the NT*, entry for *1747 ἔλεγχος*. Retrieved from BibleWorks 9.0 software
29 *Holman Christian Standard Bible*, Study Bible edition (Holman Bible Publishers 2010) study note Hebrews 11:1-40, p. 2126
30 *Conviction (1650) elegchos*, Sermon Index.net, quoting Wiersbe. Retrieved from https://img.sermonindex.net/modules/articles/article_pdf.php?aid=33754 (last accessed November 3, 2021)
31 *Conviction (1650) elegchos*, Sermon Index.net, citing *Holman New Testament Commentary*. Retrieved from https://img.sermonindex.net/modules/articles/article_pdf.php?aid=33754 (last accessed November 3, 2021)

conviction of things unseen and is thus the assurance of what is hoped for.[32]

The presence of God-given faith in one's heart is conviction enough that He will keep His Word.[33]

Our next word to consider in Hebrews 11:1 is the word translated as "reality." The Greek word is *hupostasis* {hoop-os'-tas-is} which was commonly used in ancient business documents as the basis or guarantee of transactions. We see this ancient understanding in the way in which the *Amplified Bible* renders this verse by referring to assurance as "the title-deed of things hoped for."

> Now faith is **the assurance (title deed, confirmation)** of things hoped for (**divinely guaranteed**), and the evidence of things not seen [the conviction of their reality—faith comprehends as fact what cannot be experienced by the physical senses]. Hebrews 11:1 AMP, bold added

Notice in the *Amplified Bible* that which is "hoped for" is considered to be "divinely guaranteed." That truth leads us right into a discussion of Isaiah 55:8-11, our Key Scripture for this lesson. I want to hone in on verse 11. We'll begin by restating that portion of our Key Scripture.

> "… So will the words that come out of my mouth not come back empty-handed. They'll do the work I sent them to do, they'll **complete** the assignment I gave them…." Isaiah 55:8-11 MSG, bold added

---

32 Bromiley, Geoffrey W., *Theological Dictionary of the New Testament*, Abridged in One Volume (Eerdmans 1985) entry for *elencho* under *elenchos, elenxis, elegmos*, p. 222

33 *Conviction (1650) elegchos*, Sermon Index.net, quoting Wiersbe. Retrieved from https://img.sermonindex.net/modules/articles/article_pdf.php?aid=33754 (last accessed November 3, 2021)

The word "complete" (highlighted in bold) is the Hebrew word `asah` {aw-saw'}. It is also commonly rendered as "accomplish." Its central idea is "performing an activity with a distinct purpose, a moral obligation, or a goal in view."[34] It is also the Hebrew word used in Genesis for God's creative power.[35] "With the utterance the result is achieved."[36]

God's word is the "unfailing agent" of His will.[37] As we previously pointed out, Genesis makes clear that by His word God commands nature and when He does nature responds. God's "word is to have the same effect on His people that it has on nature. They must be responsive to His royal will."[38] His "words have assignments on them, they have power in them to create what He wants created."[39] If we widen our lens and return to the entire Key Scripture for this lesson we will notice that God uses the rain, seed and farmer as His comparative. That comparison is used intentionally. As scholar J. Alec Motyer points out: [40]

> The parallel between the life agency of rain and the effective word is exact. Each has a heavenly origin and power of effectiveness and neither fails.... As the rain furnishes both seed and bread, so the word of God plants the seed of ... [whatever His heart desires] in the [recep-

---

34 Baker and Carpenter, *The Complete WordStudy Dictionary of the Old Testament* (AMG Publishers 2003) word #6213, p. 876
35 See Genesis 1:7,11,12,16,25,26,31; 2:2,4,8; 3:1
36 Spence-Jones & Exell, general editors, *The Pulpit Commentary, Isaiah 55:11*. Retrieved from Hill, Gary, *The Discovery Bible*, HELPS Ministries, Inc.
37 Motyer, J. Alec, *The Prophecy of Isaiah: An Introduction & Commentary* (InterVarsity Press 1993) Isaiah 55:10-11, p. 458
38 Longman III and Garland, general editors, *The Expositor's Bible Commentary: Psalms*, Vol. 5, Revised Edition (Zondervan 2008) Psalm 147:19-20, p. 1001
39 Quoting Dutch Sheets, panel discussion aired on govictory.com/Flashpoint, January 7, 2021
40 Motyer, J. Alec, *The Prophecy of Isaiah: An Introduction & Commentary* (InterVarsity Press 1993) Isaiah 55:10-11, pp. 457-458

tive human] heart and feeds the ... [one who hears and obeys] with the blessed consequences ... [that revelation] produces.

Remember God's word is living. "The relationship of hope and faith is like a *seed* stored for the harvest."[41] *Pistis* (faith) is the implanted word in the "soil" of Abraham's heart which contains God's persuasive power. That revelation-promise from God was alive – it was like a seed with life in it. It was pregnant with God's persuasion of what was in His perfect will.

Because Abraham's heart was receptive, his heart was conducive to becoming a womb, an incubator, for God's persuasive word. Abraham's welcoming heart must then hold on to that promise until the fullness of time comes on God's Kingdom calendar. At the time specified by God, His promise will be fulfilled and Abraham's son will be born. We could say that *faith* initially connected Abraham to the promise that God had made, but *hope* was the glue that kept him connected until God fulfilled His word.

Let's see how these biblical principles of promise work together in the gospel message of salvation. We find our two faith-related concepts of *pistis* and *pisteuo* in Paul's letter to the Romans:

> But what does it say? "THE WORD IS NEAR YOU, IN YOUR MOUTH AND IN YOUR HEART"—that is, the word of **faith** [*pistis*] which we are preaching, that if you confess with your mouth Jesus *as* Lord, and **believe** [*pisteuo*] in your heart that God raised Him from the dead, you will be saved; for with the heart a person **believes** [*pisteuo*], resulting in righteousness, and with the mouth he confesses, resulting in salvation. Romans 10:8-10, bold added

Paul says God extends a promise of salvation (faith/*pistis* - revelation that can only be initiated by God). That faith is intended

---

41 Hill, Gary, *The Discovery Bible*, HELPS Ministries, Inc., [G]1680 *elpís* under Observations, 2, *Reflection*, italics in original

to elicit *pisteuo* (belief, trust). When that revelation finds its home in a person's heart their heart becomes like a womb-incubator for God's persuasive word in its seed form. That welcoming heart must then hold on to the promise of salvation until the fullness of time comes on God's Kingdom calendar. In other words, the gospel message works just like the revelation-promise that found its home in Abraham's heart. Abraham had to keep faith alive (even hoping against all hope) in order to permit that implanted seed to give full birth to the life that was in it. In the same way, every Christ-follower must persist in faith in order to permit the seed of the gospel promise to give full birth to the life contained in it.[42] That seed-promise contains the power for resurrection life! If that seed is not retained full term in the heart's womb-incubator, it cannot sprout and give birth to the fullness of the promise contained within it. As with Abraham, *faith* initially connects us to the promise God made, but *hope* is the glue that keeps us connected until God fulfills His word.

We have been focusing on the creative power that is contained in the living word of God's promise. Before we conclude this lesson, it is important to consider the nature of the God who made the promise. The *Theological Wordbook of the Old Testament* points out: "That which is hoped for is not some desideratum [something that is needed or wanted] arising from one's imagination but in God Himself and whatever He should purpose to accomplish."[43]

The prophet Isaiah deals with the "basic question of where authority and rule lie in world events. He will reply that all events originate in heaven, all individuals are stirred and guided by the Lord, all empires rise and fall at His direction: there is no other ultimate agent."[44] Isaiah declares that the Lord governs all nations (Isaiah 40:15-17), is the Ruler of all rulers (Isaiah 40:21-24) and

---

42 See the parable of the sower which compares the gospel to a seed sown by a farmer. Matthew 13:1-15; Mark 4:1-12; Luke 8:4-10

43 Harris, Archer, and Waltke, editors, *Theological Wordbook of the Old Testament* (Moody Press 1999) word #859, p. 374

44 Motyer, J. Alec, *The Prophecy of Isaiah: An Introduction & Commentary* (InterVarsity Press 1993) Isaiah 41:2-4, p. 309

The Power of Hope

has no rival god who is able to challenge or hinder Him (Isaiah 40:18-20). He is King over the entire universe!

> "… I am God, and there is no other; I *am* God, and there is no one like Me, Declaring the end from the beginning …. Saying, 'My purpose will be established, And I will accomplish [`asah*]⁴⁵ all My good pleasure' …." Isaiah 46:9-10, italics in original

Isaiah 41:8-20 pictures Yahweh as the exclusive director/administrator of *all* history.⁴⁶ That unchangeable truth serves as a guarantee for **every** promise He makes. God's nature and sovereign rule provide a solid unshakeable ground for trusting His divine promises. Faith can look seemingly unsupportive facts squarely in the face and still trust because God is worthy of trust! If we return to our Word Study on *pisteuo* (believe, trust) we will see that the very definition of this word presumes trust in the one who makes the promise. A few quick quotes from our prior Word Study will help you see what I mean:

> *Pisteuo* - "to entrust oneself to someone or something in complete confidence: [translated as] believe (in), trust, with the implication of total commitment to the one who is trusted."

The ground for all biblical hope lies in the covenantal character and integrity of Yahweh.⁴⁷ His character was revealed in Exodus 34 as He passed in front of Moses and declared:

> "The LORD, the LORD God, compassionate and gracious, slow to anger, and abounding in lovingkind-

---

45 Same word we discussed in Isaiah 55:11
46 Motyer, J. Alec, *Isaiah*, Tyndale Old Testament Commentaries (IVP Academic 1999) Isaiah 41:1-7, p. 283
47 Exodus 34:5-7; Longman III and Garland, general editors, *The Expositor's Bible Commentary: Psalms*, Vol. 5, Revised Edition (Zondervan 2008) *Reflections: The Perfections of Yahweh*, p. 271

ness and truth; who keeps lovingkindness for thousands, who forgives iniquity, transgression and sin ...." Exodus 34:6b-7a

Henri Louis Goulet, my research mentor, restates that passage in his own words like this, "YHWH! YHWH! God compassionate and gracious; slow to anger; abounding in *chesed* (loyal lovingkindness and *emet* trustworthiness); habituating *chesed* for the thousands and forgiving mistake and wrongfulness and sin."[48] That's quite a mouthful so it will be helpful to park here for a moment and look at God's self-disclosure a little more closely. When we break it down, much of what Yahweh revealed to Moses is pretty straightforward. His habit is to be compassionate, gracious, not quick to become angry and forgiving. What most likely requires a bit more elaboration is the idea of His *chesed* (also commonly transliterated as *hesed*).

Hesed is considered to be one of the richest and most theologically insightful words in the entire Old Testament. It is employed about 245 times. Attempts to adequately define this Hebrew word have filled scholarly articles, dissertations and even entire books. That fact attests both to its theological importance and yet to the difficulty of accurately and concretely pinning down the fullness of its meaning.[49] As a result, a simple Word Study cannot possibly do the word justice, but it will serve our purpose here by giving us a starting point for understanding *hesed* as it describes God's character.

---

48   Goulet, Henri Louis, *What is Biblical 'Faith'? Beyond Easy Believism and Cheap Grace,* Messianic Studies Institute Online Course, December, 2020

49   Kynes, Will, *God's Grace in the Old Testament: Considering the Hesed of the Lord,* University of Cambridge, Knowing & Doing C. S. Lewis Institute, 2010 (Ph.D. Candidate)

Word Study

*There is no one-word English equivalent for hesed. However, the Theological Wordbook of the Old Testament suggests that "'**lovingkindness**' [meaning tender and benevolent affection] is not far from the fullness of meaning" of hesed.*[50] *Hesed basically refers to acts of kindness initiated in the context of relationship and the reciprocal repayment with acts of kindness.*[51]

"Dr. [Gleason] Archer was known to have said that he thought hesed was the single most difficult biblical word to translate fully. He ended up saying the closest was the hyphenated term 'covenant-loyalty' and then went on to [explain] that it is often translated as goodness, kindness, faithfulness, etc. but that's because [it is] the outcome of God's covenant-loyalty. Because [God] is always loyal to His covenant, we perceive it as goodness, kindness, faithfulness, etc."[52]

A recurring biblical description of God's nature as He relates to His covenant partner Israel is that He *"abounds in hesed."*[53] Even

---

50   Harris, Archer Jr., and Waltke, editors, *Theological Wordbook of the Old Testament* (Moody Press 1999) word #698, p. 307
51   Tigay, Jeffrey H., *The JPS Torah Commentary: Deuteronomy*, The Traditional Hebrew Text with the New JPS Translation Commentary (The Jewish Publication Society 1996) Deuteronomy 5:10 under *showing kindness*, p. 67
52   Joan Winchell, Email to Deborah Roeger July 5, 2022. Joan's explanation is based on her first-hand knowledge.
53   See for example: Exodus 34:6; Nehemiah 9:17; Psalm 103:8; Jonah 4:2; Lamentations 3:22

when she acts unfaithfully, He acts in covenant fidelity.[54] "When [*hesed*] is used of God it denotes that deep commitment of God to His people that reaches out beyond the mere demands of reciprocal obligation such as those specified by law or custom."[55]

God's response to His promises is set by His self-revealed character and driven by His internal consistency to the character He has revealed.[56] The Bible declares that it is "for the sake of His Name" that God acts on behalf of His covenant people and keeps the promises He has made to them.[57] It is important to understand that in the culture of the ancient Hebrews a name "signifies all that is essentially true of a person."[58] In the world of the Bible, a person's name was more than an identifying label, it was "that which sums up and expresses the inner 'real' truth about a person."[59] God's character and reputation are reflected in His actions. Because God is in sovereign control of history and He *always* acts in a way that is completely consistent with His character, the Psalms can confidently declare God's faithfulness to all generations:

> For the LORD is good; His lovingkindness is everlasting And His faithfulness to all generations. Psalm 100:5

---

54 Longman III and Garland, general editors, *The Expositor's Bible Commentary: Psalms*, Vol. 5, Revised Edition (Zondervan 2008) Psalm 103:7-10, p. 759

55 Thompson, J. A., *The Book of Jeremiah*, The New International Commentary on The Old Testament (Eerdmans 1980) Jeremiah 9:22-23, p. 319

56 Block, Daniel I., *The Book of Ezekiel Chapters 1-24*, The New International Commentary on the Old Testament (Eerdmans 1997) E. Messages Of Sin And Retribution ([Ezekiel] 17:1-22:31) under *Theological Implications*, p. 658

57 See for example: Psalm 23:3; 25:11; 31:3; 79:9; 106:8; 109:21; 143:11; Isaiah 48:9; Ezekiel 20:44; 36:22. See Thompson, J. A., *The Book of Jeremiah*, The New International Commentary on The Old Testament (Eerdmans 1980) Jeremiah 14:7, p. 380 for similar list

58 Motyer, J. Alec, *The Prophecy of Isaiah: An Introduction & Commentary* (InterVarsity Press 1993) Isaiah 65:15-16d, p. 528

59 Motyer, J. Alec, *The Prophecy of Isaiah: An Introduction & Commentary* (InterVarsity Press 1993) Isaiah 66:22, p. 543

The Power of Hope

> For the word of the LORD is upright, And all His work is *done* in faithfulness. Psalm 33:4, italics in original

We need to address the "elephant in the room" before we move on. In His wisdom, God created a world that allows every person free choice. How is it possible then to have a confident expectation based on God's sovereignty if people also have free choice? How do we reconcile these two biblical truths? Chuck Smith, the founder of Calvary Chapel, says it well when he teaches there are some things God never asks us to understand or to reconcile.[60]

> We need to believe both of them through faith, because I can't keep them in balance by my [human] understanding. I don't understand how they come together. But I do believe them both. I believe God is sovereign, and I also believe I'm responsible and God holds me responsible for the choices I make. I simply trust God that both assertions of Scripture are true.

We may *desire* greater understanding, but the good news is when we trust God we don't *need* to understand. To say that differently, understanding is **not** a prerequisite to faith. The unchanging character of God permits us to hold on to our faith by choice despite what we don't comprehend. I find J. Alec Motyer's comment about the "two sides" of God's wisdom particularly insightful:[61]

> [D]ivine wisdom is hard for humans to understand because it always has 'two sides'. That is, while perfectly coherent in itself it is always more than we can see at any given time.

---

60 Smith, Chuck, *Calvary Chapel Distinctives: The Foundational Principles of the Calvary Chapel Movement* (The Word For Today Publishers 2019, 11th printing) p. 53, see also p. 119

61 Motyer, J. Alec, *The Prophecy of Isaiah: An Introduction & Commentary* (InterVarsity Press 1993) Isaiah 40:2, p. 299, citing Dhorme

Remember we are not trusting blindly. The fact of the matter is that biblical hope amounts to trusting in that which we have *yet* to experience based upon evidence gained from what we have *already* experienced. So, the first reason we can have hope is because we choose to believe the Bible when it assures us of God's Sovereignty. The second truth that enables our hope is that God remains faithful to His people because He has obligated Himself by covenant to do so.

> Understand, therefore, that the LORD your God is indeed God. He is the faithful God who keeps his covenant for a thousand generations and lavishes his unfailing love on those who love him and obey his commands. Deuteronomy 7:9 NLT

Who then has the right and privilege of standing firm in trust on the promises of God? The clear answer of the Bible is that it is one in a covenant relationship with Him and remains faithful to that covenant. We see this covenantal qualification clearly stated by David in Psalm 18.

> With the faithful [*hasid*] You prove Yourself faithful; with the blameless [*tamim*] man You prove Yourself blameless. Psalm 18:25 HCSB

Because word definitions are essential to fully understand Psalm 18:25, let's consider brief definitions for both of these Hebrew words.

With the faithful [hasid]: The word *hasid* (also transliterated *chasad*) {khaw-seed'} is a derivative word of *hesed*. One who is *hasid* is a faithful follower of Yahweh. His faithfulness is demonstrated by his actions. He makes a habit of doing

The Power of Hope

what is right (what is expected in the context of covenant relationship) in God's eyes.[62]

with the blameless [tamim] man: Blameless does not refer to being sinless, it denotes faithfulness to God.[63] In its verb form *tamim* {taw-meem'} denotes completeness which naturally moves "toward that which is ethically sound, upright" and refers to belonging completely to God.[64] *Tamim* is the standard term in the Psalms for God's servants. It could be translated as "loyal."[65]

What the psalmist is referring to here is character that is measured by faithfulness in keeping God's commands.[66] The psalmist is conveying the biblical truth that God is faithful to those who are in covenant relationship with Him and "are concerned with being 'faithful' ... 'beloved,' 'loyal'... 'blameless,' and 'pure'...."[67] This truth provides rock-solid ground for hope to all who keep God's commandments.

One final word before we move on to Lesson 4. The church in America rarely thinks in terms of our covenant relationship with God. Therefore, a quick overview may be helpful here. God made a covenant with Abraham, restated to Isaac and then restated to

---

62 *NET Bible Notes*, translator's note 73, Psalm 18:25. See: Psalm 4:3; 12:1; 16:10; 31:23; 37:28; 86:2; 97:10. See also: *Holman Christian Standard Bible*, Study Bible edition (Holman Bible Publishers 2010) *Word Study*, entry for *chesed*, p. 1009 stating the use of *chasad* in Psalm 18:25 "means *prove oneself faithful,*" italics in original

63 *Holman Christian Standard Bible*, Study Bible edition (Holman Bible Publishers 2010) study note Psalm 18:20-24 under *blameless*, p. 897

64 Harris, Archer, and Waltke, editors, *Theological Wordbook of the Old Testament* (Moody Press 1999) word #2522d, pp. 973-974

65 Kidner, Derek, *Psalms 1-72: An Introduction and Commentary*, Tyndale Old Testament Commentaries (IVP Academic 1973) Psalm 18:25, p. 111

66 *Holman Christian Standard Bible*, Study Bible edition (Holman Bible Publishers 2010) study note Psalm 18:20-24, p. 897; See for example: "May my heart be blameless regarding Your statutes so that I will not be put to shame." Psalm 119:80 HCSB

67 Longman III and Garland, general editors, *The Expositor's Bible Commentary: Psalms*, Vol. 5, Revised Edition (Zondervan 2008) Psalm 18:25-26, p. 208, Scripture references omitted

Jacob (who was renamed Israel). The patriarchs knew Him as a covenantal God. When God led the Hebrew people out of Egyptian captivity during the exodus, He was acting because He was in a covenant relationship with their forefathers.

Remember it was in Exodus that God revealed His attributes to Moses and central to His character was covenant making and covenant keeping. After all of Israel had left Egypt and traveled to the foot of Mt. Sinai, God entered into a covenant relationship with the entire nation. The people responded that they would keep that covenant, obeying all that God had commanded them. The Bible records their repeated failure to do so. Against the backdrop of the Babylonian exile, the prophet Jeremiah was the first to announce God's *renewed* covenant with Israel. That "new" covenant was described as follows:

> "Behold, days are coming," declares the LORD, "when I will make a new covenant with the house of Israel and with the house of Judah, not like the covenant which I made with their fathers in the day I took them by the hand to bring them out of the land of Egypt, My covenant which they broke, although I was a husband to them," declares the LORD. "But this is the covenant which I will make with the house of Israel after those days," declares the LORD, "I will put My law within them and on their heart I will write it; and I will be their God, and they shall be My people. They will not teach again, each man his neighbor and each man his brother, saying, 'Know the LORD,' for they will all know Me, from the least of them to the greatest of them," declares the LORD, "for I will forgive their iniquity, and their sin I will remember no more." Jeremiah 31:31-34

In his letter to the Romans, the Apostle Paul makes clear that all Gentile Christ-followers (that is you if you are not of Jewish heritage) are grafted into this new covenant God made with Israel

(Romans 11:17). What that means is that everyone who has been born again by accepting God's gift of salvation is in a covenant relationship with God. Shout Hallelujah because when you are faithful to that covenant relationship, you have the guarantee that God will fulfill every promise He makes to you!

In our next lesson, we will look at the second element of the three-stranded cord which defines biblical hope: the Promise Keeper's Appointed Time.

Hear What The Spirit is Saying to the Church: *Indeed do I invite you to shout Hallelujah! I desire my people to understand the truth that my only expectation of them is to be faithful to the covenant I have with them. When they are faithful, it allows me to be faithful. That blesses me!*

LESSON 4:

THE PROMISE KEEPER'S
APPOINTED TIME

"[B]ut when the appointed time arrived, God sent forth his Son. He was born from a woman ... so that he might redeem ... and thus enable us to be made God's sons." Galatians 4:4-5 CJB

IN OUR LAST lesson we looked at the first of the three elements which are woven together in the very essence and definition of biblical hope. In sum, we learned that before you can have hope you must first have a promise from God. "So then the faith is by a report, and the report through a saying of God."[1] Without a promise as the foundation of hope, you will dead-end into misguided optimism. We also learned that what makes hope in the promise of God so secure is who God is, His very nature is to accomplish His word. His faithfulness leaves no excuse for unbelief! In this lesson, we want to unpack the second component of hope: the Promise Keeper's appointed time.

As a young girl, I couldn't wait to curl up and read the latest *Nancy Drew* mystery as soon as I got my hands on it. While I loved them, the suspense in those mysteries often kept me on edge sometimes to the point of fear. To move past that fear, I had to keep pushing ahead page after page, chapter after chapter. I did so because from past experience I knew with certainty it would all work out in the end. However, in the pages between the beginning and the end, I was on the edge of my seat so-to-speak. On the other

---

1 Romans 10:17 YLT, *The English Young's Literal Translation of the Holy Bible* 1862/1887/1898 by J. N. Young (Public Domain)

hand, let's assume you asked the author Carolyn Keene,[2] whether those mysteries kept her on the edge of her seat wondering how it would all turn out. There is no doubt her answer would be a resolute and self-confident, "No!" Why could we be certain of her answer? Because she wrote the script. God is the same way. He is not sitting on the edge of His seat wondering if a promise He made will be fulfilled. When He speaks, He acts. He wrote the script and His script includes an appointed time in which every promise will be fulfilled.

Even so, it is important to understand that God's method of reckoning time is not the same as ours.[3] He is not time-bound in the same way that we are. The very first chapter of Genesis makes clear that time had a beginning. Because God initiated time, He is outside of time.[4] He is master over time and is not constrained in any way by it. Therefore, God can (and most likely will) speak a word of instruction or promise without indicating *when* it is to occur. Because His word is not time-bound, it sounds to us like an imminent command/promise – but in reality, it could be days, weeks, months, even years before its complete fulfillment. This is important to understand. If we don't know that God's concept of time and ours are often vastly different, it will be all too easy for the enemy to convince us of his lies. Satan will be able to confuse us with deceiving statements like, "You did not hear God speak" when you actually did, or "God is late in delivering on His promise

---

2   Mildred A. Wirt Benson used the pen name Carolyn Keene and was paid $125 per book to write the *Nancy Drew* series for *The Stratemeyer Syndicate*. Kennedy, Elizabeth, *Mildred Wirt Benson, aka Carolyn Keene Biography*, ThoughtCo., updated on January 30, 2020. Retrieved from https://www.thoughtco.com/mildred-wirt-benson-author-bio-626287 (last accessed January 25, 2022)

3   Block, Daniel I., *The Book of Ezekiel: Chapters 1-24,* The New International Commentary on the Old Testament (Eerdmans 1997) B. Prophecy – True And False ([Ezekiel] 12:21-14:11) under *Theological Implications,* p. 393

4   Hodge, Bodie, *Is God Bound By Time?* May 19, 2006, Answers in Genesis.org. Retrieved from https://answersingenesis.org/who-is-god/is-god-bound-by-time/ (last accessed August 8, 2021)

and therefore cannot be trusted" which is never true. Remember Jesus said that there is no truth in Satan, "When he lies, he speaks out of his own character, for he is a liar and the father of lies (John 8:44b ESV)."

Let's return to the promise God made to Abraham about a son who would be his heir. When God first made that promise He did not set any particular time boundary on it. It seems it could have happened at any time – perhaps even within the first nine months after the promise was given. However, we know from Scripture that Abraham waited about 24 years before God made the announcement that did carry His specific time stamp. Let's think about this for a minute. Because Abraham did not know *when* God would do what He said he would do, Abraham would have awakened, lived his life that day and retired at the end of the day more than 8,700 times[5] not knowing if *that* would be the day he would begin to see tangible evidence of God's promise. As far as Abraham knew, any one of those days could have been the day Sarah announced she was expecting the child of promise. After about 8,760 days had passed, God announced to Abraham that Isaac would be born in a year (Genesis 18:10).

> "… Is anything too difficult for the LORD? **At the appointed time** I will return to you, at this time next year, and Sarah will have a son." Genesis 18:14, bold added

Afterwards the author of Genesis tells us that God was right on time in fulfilling that promise to Abraham and Sarah:

> So Sarah conceived and bore a son to Abraham in his old age, **at the appointed time** of which God had spoken to him. Genesis 21:2, bold added

In both verses, the phrase "at the appointed time" (highlighted in bold) is a translation of the Hebrew noun *mow`ed* {mo-ade'} or *mo`ed* {mo-ade'}. It derives from the verb *ya'ad* meaning to

---

[5] Twenty-four years multiplied by 365 days per year is 8,760 days.

appoint or fix.[6] When God reiterated the promise to Abraham it came with a God-ordained time stamp – God's set time for fulfillment. When God reveals the desire of His heart by making a promise it is always fulfilled according to *His* prescribed timetable. However, the Bible makes repeatedly clear that God does not always indicate the set time for fulfillment. He often simply reveals His promise and leaves us in His *Hope Waiting Room* until the fullness of time has come. Let's consider three biblical examples: Joseph, Moses and David.

JOSEPH

- As a youth, Joseph was given two dreams in which God revealed his prophetic destiny.

   > Then Joseph had a dream, and when he told it to his brothers, they hated him even more. He said to them, "Please listen to this dream which I have had; for behold, we were binding sheaves in the field, and lo, my sheaf rose up and also stood erect; and behold, your sheaves gathered around and bowed down to my sheaf." Then his brothers said to him, "Are you actually going to reign over us? Or are you really going to rule over us?" So they hated him even more for his dreams and for his words. Genesis 37:5-8

   > Now he had still another dream, and related it to his brothers, and said, "Lo, I have had still another dream; and behold, the sun and the moon and eleven stars were bowing down to me." He related *it* to his father and to his brothers; and his father rebuked him and said

---

6   *Numbers 9 Commentary*, Precept Austin. Retrieved from https://www.preceptaustin.org/numbers-9-commentary (last accessed August 8, 2021)

> to him, "What is this dream that you have had? Shall I and your mother and your brothers actually come to bow ourselves down before you to the ground?" His brothers were jealous of him, but his father kept the saying *in mind*. Genesis 37:9-11, italics in original

- The Bible gives us two reference points concerning Joseph's age. The first is found in Genesis 37:2 and the other is located in Genesis 41:46. Let's consider both references, but place a few recorded events in between them.

> These are *the records of* the generations of Jacob. Joseph, when he was **seventeen years of age**, was pasturing the flock with his brothers, while he was *still* a youth, along with the sons of Bilhah and the sons of Zilpah, his father's wives. And Joseph brought back a bad report about them to their father. Genesis 37:2, italics in original, bold added

- As we've noted Joseph had his first dream; then he had a second dream (Genesis 37:5-7;9-11).
- Joseph's brothers sold him as a slave to a caravan of Ishmaelites on their way to Egypt (Genesis 37:28).
- Joseph was purchased by Potiphar from the Ishmaelites. Potiphar was an officer of Pharaoh and captain of the guard. Joseph became a faithful servant in his household (Genesis 39:1-6).
- Joseph was falsely accused of assaulting Potiphar's wife and sent to prison (Genesis 39:12-20).
- Joseph interpreted a dream for Pharaoh and was elevated to his right-hand position at the age of 30 (Genesis 41:46).

> Now Joseph **was thirty years old** when he stood before Pharaoh, king of Egypt. And Joseph went out from the presence of Pharaoh and went through all the land of Egypt. Genesis 41:46, bold added

- From the biblical account, it seems probable that it was about 13-14 years between Joseph's dreams and the time he entered Pharaoh's service. It was some time after that when his brothers actually bowed down at his feet. One biblical timeline suggests about another 10 years had passed.[7] All in all, it appears from the biblical record that about 24 years could have elapsed between the prophetic dreams God gave Joseph and the time of their literal fulfillment.
- The psalmist shares God's perspective on the matter:

  > Until the time came to fulfill his dreams, the LORD tested Joseph's character. Psalm 105:19 NLT

- The earlier dreams of his exalted family status ultimately proved to be God's word of promise. However, the fulfillment came only after a lengthy period of trial. God was purposefully using Joseph's extended waiting season to shape Joseph's character so he could handle the assignment God had for him.

MOSES

- Our review of Moses begins at his birth. It was recorded without much fanfare in Exodus 2.

  > Now a man from the house of Levi went and married a daughter of Levi. The woman

---

[7] *The Biblical Timeline* entry for *Joseph*, thebiblicaltimeline.org. Retrieved from http://www.thebiblicaltimeline.org/joseph (last accessed August 8, 2021)

The Power of Hope

> conceived and bore a son; and when she saw that he was beautiful, she hid him for three months. Exodus 2:1-2

- The text surrounding Moses' birth does not provide any explanation for the author's comment that his mother "saw that he was beautiful ["*tob*" or "*tov*" in Hebrew]." Scholar Bruce Waltke summarizes *tob* as referring to whatever/whoever is "desirable because it/he serves the purpose for which it [/he] was made."[8]
- So, Moses began well with a purposeful God-ordained future but with no time stamp indicating the precisely appointed time God has in mind. We are left to assume Moses has a heart for that destiny when we are told that at the age of 40 he killed an Egyptian taskmaster who was beating a Hebrew slave. Once again Scripture gives us two points of reference regarding the age of Moses. We will again put these two side by side with a few significant timeline events in between.

> Moses was educated in all the learning of the Egyptians, and he was a man of power in words and deeds. But **when he was approaching the age of forty**, it entered his mind to visit his brethren, the sons of Israel. And when he saw one *of them* being treated unjustly, he defended him and took vengeance for the oppressed by striking down the Egyptian. And he supposed that his brethren understood that God was granting them deliverance through him, but they did not understand. Acts 7:22-25, italics in original, bold added

---

8 Waltke, Bruce K., *The Book of Proverbs: Chapters 1-15*, The New International Commentary on the Old Testament (Eerdmans 2004) Theology under *b. The Wise and Righteous, (1) The Wise and Righteous and Other Correlative Terms*, p. 99, citing K.-D. Schunck, *TDOT*, 5:298, s.v. *tob*

- Moses fled to Midian where he married Zipporah, had two sons and was the shepherd of his father-in-law's sheep (Exodus 2:15-22, 3:1).

   "**After forty years had passed**, an ANGEL APPEARED TO HIM IN THE WILDERNESS OF MOUNT SINAI, IN THE FLAME OF A BURNING THORN BUSH...." Acts 7:30, uppercase text in original, bold added

- At the burning bush Yahweh commissioned Moses to return to Egypt. He was instructed to confront Pharaoh and lead Abraham's descendants out of Egypt to the land God had promised to them.

   Moses was eighty years old and Aaron eighty-three, when they spoke to Pharaoh. Exodus 7:7, bold added

- Like Joseph, Moses was separated from his own people. During that season, Yahweh molded and shaped him into the leader He desired. That took 40 years so he was 80 years old when he stepped into his destiny as Israel's leader for the exodus. Moses then walked out God's perfect plan in God's appointed time, fulfilling the purpose for which He was created.

DAVID

- God directed Samuel to anoint David as the king of Israel when David was young (1 Samuel 16:13). After he was anointed, David waited about 15 years for the kingly crown to be placed on his head.
- Commentators generally suggest David was between 10 and 15 years old when he was anointed by Samuel. We are given a clue as to his age in 1 Samuel 17 which describes

David slaying Goliath. Those events appear to take place some undisclosed amount of time *after* David was commissioned as king. Even so, David is described by both King Saul and Goliath as being a "youth."

> Then Saul said to David, "You are not able to go against this Philistine to fight with him; for you are *but* a **youth** while he has been a warrior from his youth." 1 Samuel 17:33, italics in original, bold added

> When [Goliath] looked and saw David, he disdained him; for he was *but* a **youth**, and ruddy, with a handsome appearance. 1 Samuel 17:42, italics in original, bold added

- The Hebrew word that is translated as "youth" (highlighted in bold) in both 1 Samuel 17:33 and 1 Samuel 17:42 is *na`ar* {nah'-ar}. It usually describes an older teenager, one who is old enough to get married.[9] At some point in Jewish history the minimum age for a boy to marry under Jewish law was set at 13 years old, presumably reflecting past prac-

---

9 Constable, Thomas L., *Expository Notes of Dr. Thomas Constable*, 1 Samuel 17 Verses 31-40. Retrieved from https://www.studylight.org/commentaries/eng/dcc/1-samuel-17.html (last accessed August 8, 2021). The *Theological Wordbook of the Old Testament* defines *na`ar* as primarily referring to "a youngster of ages between weaning and (especially) marriageable young manhood." Harris, Archer, and Waltke, editors, *Theological Wordbook of the Old Testament* (Moody Press 1999) word #1389a, p. 586; *The Complete WordStudy Dictionary of the Old Testament* points out that *na`ar* is used "for one old enough to serve in battle ... [or] to a young male servant." Baker and Carpenter, *The Complete WordStudy Dictionary of the Old Testament* (AMG Publishers 2003) word #5288, p. 742

tice. In the second century B.C. the Talmud recommended a male marry at age 18, or somewhere between 16 and 24.[10]
- As a youth, David was brought in from the fields to serve in King Saul's court playing soothing music at the King's command (1 Samuel 16:21-22).
- Later Saul released him from that service but made him a commander in his army (1 Samuel 18:13).
- David was exceedingly successful in battle and Saul gave David his daughter to marry (1 Samuel 18:14-30).
- David fled from Saul's service when Saul threatened to harm him because the people were exalting David more than Saul (1 Samuel 18-20).
- From that time until he was crowned King over Judah (2 Samuel 2:7), David lived a life on the run from Saul, led a band of misfits, fought and won many battles (1 Samuel 21-30) and twice spared Saul's life (1 Samuel 24; 26).
- Like Joseph and Moses, David was set apart by God and refined by the fire of testing before the appointed time for His promise to be fulfilled.
- The first crown David wore was as King over the tribe of Judah. The Bible provides us with the detail that when he was finally crowned King over all of Israel he was 30 years old.[11]

> David was **thirty years old** when he became king, *and* he reigned forty years. 2 Samuel 5:4, italics in original, bold added

Although it is somewhat lengthy, I am adding a quote here from Bill Johnson's book, *Strengthen Yourself in the Lord*. It is a

---

10   *Marriage in Judaism*, jewishvirtuallibrary.org. Retrieved from https://www.jewishvirtuallibrary.org/marriage-in-judaism (last accessed April 12, 2022)

11   Initially, David was king over Judah, his own tribe. He reigned 7 ½ years over that tribe (2 Samuel 2:1-11). He was later anointed king over all Israel (2 Samuel 5:1-5). Then the throne was moved to Jerusalem and there he ruled for 33 years. Altogether his reign totaled 40 years.

very insightful characterization of what God was accomplishing in David when he permitted the challenges David faced between the time of his anointing and the perfectly appointed time the King's crown was placed on his head.

> ... the tests that David endured were tests that specifically addressed his ability to keep his focus on his identity and purpose. He was tested by coming into circumstances that directly contradicted God's Word over his life. His job was to ignore the enemy's agenda and develop the strength of character that God was after. It was like God was saying, "OK David, I've called you as a man after my own heart and anointed you to be the king of Israel. That is your destiny. Will you be a king with my heart when the man currently in your position is attacking you, chasing you and doing everything to keep you from your destiny? Will you be that king when the Jews you are supposed to rule intend to turn you over to the enemy? Will you be that king when your army consists of a bunch of losers? Will you be that king when your palace is a cave in the wilderness? And will you be that king when your closest friends disown you and threaten your life? If you can strengthen yourself in Me, then you can be trusted to be that king when all the circumstances line up."[12]

The way we know David believed God's promise of kingship was by David's actions.[13] God required David to keep acting on that promise for about 15 years before it was actualized for all the world to see. Like Joseph and Moses, David models for us biblical hope during a lengthy and difficult waiting season. These biblical accounts illustrate that it is often necessary to stay in the boat and ride out the storms God permits in order to be in the proper posi-

---

12 Johnson, Bill, *Strengthen Yourself in the Lord* (Destiny Image Publishers 2007) pp. 39-40
13 Johnson, Bill, *Strengthen Yourself in the Lord* (Destiny Image Publishers 2007) p. 40

tion at the appointed time. Nothing short of that obedient waiting enables promise fulfillment to manifest itself.

We've established the truth that every promise God makes has a set time for its fulfillment. As our Key Scripture indicates, that fact was true even for the birth of His Son!

> [B]ut **when the appointed time arrived**, God sent forth his Son. He was born from a woman .... Galatians 4:4-5 CJB, bold added

The next thing I want to look at is the fact that a critical element concerning God's set times in the Bible is the biblical principle that "time comes." There are at least 64 biblical references from Exodus to Revelation that the time had (or will) come. Let's consider a few of them.

> "... Now go, lead the people to the place I spoke of, and my angel will go before you. However, **when the time comes** for me to punish, I will punish them for their sin." Exodus 32:34 NIV, bold added

> You will arise and have compassion on Zion, for **it is time** to show favor to her; the **appointed time has come**. Psalm 102:13 NIV, bold added

> "I, the LORD, have spoken! The **time has come**, and I won't hold back. I will not change my mind, and I will have no pity on you. You will be judged on the basis of all your wicked actions, says the Sovereign LORD." Ezekiel 24:14 NLT, bold added

> The two kings, with their hearts bent on evil, will sit at the same table and lie to each other, but to no avail, because an end will still **come at the appointed time**. Daniel 11:27 NIV, bold added

"The **time has come**," he said. "The kingdom of God is near. Repent and believe the good news!" Mark 1:15 NIV, bold added

But the **time will come** when the bridegroom will be taken from them, and on that day they will fast. Mark 2:20 NIV, bold added

Be on guard! Be alert! You do not know when **that time will come**. Mark 13:33 NIV, bold added

God has an appointed time for all things in His Kingdom. Everything moves in a forward direction towards *that* set time, that strategically chosen time on God's calendar. This biblical reality is more than a minor piece of interesting Bible trivia! If you can grasp this truth it will entirely reorient your ability to hold on to hope in the waiting seasons of life.

When we are waiting for something it is common in our English language to speak of "time going by." We say things like, "there went another day!" On the other hand, God's Kingdom speaks of "time coming towards its fulfillment." A few simple word definitions will highlight that these two perspectives take our thoughts in opposite directions!

Word Study

*To say something **goes** means it leaves, departs, comes to an end, ceases to exist, disappears, is used up, it passes into a specified state, especially an undesirable one.*

*To say something **comes** means it joins in a specific activity, moves or travels towards or into a place which is thought of as near or familiar to the speaker, it arrives, reaches, or extends to a specified point.*

I encourage you to prayerfully ponder these two definitions until you *see* (with spiritual understanding) the difference. They are in fact opposites – one keeps you focused in forward movement and the other leads to what repeatedly seems like a dead end. With each subsequent dead-end hope diminishes. The truth, however, is that when you have a promise from God *every* day you live brings you another day closer to that appointed time God has inscribed on His calendar with a permanent marker.

We have already noted that even the birth of the Messiah was in fulfillment of its set time! We will conclude our lesson with that promise fulfilled *right on-time*. Because God loves to reveal His secret counsel to His prophets, approximately seven hundred years before Christ was born His place of birth was disclosed:

> "But as for you, Bethlehem Ephrathah, *Too* little to be among the clans of Judah, From you One will go forth for Me to be ruler in Israel. His goings forth are from long ago, From the days of eternity." Micah 5:2, italics in original

About the same time, Isaiah prophetically revealed the reality of His human birth and His divine nature (Isaiah 9:6-7). Isaiah also announced that one of the names He would be given is *Immanuel*, meaning God with us:

> Therefore the Lord Himself will give you a sign: Behold, a virgin will be with child and bear a son, and she will call His name Immanuel. Isaiah 7:14

Then at the appointed time, in the first century A.D., Christ initiated His earthly ministry with these words:

> ... "**The time is fulfilled**, and the kingdom of God is at hand; repent and believe in the gospel." Mark 1:15, bold added

They were echoed a few decades later by the apostle Paul who wrote:

> But **when the set time had fully come**, God sent his Son, born of a woman, born under the law. Galatians 4:4 NIV, bold added

Israel waited expectantly for God's appointed time of the Messiah's birth. Jesus came from the Father.[14] He knew and understood the Father's appointed times. As a result, Scripture makes clear that during His earthly ministry Jesus moved according to the Father's set times.

> On the first day of the Festival of Unleavened Bread, the disciples came to Jesus and asked, "Where do you want us to make preparations for you to eat the Passover?" He replied, "Go into the city to a certain man and tell him, 'The Teacher says: **My appointed time is near**. I am going to celebrate the Passover with my disciples at your house.'" Matthew 26:17-18 NIV, bold added

> Jesus said to her, "[Dear] woman, what is that to you and to Me? **My time** [to act and to be revealed] **has not yet come**." John 2:4 AMP, bold added

> So Jesus said to them, "**My time has not yet come**; but any time is right for you...." John 7:6 AMP, bold added

> "... Go up to the festival yourselves. I'm not going up to the festival yet, because **My time has not yet fully come**." John 7:8 HCSB, bold added

---

14 John 16:28

So they were eager to arrest Him; but no one laid a hand on Him, because **His time had not yet come.** John 7:30 AMP, bold added

So certain is the biblical understanding of God's faithfulness to do what He says He will do that it often speaks in past tense as though fulfillment had already happened![15] Because I can trust God and His appointed times, I do not need to know how or when God is going to fulfill His promise! Hope endures according to His set timetable. "*Biblical* hope rests on knowing God's plan never has *unnecessary delays* (such are only apparent). Accordingly, *in hope* believers triumphantly continue on despite what *appears* to be '*no or slow*' fulfillments. *God's plan is never late. His timetable* (unlike ours) always elevates the *eternal* over the transient (what is passing)."[16] "Hope is never ill, when faith is well."[17] I would add that in God's Kingdom hope is never wasted!

We have considered the first two elements of biblical hope. In our next lesson, we will tackle the third and final strand of that twisted cord: the fact that hope always refers to a specific type of waiting – waiting that is patient, confident and expectant.

Hear What The Spirit is Saying to the Church: *It is the desire of my heart that my church learns my character and truly believes I am trustworthy in all things. I am never late!*

---

15 Motyer, J. Alec, *Isaiah*, Tyndale Old Testament Commentaries (IVP Academic 1999) Isaiah 9:1-7, p. 99, referring to the practice of using past tense as a "Hebrew idiom."
16 Hill, Gary, *The Discovery Bible*, HELPS Ministries, Inc., [G]1680 *elpís* under *Summary*, italics in original
17 Detzler, Wayne A., *New Testament Words In Today's Language* (Victor Books 1986) entry for *hope*, p. 219, quoting John Bunyan (1628-88) who was imprisoned and persecuted for his faith in Christ

LESSON 5:

PATIENT, CONFIDENT, EXPECTANT WAITING

"But if we hope for what we do not see, with perseverance we wait eagerly for it." Romans 8:25

WE ARE READY to delve deeper into the concept of waiting which is necessary for the fulfillment of the promise. The first two elements of hope (the subject of Lessons 3 and 4 respectively) depend in large part on the choices the *Lord* makes in that the promise and the timing are initiated by Him. However, this third component of biblical hope is entirely dependent on the choices *we* make!

In His omniscience, God "calls those things which do not exist as though they did."[1] As we have already noted, the Bible often speaks of God's promises in past tense because they are so certain to become reality. Our biblical mandate as Christ-followers is to hold onto the future promises of God with that kind of sureness until we are able to experience the reality of that hope at the appointed time. In fact, as we will learn before our study concludes, hope allows us to reach forward into the future, grab hold of that joy of blessing and pull it towards us so that we can rejoice in it today!

Biblical hoping means to *wait!* The Bible never promises "that the full adequacy of Christ as Savior *guarantees* the perseverance of true believers. On the contrary, His adequacy provides the sufficient *means* for them to persevere and the all-compelling *reason*

---

1   Romans 4:17 NKJV

for them to give diligence thereunto."[2] In this lesson, I want to begin to explore how patient waiting with confident expectation works to help Christ-followers persevere until the appointed time of fulfillment. We are going to see that the characteristics that describe one who hopes in the Lord include: perseverance, diligence, steadfastness, loyalty, trustworthiness, resolve, patience, fortitude, endurance, and stamina.

Let's start with the biblical truth that we are called not only to an initial belief/trust but to a faith that crosses the finish line no matter what! Many Scriptures support this truth, but we will be able to accomplish our purpose here by limiting our overview to the book of Revelation. Our task will be easily achieved because overcoming is a persistent theme of the seven letters to the churches found in Revelation Chapters 2 and 3. Let's look at those seven overcoming promises in order (bold added to each):

1. Letter to Ephesus – The one who **overcomes** will be granted the privilege of eating from the tree of life. Revelation 2:7b
2. Letter to Smyrna – The one who **overcomes** will not experience the second death. Revelation 2:11b
3. Letter to Pergamum – The one who **overcomes** will be given hidden manna and a white stone with a new name. Revelation 2:17b
4. Letter to Thyatira – The one who **overcomes** and remains faithful to God's commands will be given authority over the nations and the right to rule over them just as Jesus has received authority from His Father. Revelation 2:26-27
5. Letter to Sardis – The one who **overcomes** will be clothed in white garments. The overcomer's name will never be erased from the book of life. Jesus will confess that person's name before His Father and before the angels. Revelation 3:5

---

2   Cockerill, Gareth Lee, *The Epistle to the Hebrews*, New International Commentary on the New Testament (Eerdmans 2012) Hebrews 3:6b, pp. 170-171, italics in original

6. Letter to Philadelphia – The one who **overcomes** will become a pillar in the new temple and will never go out from that temple. Jesus will write a new name on that person. Revelation 3:12
7. Letter to Laodicea – The one who **overcomes** will be given the right to sit with Jesus on His throne. Revelation 3:21

In each case, the word translated as "overcomes" is the Greek word *nikao* {nik-ah'-o} which refers to one who has overcome by conquering. Accordingly, another common way in which *nikao* is frequently translated is with the word "victorious." The verb itself implies a battle and indicates triumphing in battle.[3] Biblically *nikao* refers to overcoming whatever resists the promises or the preferred will of God.[4]

It is undeniable that overcoming involves a battle. As we saw in the examples of Joseph and Moses and David, that battle takes place in the waiting season. In God's Kingdom, waiting on Him is never *wasted* time, it is *invested* time![5] Proper waiting is a God-ordained spiritual battle strategy to enable our victory in that inevitable battle.

There are three key descriptive words regarding the type of waiting demanded when we find ourselves in the *Hope Waiting Room*. Each word is important to our understanding. The first is the word "patient," the second is the word "confident" and the third word is "expectant." Let's quickly review the definitions of the Hebrew and Greek hope words we studied in Lesson 2. As we do, notice how each of these key waiting terms overlap in these definitions. The key terms will be highlighted in bold text to make them easy to identify.

---

3   Hill, Gary, *The Discovery Bible*, HELPS Ministries, Inc., [G]3528 *nikáō*, citing K. Wuest; Zodhiates, Spiros, *The Complete Word Study Dictionary: New Testament* (AMG Publishers 1992) word #3528, p. 1011
4   Hill, Gary, *The Discovery Bible*, HELPS Ministries, Inc., [G]3528 *nikáō*
5   Personal Journal May 17, 2021

- The Greek noun *elpis* means sure confidence, a favorable and **confident expectation** based on solid certainty.
- *Batah* (Hebrew) is a Hebrew verb that indicates trust and **confidence**.[6]
- Hebrew verb *yachal* carries the idea of trust and **confident expectation** resulting in **patient waiting**.[7]
- *Qavah* (Hebrew) is a root word meaning "**to wait** or look for **with eager expectation**."[8] In refers to "**enduring patiently** in **confident hope** that God will decisively act" on behalf of His people.[9]
- Figuratively *tiqvah* (Hebrew) refers to "an attitude of anticipation with the **expectation** that something will happen."[10]

What we are learning is that biblical hope always involves a very specific kind of waiting. Hope in the Bible refers to patiently waiting, patiently anticipating and even patiently enduring while maintaining a desire and confident expectation for the good God promised.[11] It is a resting belief evidenced by "quietness, the absence of frenzy and [the absence of] restless anxiety."[12] This type of trust is possible because the expected outcome is not based on our own

---

6 Baker and Carpenter, *The Complete WordStudy Dictionary of the Old Testament* (AMG Publishers 2003) word #982, p. 128

7 Harris, Archer, and Waltke, editors, *Theological Wordbook of the Old Testament* (Moody Press 1999) word #859, p. 373

8 Harris, Archer, and Waltke, editors, *Theological Wordbook of the Old Testament* (Moody Press 1999) word #1994, p. 791

9 Harris, Archer, and Waltke, editors, *Theological Wordbook of the Old Testament* (Moody Press 1999) word #1994, p. 791

10 Baker and Carpenter, *The Complete WordStudy Dictionary of the Old Testament* (AMG Publishers 2003) word #8615, p. 1243

11 Bromiley, Geoffrey W., *Theological Dictionary of the New Testament* (Eerdmans 1985) entry for *elpis* under E. *The Early Christian Concept of Hope*, p. 231

12 Motyer, J. Alec, *The Prophecy of Isaiah: An Introduction & Commentary* (InterVarsity Press 1993) Isaiah 30:15-17, p. 249

The Power of Hope 79

perceptions and abilities, rather it is firmly rooted in confidence in our reliable God and what He will do.[13]

In a manner of speaking, when God gives a promise with a future appointed time, He opens the door to His *Hope Waiting Room* and invites us to take a comfortable seat. Our contentment in waiting is evidence that we are being led by His Spirit.

We have noted three words, all of which are important traits of one who is seated in God's Waiting Room: patience, confidence and expectation. We want to dig deeper into these words one at a time beginning with patience. In the remainder of this lesson watch for the words in the Scripture quote which have an * asterisk placed beside them. They will be words we have already studied and should by now be familiar. In this way, you will more readily see how in biblical thought the concepts of faith · hope · patience · waiting · expectation flow seamlessly from one to the other.

Waiting Room Patience: There are two Greek words translated as "patience" in the New Testament: *hypomone* {hoop-om-on-ay'} and *makrothymia* {mak-roth-oo-mee'-ah} (also transliterated as *makrothumia*). Between these two words, the Greek language generally covers patience as it relates to other persons and patience in respect to enduring challenging things or challenging circumstances.[14] We will encounter sandpaper people who will test us as we wait. We will also routinely face difficult things and circumstances in God's *Hope Waiting Room*. As a result, it is well worth our time to consider both of these words.

> **Patient endurance** [*hypomone*] is what you need now, so that you will continue to do God's will. Then you will receive all that he has promised. Hebrews 10:36 NLT, bold added

---

13 Bromiley, Geoffrey W., *Theological Dictionary of the New Testament* (Eerdmans 1985) entry for *elpis* under E. *The Early Christian Concept of Hope*, p. 231; Harris, Archer, and Waltke, editors, *Theological Wordbook of the Old Testament* (Moody Press 1999) word #859, p. 373
14 Zodhiates, Spiros, *The Complete Word Study Dictionary: New Testament* (AMG Publishers 1992) word #3115, p. 938

Consider it all joy, my brothers and sisters, when you encounter various trials, knowing that the testing of your faith [*pistis*]* produces **endurance** [*hypomone*]. And let **endurance** [*hypomone*] have *its* perfect result, so that you may be perfect and complete, lacking in nothing. James 1:2-4, italics in original, bold added. [Remember the asterisk* marks a word we have previously studied.]

Word Study

*As noted in Hebrews 10:36 the phrase **patient endurance** and in James 1:2-4 the word **endurance** (used twice) are all translations of the Greek word hypomone {hoop-om-on-ay'} (also transliterated as hupomone). Biblically hypomone describes a person who does not waver or vacillate. He stands on God's promise and refuses to budge even during great trials and suffering.*[15]

In a military context, hypomone refers to soldiers who were expected to maintain their positions even in intense combat. Their goal was to outlast the enemy's resistance.[16] *Hypomone is demonstrated when a person faces great trials and survives every scheme of the enemy by refusing to give up!*[17]

Hypomone "turns down every opportunity to quit."[18]
In today's language, it refers to "staying power or hang in

---

15 Renner, Rick, *Sparkling Gems from the Greek* (Harrison House Publishers 2003) August 9, p. 578
16 *Romans 5:3 Commentary*, Precept Austin, citing Morris. Retrieved from https://www.preceptaustin.org/romans_53-5 (last accessed November 10, 2021); Renner, Rick, *Sparkling Gems from the Greek* (Harrison House Publishers 2003) March 10, p. 147
17 *Hypomone* is demanded of every Christ-follower. Daniel was warned that we have an enemy who seeks to wear us out! See: Daniel 7:25 AMP
18 Renner, Rick, *Sparkling Gems from the Greek Volume II* (Harrison House Publishers 2016) October 19, p. 951

The Power of Hope

> there power."[19] *William Barclay calls hypomone the spirit which can bear things with blazing hope!*[20]

Hypomone is a very strong word in the New Testament. "It depicts a person who knows he is in the right place – hence, regardless of the pressure, assaults, or restraints that are forced upon him, he has decided that he will not *bend, bow* or *break* under that pressure. He has simply decided that this is his spot, and nothing is going to move him from it…. *for any reason.*"[21] This type of tenacious waiting results in a steadfastness that will ensure a victorious finish despite delays and setbacks no matter how long or how difficult the waiting season is![22]

The second word frequently translated as "patience" in the New Testament is the word *makrothymia*. James highlights the prophets of the Old Testament era for the patient faith they displayed in the face of often overwhelming adversity and pressure.

> For examples of **patience** [*makrothymia*] in suffering, dear brothers and sisters, look at the prophets who spoke in the name of the Lord. James 5:10 NLT, bold added

James focuses on the faithful prophets in Israel's past. He highlighted them because they illustrate "how ordinary people who

---

19 Renner, Rick, *Sparkling Gems from the Greek Volume II* (Harrison House Publishers 2016) October 19, p. 951
20 Hill, Gary, *The Discovery Bible*, HELPS Ministries, Inc., [G]5281 *hypomonē* under *Key quotes,* quoting William Barclay, *A New Testament Word Book* (London 1955) p. 60
21 Renner, Rick, *Sparkling Gems from the Greek Volume II* (Harrison House Publishers 2016) July 6, p. 621, italics in original
22 Robertson, A. T., *Robertson's New Testament Word Studies*, 1 Thessalonians entry for *Verse 3* under *Patience of hope.* Retrieved from https://www.studylight.org/commentaries/eng/rwp/1-thessalonians-1.html (last accessed August 8, 2021)

shared the common human experience of suffering became extraordinary through their persevering faith in the face of adversity."[23]

The author of Hebrews links patience together with faith and hope.

> We want each of you to show this same diligence to the very end, so that what you hope [*elpis*]* for may be fully realized. We do not want you to become lazy, but to imitate those who through faith [*pistis*]* and **patience** [*makrothymia*] inherit what has been promised. Hebrews 6:11-12 NIV, bold added. [Notice our now familiar words for hope [*elpis*] and faith [*pistis*] marked by the *asterisk.]

As noted, the highlighted word "patience" in both the James and Hebrews quotes is the Greek word *makrothymia* {mak-roth-oo-mee'-ah}. A Word Study will be helpful.

Word Study

*Translated as **patience**, the Greek noun makrothymia {mak-roth-oo-mee'-ah} is a compound word from makros referring to long, distant, far off, large + thumos meaning temper, passion, emotion.*[24]

It denotes the capacity to suffer wrong and withhold retaliation. It is the ability to restrain feelings or bear up under the oversights and wrongs inflicted by others without retaliating.

Makrothymia refers to "a conquering patience."[25] *It "could be translated 'large emotions,' signifying wells of*

---

23 McCartney, Dan G., *James*, Baker Exegetical Commentary on the New Testament (Baker Academic 2009) James 5:10-11, p. 243
24 *Colossians 3:12-14 Commentary*, Precept Austin. Retrieved from https://www.preceptaustin.org/colossians_312-25 (last accessed August 8, 2021)
25 *Colossians 3:12-14 Commentary*, Precept Austin, citing Barclay, *Daily Study Bible*, Colossians 1 Comments. Retrieved from https://www.pre-

> *endurance that will not dry up, no matter how much is drawn from them."*[26]

"*Makrothymia* is the steadfastness of faith and hope which is not vexed by waiting. Its basis is the promise of the righteous God."[27] A Greek historian who lived at the same time as Jesus took note of the determined patience [*makrothymia*] of those who were living in a city under siege[28] and decided to plant turnips. Their hope was for those turnips (which take up to two months to mature) to ripen in time so they could be eaten before the city was defeated.[29] The citizens of that city were engaging in what they hoped would be conquering patience. In Hebrews 6:15 the related verb *makrothymeo* is used in reference to Abraham's patient faith in God while enduring the pressure of his trying circumstances.

> And so, having **patiently waited**, [Abraham] obtained the promise. Hebrews 6:15, bold added

For the Christ-follower Paul identifies the source of this type of enduring patience as the Holy Spirit.

---

ceptaustin.org/colossians_312-25 (last accessed August 8, 2021)

26 *Colossians 3:12-14 Commentary*, Precept Austin, citing Briscoe, D. S., & Ogilvie, L. J., *The Preacher's Commentary Series: New Testament* (Thomas Nelson 2003). Retrieved from https://www.preceptaustin.org/colossians_312-25 (last accessed August 8, 2021)

27 Bromiley, Geoffrey W., *Theological Dictionary of the New Testament* (Eerdmans 1985) entry for *makrothymia* under *D. The NT. 3. The Catholic Epistles*, p. 551

28 In ancient times when an enemy army encountered a city that refused to surrender and could not be overtaken by quick assault they would blockade that city in a prolonged assault called siege warfare. The blockade would prevent food supplies from entering that city in hopes of either causing the inhabitants to surrender or starve to death.

29 Hoehner, Harold W., "Romans," in *The Bible Knowledge Word Study Acts-Ephesians*, edited by Darrell L. Bock (Victor 2002) Romans 2:4 under *Patience (makrothymias)*, p. 137

But the fruit of the Spirit is love, joy, peace, patience [*makrothymia*], kindness, goodness, faithfulness, gentleness, self-control .... Galatians 5:22-23

Christ-followers who exhibit *makrothymia* in the waiting room "will have refreshing water to sustain continual effectiveness even in the face of unrelenting pressures. Those with such patience and faith are those who receive or 'inherit the promises.'"[30]

As we can see, biblical patience is more than being "able to remain calm and not become annoyed when waiting for a long time or when dealing with problems or difficult people."[31] When the New Testament authors refer to "patience" they are referring to a staying power – a power that keeps and holds under pressure no matter what trials you face. A follower of Christ who is patient in the waiting season "is *thoroughly committed* to maintaining his position. He will stay in that spot as long as it's necessary for him to achieve victory.... [He holds on to] a faith that manifests as a tough, resistant, persistent, obstinate, stubborn, tenacious spirit that refuses to let go of what it wants or believes."[32] This type of faith "has focused desire. It knows what it wants. It doesn't vacillate. It never moves."[33] As we are learning, biblical patience can be described as faith that stands still in one spot without complaint until that which God has promised is revealed.

<u>Waiting Room Confidence:</u> We will turn to three of Paul's epistles where he expresses confidence in God so we

---

30 *Colossians 3:12-14 Commentary*, Precept Austin, citing Briscoe, D. S., & Ogilvie, L. J., *The Preacher's Commentary Series: New Testament* (Thomas Nelson 2003). Retrieved from https://www.preceptaustin.org/colossians_312-25 (last accessed August 8, 2021)
31 *Merriam-Webster.com Dictionary*, entry for *English Language Learners Definition of patient (Entry 1 of 2)*. Retrieved from https://www.merriam-webster.com/dictionary/dictionary/patient (last accessed August 8, 2021)
32 Renner, Rick, *Sparkling Gems from the Greek Volume II* (Harrison House Publishers 2016) February 5, p. 138, italics in original
33 Renner, Rick, *Sparkling Gems from the Greek Volume II* (Harrison House Publishers 2016) February 5, p. 138, italics in original

can see how intimately biblical confidence and biblical hope are connected. To the church at Philippi Paul wrote:

> *For I am* **confident** of this very thing, that [God] who began a good work in you will perfect it until the day of Christ Jesus. Philippians 1:6, italics in original, bold added

In Philippians 1:6, the word "confident" (highlighted in bold) is the Greek word *peitho* {pi'-tho}. This should be a familiar word to us from Lesson 3. There we learned that in most cases *peitho* means "[t]o persuade, particularly to move or affect by kind words or motives.... Generally, to persuade another to receive a belief, meaning to convince ...."[34]

Turning to Paul's letters to the Ephesians and the Corinthians, we find two more statements from Paul about confidence from the same source.

> *This was* in accordance with the eternal purpose which He carried out in Christ Jesus our Lord, **in whom** we have boldness and **confident** access through faith [*pistis*]* in Him. Ephesians 3:11-12, italics in original, bold added. [Notice our familiar word for faith [*pistis*] marked by the *asterisk.]

> Such **confidence** we have through Christ toward God. 2 Corinthians 3:4, bold added

In these two quoted verses, both "confident" and "confidence" (highlighted in bold) are translations of *pepoithesis* {pep-oy'-thay-sis}, a derivative of the Greek word *peitho*. It refers to a "state of certainty about something to the extent of placing reliance on" it.[35] It is noteworthy that in Ephesians 3:12, Paul is not referring

---

34 Zodhiates, Spiros, *The Complete Word Study Dictionary: New Testament* (AMG Publishers 1992) word #3982, p. 1134
35 Bauer-Danker, *Greek-English Lexicon of the NT* (*BDAG*), entry for 5788 πεποίθησις. Retrieved from BibleWorks 9.0 software

to the run-of-the-mill type of confidence. In the original Greek, Paul used a form of the word *pepoithesis* which "depicts *absolute confidence* — that is, one who is *doubly persuaded*. You could say that this person is *convinced to the core* — rock-solid *certain* about what he believes or feels. He is so *completely persuaded* and *trustful* of what he believes that no element of doubt remains."[36]

The natural question is *who* has done the persuading that Paul references in both of these confident assertions? Our quote from Ephesians 3 answers that question. Look back at the phrase "in whom" (highlighted in bold). It is easy to see that phrase refers back to Jesus who was just mentioned by Paul. This type of confidence is not based on ourselves, it is found in our relationship with Jesus Christ through the enabling power of Holy Spirit. Paul is referring to persuasion that is authored/produced by the Holy Spirit through faith.[37]

Waiting Room Expectation: Three Greek words used in the New Testament when referring to acceptance, waiting and expectation are: *ekdechomai* {ek-dekh'-om-ahee}, *apekdechomai* {ap-ek-dekh'-om-ahee} and *prosdechomai* {pros-dekh'-om-ahee}. Notice that all three are compound words which result from combining a prefix with the verb *dechomai* {dekh'-om-ahee}. That fact allows us to quickly see that these three words are closely related to each other. Because these words all derive from the verb *dechomai* {dekh'-om-ahee} it is helpful to delve into the meaning of that root word first.

Word Study

In the Greek language dechomai {dekh'-om-ahee} is a verb that refers to a deliberate and ready acceptance of

---

36 Renner, Rick, *Sparkling Gems from the Greek Volume II* (Harrison House Publishers 2016) February 22, p. 192, italics in original

37 Hill, Gary, *The Discovery Bible*, HELPS Ministries, Inc., Cognate: [G]4006 *pepoíthēsis*, "properly, *persuasion*; used ... more commonly of *Spirit-produced persuasion* (2 Cor 3:4; Ep. 3:13)," italics in original

> *something offered. In the Bible, it is usually translated as* **accept, receive,** *or* **welcome.**
>
> *Included within the definition of dechomai is the idea of "not refusing" or "not rejecting" – receiving favorably and embracing that which has been offered.*[38]
>
> *Because it conveys the idea of a reception that is both voluntary and welcome, it pictures the Christ-follower "putting out the welcome mat" for truth offered by God.*[39]

When you welcome and receive the promises of God in the same way in which you receive and welcome your good friend whom you have invited into your home, *dechomai* describes your actions. In other words, *dechomai* pictures a welcoming voluntary and willing agreement with what God says.[40]

Now that we understand the word that is the basis of each of the other three Greek words we are considering, let's look at examples of how each word is used in Scripture. We'll begin with *ekdechomai* {ek-dekh'-om-ahee}.

The author of Hebrews chose the word *ekdechomai* to describe the truth that Christ is waiting expectantly at the right hand of His Father. Hebrews 10:13 specifies that the resurrected Jesus is waiting for a promise His Father made. It is the promise recorded in Psalm 110:1 and repeated by Jesus in Matthew 22:44.

> [The resurrected Christ] is now **waiting** until His enemies are made His footstool. Hebrews 10:13 HCSB, bold added

---

38 Thayer, Joseph, *Thayer's Greek-English Lexicon of the New Testament*, entry for *Strong's NT 1209 dechomai*. Retrieved from https://biblehub.com/thayers/1209.htm (last accessed August 8, 2021)

39 *James 1:21 Commentary*, Precept Austin. Retrieved from https://www.preceptaustin.org/james_121 (last accessed August 8, 2021)

40 *James 1:21 Commentary*, Precept Austin. Retrieved from https://www.preceptaustin.org/james_121 (last accessed August 8, 2021)

The LORD said to my Lord: "Sit at My right hand Until I make Your enemies a footstool for Your feet."
Psalm 110:1

'THE LORD SAID TO MY LORD, "SIT AT MY RIGHT HAND UNTIL I PUT YOUR ENEMIES BENEATH YOUR FEET."'
Matthew 22:44, uppercase text in original

WORD STUDY

In Hebrews 10:13, the verb **waiting***, which is highlighted in bold, is a translation of the Greek word ekdechomai {ek-dekh'-om-ahee}. As has been mentioned, it is a compound word that combines ek meaning from + dechomai meaning to receive kindly, accept deliberately and readily.*

Ekdechomai denotes that Jesus is remaining in a place or state while awaiting a future event He expects to happen.[41] *By definition, this is an earnest expectation emphasizing waiting which "is deeply (personally) engaged, actively waiting – welcoming the anticipated end-conclusion."*[42]

Here the expectant waiting describes what Christ is doing and the future event He is expecting is the realization of His sovereign Kingship. His Father has promised Him that all things shall be completely subdued under His authority.

---

41 *Hebrews 10:11-13 Commentary*, Precept Austin. Retrieved from https://www.preceptaustin.org/hebrews_1011-13 (last accessed August 8, 2021)
42 Hill, Gary, *The Discovery Bible*, HELPS Ministries, Inc., [G]1551 *ekdéxomai*, italics in original ignored

The Power of Hope

Jesus becomes our model for how to wait in expectation of a promise we are convinced will be fulfilled. Understandably then, James uses *ekdechomai* when he exhorts Christ-followers to be patient as they expectantly wait for the return of the Lord. He points to the farmer as an example of one who patiently waits in anticipation.

> Therefore be patient [*makrothymeo*],* brethren, until the coming of the Lord. The farmer **waits** [*ekdechomai*] for the precious produce of the soil, being patient [*makrothymeo*]* about it, until it gets the early and late rains. You too be patient [*makrothymeo*];* strengthen your hearts, for the coming of the Lord is near. James 5:7-8, bold added. [Notice our familiar word for patience [*makrothymeo*] marked by the *asterisk.]

James points to the farmer's patient waiting for the rain his crops need for growth. He uses that type of familiar waiting as an example of how Christ-followers should wait patiently for the second coming of Jesus.

Our second word *apekdechomai* {ap-ek-dekh'-om-ahee} is a compound of three words in the Greek: *apo* which generally "designates movement 'from' an object" in the sense of separation[43] + *ek* which can signify "an exit 'from within' something which there had earlier been a close connection"[44] + *dechomai* which as noted in our Word Study is a verb referring to a deliberate and ready acceptance of something offered. The composite word denotes an attitude of

---

43 Wenstrom, William E., Jr., *Greek Word Studies* (William E. Wenstrom, Jr. Bible Ministries 2002) entry for *Apo*. Retrieved from https://www.wenstrom.org/downloads/written/word_studies/greek/apo.pdf (last accessed July 28, 2022)

44 Wenstrom, William E., Jr., *Greek Word Studies* (Wenstrom.org no publication or copyright date given) entry for *Ek*. Retrieved from https://www.wenstrom.org/downloads/written/word_studies/greek/ek.pdf (last accessed July 28, 2022)

intense yearning and eager waiting.⁴⁵ An author may choose to use this preposition simply for emphasis.

> But we who live by the Spirit **eagerly wait** [*apekdechomai*] to receive by faith [*pistis*]* the righteousness God has promised to us. Galatians 5:5 NLT, bold added. [Notice our familiar word for faith [pistis] marked by the *asterisk.]

> But if we hope [*elpizo*]* for what we do not see, with perseverance [*hypomone*]* we **wait eagerly** [*apekdechomai*] for it. Romans 8:25, bold added. [Notice our familiar words for hope [*elpizo*] and perseverance (i.e. patient endurance) [*hypomone*] marked by the *asterisk.]

As noted, the phrases "eagerly wait" (Galatians 5:5) and "wait eagerly" (Romans 8:25, our Key Scripture for this lesson) which I have highlighted in bold are translations of the word *apekdechomai*. Both of these verses are excellent examples of exactly what we have been talking about.

We have already noted that *apekdechomai* {ap-ek-dekh'-om-ahee} is a compound of three words in Greek. The prefix *apo* + the prefix *ek* are added to the root word *dechomai*. Before we move on, I'd like to highlight just a few additional points noted in the *Theological Dictionary of the New Testament* about these two prefixes as used in this context.⁴⁶

---

45 Wenstrom, William E., Jr., *Greek Word Studies* (Wenstrom.org 2016) entry for *Apekdechomai*. Retrieved from https://www.wenstrom.org / downloads/written/word_studies/greek/apekdechomai.pdf (last accessed August 8, 2021)

46 Wenstrom, William E., Jr., *Greek Word Studies* (Wenstrom.org 2016) entry for *Apekdechomai*. Retrieved from https://www.wenstrom.org / downloads/written/word_studies/greek/apekdechomai.pdf (last accessed August 8, 2021); *Philippians 1:18-20 Commentary*, Precept Austin, citing Vincent. Retrieved from https://www.preceptaustin.org/philippians_118-24 (last accessed August 8, 2021)

The Power of Hope

- The prefix *apo* emphasizes the distance in time till the fulfillment of what is hoped for. As a result, it adds the idea of waiting with compelled perseverance.
- *Apo* also denotes withdrawing attention from whatever is inferior to that for which you are waiting. In other words, it refers to turning away from something lesser in order to lay hold of something greater. In this regard, *apo* indicates an intense hope with a laser-like focus.
- The preposition *ek* intensifies the existing meaning of the word so that the composite word conveys an attitude of yearning intensely and waiting eagerly.

The *Theological Dictionary of the New Testament* concludes: "On the basis of the gospel that is already received (*dechomai*), *apekdechomai* thus characterizes Christian life as one of expectation of the great climax which gives not only this life but also the whole of creation its meaning."[47]

Our last word *prosdechomai* is found in Scriptures which refer to living in expectation of the Kingdom of God, resurrection hope and as well as in reference to an attitude that is motivated by the promise of Jesus' return.

Word Study

Prosdechomai {pros-dekh'-om-ahee} combines pros which in this context implies motion or direction toward + dechomai a deliberate and ready reception.[48]

---

47 Bromiley, Geoffrey W., *Theological Dictionary of the New Testament*, Abridged in One Volume (Eerdmans 1985) entry for *dechomai* under *ek-*, *apekdechomai*, p. 147

48 *Titus 2:13 Commentary*, Precept Austin. Retrieved from https://www.preceptaustin.org/titus_213-15 (last accessed August 8, 2021)

> *It essentially "expresses expectant waiting where a person is ready and willing to receive all that is hoped for. This is active 'looking-for-and-waiting!'"*[49]
>
> *The main idea of prosdechomai in the New Testament is to expectantly await, often reflecting eagerness.*[50]

Joseph of Arimathea was living in eager *expectation* of the Kingdom of God:

> Joseph of Arimathea came, a prominent member of the Council, who himself was **waiting** [*prosdechomai*] for the kingdom of God; and he gathered up courage and went in before Pilate, and asked for the body of Jesus. Mark 15:43, bold added

Another way to translate *prosdechomai* is with the phrase "looking forward to" as shown in the following Scripture quotes:

> Joseph of Arimathea, a prominent member of the Sanhedrin who was himself **looking forward to** [*prosdechomai*] the kingdom of God, came and boldly went in to Pilate and asked for Jesus' body. Mark 15:43 HCSB, bold added

> There was a man in Jerusalem whose name was Simeon. This man was righteous and devout, **looking forward to** [*prosdechomai*] Israel's consolation,[51] and the Holy Spirit was on him. Luke 2:25 HCSB, bold added

---

49 Hill, Gary, *The Discovery Bible*, HELPS Ministries, Inc., [G]4327 *prosdéxomai*, italics in original
50 Bromiley, Geoffrey W., *Theological Dictionary of the New Testament*, Abridged in One Volume (Eerdmans 1985) entry for *dechomai* under *prosdechomai*, p. 148; *ESV Study Bible* (Crossway Books 2008) study note Titus 2:13, p. 2350
51 The "consolation" [could also be translated as "restoration" or "deliverance"] of Israel. It "refers to Simeon's hope that the Messiah would come

The Power of Hope

> Coming up to them at that very moment, [Anna] gave thanks to God and spoke about the child to all who were **looking forward to** [*prosdechomai*] the redemption of Jerusalem. Luke 2:38 NIV, italics in original, bold added

We need to stop here for a moment so we can shout *Hallelujah*! The good news of the gospel is that the Messiah has come and the extended period of waiting is over! God honored the persevering expectation of both Anna and Simeon – they each saw the promised Messiah with their own eyes!

Paul employed the word *prosdechomai* in his defense before Felix, the Roman appointed governor of Judea. In Paul's self-defense he described the hope of the promised future bodily resurrection he and his Jewish brothers shared.

> And I have a hope [*elpis*]* in God, which these [Jewish brothers of mine] also **accept** [*prosdechomai*], that there is going to be a resurrection, both of the righteous and the unrighteous. Acts 24:15 HCSB, bold added. [Notice our familiar word for hope [*elpis*] marked by the *asterisk.]

As we have seen, *prosdechomai* is used to refer to things which are still in the future. In that regard it denotes remaining in a present place and/or state because of *expectation* of that future event.[52] It conveys an attitude of waiting that is intensely counting

---

and deliver the nation (Isa 40:1; 49:13; 51:3; 57:18; 61:2; 2 Bar 44:7)." *NET Bible Notes*, study note 71, Luke 2:25

52 Wenstrom, William E., Jr., *Greek Word Studies* (Wenstrom.org 2016) entry for *Prosdechomai*, citing Louw and Nida, *Greek-English Lexicon of the New Testament Based on Semantic Domains*, Volume 2, pp. 729-730. Retrieved from https://www.wenstrom.org/downloads/written/word_studies/greek/prosdechomai.pdf (last accessed April 12, 2022)

on, earnestly expecting with the distinct sense of welcoming now that for which we wait.[53]

We will bring this lesson to a close by adding one more Greek word to the "waiting" word group we have been exploring. I want to take the time to add it because it presents an unforgettable word picture that captures the essence of biblical hope and expectation in the waiting seasons of life. The word is *apokaradokia* {ap-ok-ar-ad-ok-ee'-ah} which is a close synonym to *apekdechomai*. It denotes attentive, persistent, or intense expectation and is sometimes translated as being "with anticipation."[54]

We find the word *apokaradokia* when Paul is writing to the church at Philippi about his earnest, persistent expectation as he looked to the future:

> It is my own **eager expectation** and hope [*elpis*],* that [looking toward the future] I will not disgrace myself *nor* be ashamed in anything, but that with courage *and* the utmost freedom of speech, even now as always, Christ will be magnified *and* exalted in my body, whether by life or by death. Philippians 1:20 AMP, italics in original, bold added. [Notice once again our familiar word for hope [*elpis*] marked by the *asterisk.]

In Philippians 1:20 the phrase "eager expectation" (highlighted in bold) is the word *apokaradokia*. When Paul used this same word in Romans 8:19, J. B. Phillips translated it as creation eagerly waiting "on tiptoe."[55] This intense expectation fosters earnest longing which can be illustrated by an Olympic runner stretching

---

53 *Jude 21 Commentary*, Precept Austin. Retrieved from https://www.preceptaustin.org/jude_21_commentary (last accessed August 8, 2021)
54 Zodhiates, Spiros, *The Complete Word Study Dictionary: New Testament* (AMG Publishers 1992) word #603, p. 225; Hill, Gary, *The Discovery Bible*, HELPS Ministries, Inc., [G]603 *apokaradokia*
55 " ... The whole creation is on tiptoe to see the wonderful sight of the sons of God coming into their own.... (Romans 8:19-21 PHILLIPS)." Schreiner, Thomas R., *Romans*, Baker Exegetical Commentary on the New Testament, 2nd edition (Baker Academic 1998, 2018) Romans 8:19,

forth his head as he anticipates crossing the finish line.[56] Noticeably it is a picture of one who leads with his head, his hands and his heart all of which cross the finish line before his feet do.[57] That's a wonderfully powerful (and hopefully unforgettable) picture of biblical expectation!

At the outset of this lesson, I said I wanted to begin to explore how patient waiting with confident expectation works to help Christ-followers persevere until the set time of fulfillment. The word definitions themselves have put our feet in the starter position for greater understanding. In the next lesson, I want to dig a little deeper into the biblical truth that there is *power* in hope!

Hear What The Spirit is Saying to the Church: *In the microwave world in which you live, I know it is hard to wait patiently. But I tell you I am able and willing to supply all you need as you look to Me!*

---

p. 426, affirming that Phillips has "aptly" rendered *apokaradokia* with the phrase "on tiptoe."

56 Hill, Gary, *The Discovery Bible*, HELPS Ministries, Inc., [G]603 *apokaradokía*

57 I credit Linda Murry-Figueroa (Fall 2021 Calvary Chapel Melbourne Women's Bible Study) with recognizing that fact in the graphic illustration I used of a stretched-out runner reaching for the finish tape.

Lesson 6:

The Strength Gained Through Hope Filled Waiting

 "[B]ut those who hope in the Lord will renew their strength. They will soar on wings like eagles; they will run and not grow weary, they will walk and not be faint." Isaiah 40:31 NIV

OUR STUDY IS CALLED *The Power of Hope*. The undeniable truth of Scripture is that overcoming involves a battle and that battle takes place in the waiting season between promise and fulfillment. Through revelation, which always has an appointed time, God throws us a lifeline. That lifeline can become hope which sustains, upholds and even nourishes us when we wholeheartedly embrace it with the kind of waiting described in our last lesson.

Proper waiting is a very strategic and effective weapon God has given us to enable our victory in the inevitable battles we will face. As we will see in this lesson, proper hopeful waiting supplies strength for the weary. We will begin our discussion by considering how hope that is drawn out of someone makes their heart sick. To do so will require a fresh look at a familiar verse in Proverbs.

> Hope deferred makes the heart sick ... Proverbs 13:12a

To begin with, the word "hope" in Proverbs 13:12 is a Hebrew word that comes from *yahal*. In fact, one scholar notes that the word used here in Proverbs 13 "designates the action of the verb" *yahal*.¹ You may recall that in Lesson 2 we said *yahal* can refer to showing a waiting attitude or waiting in anticipation. The author of Proverbs points out that when our anticipatory waiting is "deferred" it makes our heart sick. We will begin by looking at what it means to have a "sick" heart and then we will look closely at the word deferred.

The word "sick" in Proverbs 13:12 is the Hebrew word *chalah* {khaw-law'}. This verb can refer to physical sickness which leads to weakness, but it is also used biblically in the sense of someone being "sick of heart" or "mind."² The meaning is a heart or mind that becomes sorrowful, weak, or grieved – perhaps even to the point of being debilitated or depleted of its spiritual strength.³

A Word Study will help us with the word deferred.

WORD STUDY

*In Proverbs 13:12 the word **deferred** is the Hebrew word mashak or masak {maw-shak'} which "essentially means 'to draw' (i.e., 'to cause to move in a particular direction by or as by a pulling force').*"⁴

---

1 Waltke, Bruce K., *The Book of Proverbs: Chapters 1-15,* The New International Commentary on the Old Testament (Eerdmans 2004) Proverbs 10:28, p. 477

2 Harris, Archer, and Waltke, editors, *Theological Wordbook of the Old Testament* (Moody Press 1999) word #655, p. 287

3 On the other hand, "desire fulfilled is a tree of life (Proverbs 13:12b)." Here the tree of life is a metaphor for that which is "the antithesis of sickness; [the one whose desire is fulfilled] is transferred from the realm of sickness and death into the realm of health and life. The fruit of that tree revitalizes energies, renews courage to live and to plan for the future, and extends life forever." Waltke, Bruce K., *The Book of Proverbs: Chapters 1-15,* The New International Commentary on the Old Testament (Eerdmans 2004) Proverbs 13:12, p. 563

4 Waltke, Bruce K., *The Book of Proverbs: Chapters 1-15,* The New International Commentary on the Old Testament (Eerdmans 2004) Proverbs 10:28, footnote 80, p. 477

> *According to the Theological Wordbook of the Old Testament, this Hebrew verb is used 36 times in the Old Testament with a variety of nuances attached to it.*[5] *For example, it is found in the context of pulling something up or out of a receptacle or place; drawing back a bow string; luring someone; to delay or prolong in the sense of drawing out time; to be patient; or drawing out sound from a ram's horn.*

Mashak is used in its concrete sense in Genesis 37:28, its first recorded use in the Bible, which refers to the fact that Joseph was *drawn up out of* the cistern where his brothers had thrown him.

> Then Midianite traders passed by. And **they drew Joseph up** [*mashak*] and lifted him out of the pit, and sold him to the Ishmaelites for twenty shekels of silver. They took Joseph to Egypt. Genesis 37:28 ESV, bold added

This literal use of the word *mashak* provides us with a good picture of its figurative use in Proverbs 13:12. In our Proverbs verse, *mashak* refers to drawing out time in the sense of prolonging or extending it. Its use "does not imply a revised time schedule but *a never-ending extension* of time."[6] The proverb states the truth that when the fulfillment of the promise (the thing that you are hoping for) seems to have never-ending extensions of time then the heart can become sick.

However, the reality of true biblical hope is that time does *not* adversely affect it! No matter how many extensions of time the one hoping needs to endure, hope that is exercised has staying power! The only way that delayed hope can make someone heart-

---

5   Harris, Archer, and Waltke, editors, *Theological Wordbook of the Old Testament* (Moody Press 1999) word #1257, p. 532

6   Waltke, Bruce K., *The Book of Proverbs: Chapters 1-15,* The New International Commentary on the Old Testament (Eerdmans 2004) Proverbs 13:12, pp. 562-563, italics added

sick is for sustaining hope to be voluntarily laid down. In other words, the one hoping has allowed it to be drawn out of him by the circumstances. When that happens, hope is forfeited and, in *that* case, the heart of the one hoping becomes "sick" – *challah*. It is weakened, grieved, depleted of its strength. Said differently, the heart is *not* automatically weakened or made sick or grieved simply because of what appears to be a delay in promise fulfillment. It is only when hope is forfeited and no longer exists in the heart that the heart is adversely affected.

Do you recall in the last lesson we learned that of the three interwoven elements of hope, the first two are largely dependent on choices God makes; however, when it comes to that third element, waiting in the *Hope Waiting Room*, the responsibility shifts to us? The only way we ever have hope is that we choose to hope! Once we have chosen it, hope cannot be stolen by the enemy. On the other hand, it can be forfeited. To say that hope has been drawn out is to say it has been abandoned, it has been laid down by choice. It denotes hope which has been surrendered because it is no longer the path we have chosen to walk. In Lesson 4 we noted that: "Hope is never ill, when faith is well."[7] However, when hope is surrendered, the heart becomes depleted of its spiritual strength and is therefore fearful and weighed down. It can become grieved, despairing and despondent.

Elijah is an example of someone whose very identity was well established in unwavering hope. However, there came a moment in time when he chose to lay down the hope that had sustained him. He had just defeated the prophets of Baal in one of the most spectacular displays of God's power recorded in the Bible. One wonders if Elijah may have thought that the time of fulfillment for all that he was hoping for had finally arrived. That was not the case. The celebration of the Mt. Carmel victory was short-lived

---

7   Detzler, Wayne A., *New Testament Words In Today's Language* (Victor Books 1986) entry for *Hope*, p. 219, quoting John Bunyan (1628-88) who was imprisoned and persecuted for his faith in Christ

The Power of Hope

and Elijah was facing death threats from Jezebel.[8] Elijah walked in great confident expectation over the course of an extended waiting season. Hope has sufficient power to sustain us through the most unbelievable hardships. Hope enables boldness in the face of opposition. However, when we lose hope because we choose to abandon it, then discouragement, fear and despair (all tools that Satan uses against us in spiritual warfare) rush in quickly to fill the spiritual void!

When Elijah allowed the voice of Jezebel to become louder than God's voice, when he shifted the magnifying glass in his hand away from God and onto Jezebel then fear arose. Hope became deferred and he ran for his life. The boldness that had previously come easily to Elijah was empowered by his hope in God; however, with the loss of his hope came the loss of his boldness![9] Because he had surrendered his hope, he ran in fear and discouragement. Being disillusioned his eyes were no longer on God, they had shifted to himself and his present circumstances.

We might be quick to defend Elijah – after all, wouldn't *anyone* in his shoes do the very same thing? He seemed to have no other choice. The reality, however, is that assumption is entirely inconsistent with what the Bible teaches us.

Let's consider some examples in Scripture of those who experienced unthinkable hardships and such extended delays in hope fulfillment that what they were hoping for was not even realized in their lifetime. They are highlighted in the Bible as admirable examples of ones who had faith and steadfastly maintained their hope – ones we are encouraged to imitate. Let's turn to a chapter in the book of Hebrews which is commonly and notably referred to as, "The Hall of Faith." In that chapter men and women of great

---

8   See: 1 Kings 18:16-19:4
9   Personal Journal December 23, 2020. God taught me this truth when I faced the temptation to lay down my hope because the promise seemed to be delayed.

and mighty exploits are listed one after another. The first two verses in Chapter 11 commends them for their faith/hope.[10]

> Now faith is the assurance of *things* hoped for, the conviction of things not seen. For by it the men of old gained approval. Hebrews 11:1-2, italics in original

But then we read surprising statements like:

> All these *died* in faith, **without receiving the promises**, but having seen them and having welcomed them from a distance, and having confessed that they were strangers and exiles on the earth. Hebrews 11:13, bold added

> And all these, having gained approval through their faith, **did not receive what was promised**. Hebrews 11:39, bold added

Talk about examples of "hope deferred!" Going to your grave with yet unrealized promises from God has to be the epitome of "a never-ending extension of time." Yet they are recorded in the annals of history as great men and women of faith-filled hope! Each one crossed the finish line of this life still hoping!

Abraham is among those listed as still living by faith when he died, not having received every thing that he was promised. Hebrews 11:13 provides a clue as to how this type of hope was possible. Scholar Gareth Lee Cockerill explains it this way: [11]

> ... it is important not to forget in what way they did participate in what God had promised. They did "see" its certain reality and future fulfillment with the eyes of faith.... the people of faith hear and obey the word of God

---

10 For a discussion of Hebrews 11:1 see Lesson 3
11 Cockerill, Gareth Lee, *The Epistle to the Hebrews*, New International Commentary on the New Testament (Eerdmans 2012) Hebrews 11:13, pp. 549-550

because they "see." "By faith" they "see," that is, they give their full attention to and live in accord with, both the "unseen" present power of God and the not yet visible future fulfillment of his promises.... [they] set the pattern for God's people. It is living by this "vision" that makes them people of faith and sustains their perseverance.

By fixing their eyes firmly on the God who made the promises the men and women listed in Hebrews 11 chose hope and never changed their minds. They took that hope-filled confident expectation to the grave with them! That inner conviction they had was not based on what they could physically see around them, it was based on God who is faithful. Most certainly when the going got rough they must have "fed on *His* faithfulness."[12] Those faithful hope-ers realized that hope works on God's timetable. They most likely understood that God views the generations as being connected such that if He chooses to fulfill the promise He made to them through their descendants it was as if God fulfilled it through them.[13]

When we are parked in God's *Hope Waiting Room* we have a bullseye target on our back and battle ensues. The reason is twofold. First God is choosing that time to test our faith so that we can ultimately learn to endure and become mature in our faith (this is the promise of James 1:3-4). On the other hand, Satan seeks to take advantage of that battlefield for our harm. But here is the truth of the matter: Satan is entirely defenseless against hope! God has not given him the power to defeat hope. Therefore, his only option in the face of hope is to try to encourage the one who is hoping to forfeit his hope. If Satan succeeds in his temptation and hope is laid down (willingly surrendered by the hope-er) then

---

12 Psalm 37:3 NKJV
13 Sheets and Ford III, *History Makers: Your Prayers Have the Power to Heal the Past and Shape the Future* (Bethany House Publishers 2004) as cited in Give Him 15, February 14, 2021. Retrieved from http://gh15database.com

Satan's power is restored! No wonder the evil one works so hard to tempt us to lay down hope![14]

The key to every hope-er's overcoming victory is stated clearly in Hebrews 6:12, "[Be] imitators of those who through faith [*pistis*] and endurance inherit the promises." When we choose to keep our feet on the path of promise and endurance they walked, then we will be able to realize the true power found in hope.

We will spend the remainder of this lesson on our Key Scripture. Although it was written in an entirely different context, it is fitting to suggest it could just have easily been applied to those faith heroes whose names are listed in the Hall of Faith. Our Key Scripture translation is NIV, I'll restate the verse here in ESV, showing that the word "hope" in the NIV can properly be translated as "wait."

> [B]ut they who **wait** for the LORD shall renew their strength; they shall mount up with wings like eagles; they shall run and not be weary; they shall walk and not faint. Isaiah 40:31 ESV, bold added

We will begin by considering the context in which this assurance of renewed divine strength was given. As we will see, God presented this promise about renewing strength to His covenant people at a time when He knew they needed their hope refreshed. In the chapter immediately preceding Isaiah 40, the prophet had warned about the future rise of Babylon – a nation that would be used by God to punish Judah for her apostasy and her unrepented sins. Isaiah prophesied between 740-680 B.C. However, it was not until 605, 597 and 586 B.C. respectively that Babylon fulfilled the prophecies against Judah and Jerusalem.[15] Even so, almost as soon as those words of warning in Chapter 39 left Isaiah's mouth he

---

14 Personal Journal December 23, 2020
15 *Isaiah 40:31 Commentary*, Precept Austin. Retrieved from https://www.preceptaustin.org/isaiah_4031_commentary (last accessed August 8, 2021)

spoke to Judah as if the Babylonian exile was almost over.[16] Given the coming disaster, hopelessness was inevitable.[17] God's revelation came at precisely the time when His covenant people needed hope for the future! God knows that the only cure for one without hope, the only comfort for a discouraged heart, is *current faith* and *future hope* in Him alone.[18] And that is exactly the message He delivered to His people through His prophet Isaiah!

God's encouraging message is an astounding review of His nature. "He is *the everlasting God*, therefore there is no time when He is not; *the ends of the earth* are his, therefore there is no place where he is not; [he is] *not ... tired or weary*, his strength does not flag, deficiency of inner resources cannot limit him, nor can lack of *understanding*."[19] The conclusion of God's message then is to consider how absurd it would be to lose "faith in One who, in relation to earth, is all-powerful ([Isaiah 40:]12), all-wise ([vv.] 13-14), dominant ([vv.] 15-17), with no god to challenge, check or rival him ([vv.] 18-20), King of kings ([vv.] 21-24), sovereignly in charge of his world down to the smallest detail so that everything is in its place, nothing overlooked, nothing lost!"[20] In Isaiah 40:26 God points to the heavens and His masterful blueprint for movement of the stars to illustrate how exact and perfect His direct day-to-day management of the world is.[21] Surely if He can manage what takes place in the heavens He is more than able to take care of what concerns His covenant people on earth!

---

16 *NIV Study Bible* (Zondervan Publishing 1995) study note Isaiah 40:1-66:24, p. 1064
17 Motyer, J. Alec, *The Prophecy of Isaiah: An Introduction & Commentary* (InterVarsity Press 1993) Isaiah 40:27-31, p. 307
18 *Isaiah 40:31 Commentary*, Precept Austin. Retrieved from https://www.preceptaustin.org/isaiah_4031_commentary (last accessed August 8, 2021)
19 Motyer, J. Alec, *Isaiah*, Tyndale Old Testament Commentaries (IVP Academic 1999) Isaiah 40:28, p. 282, italics in original
20 Motyer, J. Alec, *Isaiah*, Tyndale Old Testament Commentaries (IVP Academic 1999) Isaiah 40:27, p. 282
21 Motyer, J. Alec, *Isaiah*, Tyndale Old Testament Commentaries (IVP Academic 1999) Isaiah 40:26, p. 282

It would be easy in light of these truths to infer that God is too great to care. However, the conclusion God expects His people to reach is that "[H]e is too great to fail!"[22] It is in light of this truth that God encourages His people to trust Him, to not lose hope no matter what. We may not understand His ways, but we should never doubt His capacity. We should confidently expect that as we become tired and weary in the days ahead we can refuel our hope by coming to His 24/7 Gift Exchange Counter. There we can exchange the little strength we have for His great unending strength!

Now let's walk through our Key Scripture together. I'll restate it here for your convenience:

> [B]ut those who hope in the LORD will renew their strength. They will soar on wings like eagles; they will run and not grow weary, they will walk and not be faint. Isaiah 40:31 NIV

those who hope in the LORD: Notice that the promise God makes is for a select group of people. It is limited to "those who hope in Him." As we've seen, the word "hope" in this verse can be translated as "wait." It can also be rendered "trust." It is the Hebrew word *qavah* {kaw-vaw'} [see Lesson 2 Word Study] which expresses the idea of waiting hopefully. The form of the word employed here points "to a maintained relationship."[23] These hope-ers are people who maintain their relationship with Yahweh. The word *qavah* provides us with a picture that illustrates *how* that relationship is sustained.[24] As we learned in Lesson 2 *qavah* refers to the type of twisting and binding used in the ancient art of rope making. A heavy cord or rope was formed by twisting, braiding or in some

---

22 Motyer, J. Alec, *The Prophecy of Isaiah: An Introduction & Commentary* (InterVarsity Press 1993) Isaiah 40:27-31, p. 307
23 Motyer, J. Alec, *Isaiah*, Tyndale Old Testament Commentaries (IVP Academic 1999) Isaiah 40:29-31, p. 283
24 Bentorah, Chaim, *Hebrew Word Study*, entry for *PATIENTLY WAITING CHAKAH* חכה. Retrieved from https://www.chaimbentorah.com/2021/01/hebrew-word-study-patiently-waiting/ (last accessed October 27, 2021)

manner tightly binding together thin strands of natural fibers. Individually those thin fiber strands were very fragile and could break easily. However, by binding them together they become stronger. In the same way, the hope-ers who are promised renewed strength in Isaiah 40:31 are weak individually but strengthened by spiritually binding themselves to Yahweh. The more figuratively they bind themselves to Him, the more confidence and trust they have in Him while they wait. In this way, they maintain their right relationship with Yahweh and keep themselves in position to receive what He has promised.

will renew their strength: We will be helped here by two Word Studies.

> ### WORD STUDY
>
> *The word **renew** is the Hebrew verb chalaph {khawlaf'} which can mean to pass through, move on, change, or renew.[25] Figuratively it can refer to a change in form or a transition from one state or stage to another (like exchanging one for the other). "This root envisions the after-effect (results) of moving on or a change of state."[26]*

Concretely *chalaph* refers to changing clothes, i.e., taking off the old and putting on the new as in Genesis 41:14. Its use in Isaiah 40:31 pictures *taking off* weakness and *putting on* God's strength.[27] The idea conveyed is to "'keep putting on fresh strength.'

---

25 Harris, Archer, and Waltke, editors, *Theological Wordbook of the Old Testament* (Moody Press 1999) word #666, p. 291; Baker and Carpenter, *The Complete WordStudy Dictionary of the Old Testament* (AMG Publishers 2003) word #2498, p. 343
26 Hill, Gary, *The Discovery Bible*, HELPS Ministries, Inc., [H]2498 ḥālaph
27 *Isaiah 40:31 Commentary*, Precept Austin. Retrieved from https://www.preceptaustin.org/isaiah_4031_commentary (last accessed August 8, 2021)

[This strength] is a different strength, as if people become eagles, a strength brought about by transformation; it is divine strength, a strength like the Lord's own that does not *weary* or *faint*."[28]

> ## WORD STUDY
>
> The word **strength** is the Hebrew noun koach *{ko'-akh} (also transliterated as koah or kowach). Its overall primary meaning is strength, power.*[29] *Koach can speak of capacity to endure, potency, or capacity to produce – often in the sense of physical strength.*[30] *It can also "connote general ability to cope with situations."*[31]
>
> *In Isaiah 40:31, koach refers to strength conferred by God.*[32] *In fact, the overwhelming majority of biblical uses of koach refers either to the power of God or the strength He gives to people.*[33]

---

28 Motyer, J. Alec, *Isaiah,* Tyndale Old Testament Commentaries (IVP Academic 1999) Isaiah 40:29-31, p. 283, italics in original

29 *Isaiah 40:31 Commentary*, Precept Austin, citing *NIDOTTE* (*New International Dictionary of Old Testament Theology and Exegesis*). Retrieved from https://www.preceptaustin.org/isaiah_4031_commentary (last accessed August 8, 2021)

30 Harris, Archer, and Waltke, editors, *Theological Wordbook of the Old Testament* (Moody Press 1999) word #436, pp. 436-437

31 Harris, Archer, and Waltke, editors, *Theological Wordbook of the Old Testament* (Moody Press 1999) word #436, pp. 436-437

32 Motyer, J. Alec, *The Prophecy of Isaiah: An Introduction & Commentary* (InterVarsity Press 1993) Isaiah 40:31, p. 308

33 *Isaiah 40:31 Commentary*, Precept Austin, citing *TDOT* 7:128. Retrieved from https://www.preceptaustin.org/isaiah_4031_commentary (last accessed August 8, 2021)

As applied to Yahweh, *koach* refers to the fact that He is omnipotent.[34] Exodus 15:6 declares that God's right hand (a metaphor for divine strength)[35] is majestic and glorious in strength (*koach*). In fact, the exodus is "the supreme example of divine power."[36] Yahweh's *koach* is described as having "shattered [Pharaoh's] pursuing attack."[37]

The Hebrew word *koach* ("strength") in Isaiah 40:31 is translated with the Greek word *ischus* {is-khoos'} in the LXX.[38] (Remember that's the first translation of the Hebrew Old Testament and it was written in the Greek language so it becomes a type of dictionary for translating Hebrew thought into Greek.) *Ischus* is used to describe one of God's attributes in Revelation.[39]

Paul used a Greek word that overlaps in meaning with *ischus* when he spoke of God's strength at work in Christ-followers as if we were an ordinary clay jar that contained this treasure.

> But we have this treasure in earthen vessels, that the excellence of the power [*dunamis*, overlapping definition with the word *ischus*] [40] may be of God, and not of us.
> 2 Corinthians 4:7 NKJV

---

34 Harris, Archer, and Waltke, editors, *Theological Wordbook of the Old Testament* (Moody Press 1999) word #436, pp. 436-437
35 Durham, John I., *Word Biblical Commentary: Exodus*, Volume 3 (Word Books 1987) Exodus 15:4-7, p. 206
36 Bromiley, Geoffrey W., *Theological Dictionary of the New Testament*, Abridged in One Volume (Eerdmans 1985) entry for *dynamai* under B. *The Idea of Power in the OT*, p. 187
37 Durham, John I., *Word Biblical Commentary: Exodus*, Volume 3 (Word Books 1987) Exodus 15:4-7, p. 206
38 *Ephesians 1:18-19 Commentary*, Precept Austin. Retrieved from https://www.preceptaustin.org/ephesians_1 18-19#might (last accessed July 30, 2022)
39 See Revelation 5:12, 7:12
40 "The group *ischy-* has the sense of 'ability,' 'capacity,' 'power,' or 'strength.' It **overlaps** with the dyna- group, but with greater stress on the power implied." Bromiley, Geoffrey W., *Theological Dictionary of the New Testament*, Abridged in One Volume (Eerdmans 1985) entry for *ischyo*, p. 378, bold added. Note: included in the dyna- group is the word *dunamis*.

The "power" Paul is describing to the Corinthians is the same power God speaks of in Isaiah 40:31. Let's look at how the church in Corinth most likely understood what Paul was saying. The phrase "earthen vessels" would have been very familiar in the culture of that day. Corinth was situated on an isthmus with two harbors, one leading to Asia and the other to Italy.[41] Wine and olive oil were very common exports from Corinth. Earthen clay was abundant making it the least expensive and the most practical raw material for the storage containers needed to ship wine and olive oil long distances.[42] This clay was commonly formed into terracotta *amphorae* (clay storage jars) which could hold about 6 gallons on average. During shipment residue from either the wine or oil would seep into the clay. That residue would turn rancid preventing the containers from being reused. The used clay jars (earthen vessels) were routinely smashed after the contents had been emptied because they were no longer good for anything. Given the familiarity of the Corinthians with *amphorae*, it seems very likely these earthen shipping containers provided the imagery Paul used in his "earthen vessel" metaphor. It would have supplied a well-suited picture for Paul's point that God uses human messengers to dispense His power because it puts God on display. It is obvious to the world that the power can't be from an ordinary human being, who is a mere earthen vessel, so God naturally gets the glory.

They will soar on wings like eagles: The obvious word picture here is of an eagle in majestic flight. Let's first take note that this is not the only time the Old Testament refers to Yahweh using eagle imagery. The exodus of Abraham's descendants from Egypt was the formative event in the history of Israel. When God later spoke of

---

41 *In The Footsteps of Paul, Corinth: Aphrodite of Cities.* Retrieved from https://www.pbs.org/empires/peterandpaul/ /footsteps/footsteps _6_2.html (last accessed August 8, 2021)

42 Will, Elizabeth Lyding, *The Ancient Commercial Amphora*, Archaeology 30:264-278 (1977). Retrieved from http://www.promare.org/wp-content/uploads/2016/07/EL-Will-1977-The-Ancient-Commercial-Amphora.pdf (last accessed August 8, 2021)

The Power of Hope

His miraculous deliverance He used the eagle to picture how He had carried them on eagles' wings and brought them to Himself (Exodus 19:4). Through Ezekiel's prophecy, Yahweh referred to Himself as "a great eagle with large wings and long pinons."[43]

Various reasons have been suggested as to why God compared His power exchange to a soaring eagle. For example:

- In ancient Israel, the eagle was considered to be the swiftest and most stately of birds.[44]
- In Psalm 103:5 [your youth is renewed like the eagle's] "the eagle serves as a symbol of vigor and freedom associated with the benefits of restoration to divine favor and covenantal status."[45]
- An eagle was known to be fast, a powerful force against an enemy and defensive of its young.[46]
- Throughout the ancient world, the eagle was commonly used to symbolize strength and royal splendor. It was a common military and royal symbol. Kings in the ancient

---

43 Quoting from Ezekiel 17:3. Scholar Daniel Block points out in his commentary on Ezekiel 17:22 that Yahweh reveals *He* is the great eagle referred to in Ezekiel 17:3 NKJV. Block, Daniel I., *The Book of Ezekiel Chapters 1-24,* The New International Commentary on the Old Testament (Eerdmans 1997) Ezekiel 17:22, p. 550

44 Block, Daniel I., *The Book of Ezekiel: Chapters 1-24,* The New International Commentary on the Old Testament (Eerdmans 1997) Ezekiel 1:8b-10, p. 96

45 Longman III and Garland, general editors, *The Expositor's Bible Commentary: Psalms,* Vol. 5, Revised Edition (Zondervan 2008) Psalm 103:5, p. 757

46 *How does the Bible use symbolism?* Compelling Truth, Old Testament under *Animals,* entry for *eagle,* citing Exodus 19:4; Deuteronomy 28:49; 32:11; 2 Samuel 1:23; Job 9:26; Psalm 103:5; Proverbs 23:5; 30:19; Isaiah 40:31; Jeremiah 48:40; 49:22; Ezekiel 1:10; 17:3; Daniel 7:4; Hosea 8:1; Micah 1:16; Habakkuk 1:8; Revelation 4:7. Retrieved from http://www.compellingtruth.org/biblical-symbolism.html (last accessed August 21, 2021)

Near East "were often portrayed as cherublike figures with eagles' wings."[47]

There is certainly a common thread of swiftness, power and strength that weaves through each of these explanations. The amazing thing about Hebrew thought is that we don't have to pinpoint just one of these possible backgrounds for Isaiah's use of the eagle metaphor. Ancient Hebrew thought allowed for multiple word associations to be true all at the same time!

they will run and not grow weary: Run is the Hebrew word *ruwts* {roots}. In Psalm 119 the psalmist uses the figurative sense of this word to refer to following God's commandments. Note that the psalmist recognizes that it is God who will enable him to keep those commands.

I shall **run** [*ruwts*] the way of Your commandments,
For You will enlarge my heart. Psalm 119:32, bold added

they will walk and not be faint: The word "walk" is a translation of the Hebrew verb *halak* {haw-lak'}. It is a common word that connotes the idea of movement: to go, to come, to walk.[48] "To walk with God means to go the same direction He is going in His company. It is lifelong obedience to [Him] and [uninterrupted] communion with Him."[49] In other words, *halak* is often used in a metaphoric sense such that it expresses the idea of keeping God's commandments as a habitual way of life.[50] The New Testament often uses the word walk in this figurative way. For example:

---

47 Block, Daniel I., *The Book of Ezekiel: Chapters 1-24,* The New International Commentary on the Old Testament (Eerdmans 1997) Ezekiel 17:11-12a, p. 539-540

48 Baker and Carpenter, *The Complete WordStudy Dictionary of the Old Testament* (AMG Publishers 2003) word #1980, p. 265

49 *How does the Bible use symbolism?* Compelling Truth, Old Testament under *Walk with God,* citing Genesis 5:22; 6:9; Deuteronomy 10:12; Joshua 22:5; 1 Kings 8:23; Micah 6:8. Retrieved from http://www.compellingtruth.org/biblical-symbolism.html (last accessed August 21, 2021)

50 Harris, Archer, and Waltke, editors, *Theological Wordbook of the Old Testament* (Moody Press 1999) word #498, p. 216

The Power of Hope

> [F]or **we walk by faith**, not by sight— 2 Corinthians 5:7, bold added

> So I say, **walk by the Spirit**, and you will not gratify the desires of the flesh. Galatians 5:16 NIV, bold added

> Therefore I, the prisoner of the Lord, implore you to **walk in a manner worthy of the calling** with which you have been called. Ephesians 4:1, bold added

> And this is love, **that we walk according to His commandments**. This is the commandment, just as you have heard from the beginning, that **you should walk in it**. 2 John 1:6, bold added

Returning to Isaiah 40:31, "weary" is a translation of the Hebrew verb *yaga`* {yaw-gah'} and "faint" is the Hebrew verb *ya`aph* {yaw-af'}. They are similar in meaning. Both words refer to being overcome by circumstances. The difference is that *ya'eph* refers to being overcome through a lack of inner resources (i.e., a feeling of "I don't have any more to give")[51] and *yaga* refers to being overcome through the objective difficulty of life.[52] For example, in Jeremiah 45:3 *yaga`* denotes Baruch's [Jeremiah's scribe] "loss of energy or spirit from [his] hopeless response to ... adversity."[53]

The Hebrew language often uses such synonyms in parallel to add emphasis or to complete the point the author is making. In Isaiah 40:31, our Key Scripture, the verbs *yaga`* and *ya`aph* are used in what is known as "synonymous poetic parallel." The author chose two words that are close in meaning so that together they emphasize that those who wait for Yahweh will *definitely not*

---

51 Hill, Gary, *The Discovery Bible*, HELPS Ministries, Inc., [H]61c (SN 3286) *yā'eph*
52 Motyer, J. Alec, *The Prophecy of Isaiah: An Introduction & Commentary* (InterVarsity Press 1993) Isaiah 40:30, p. 308
53 Baker and Carpenter, *The Complete WordStudy Dictionary of the Old Testament* (AMG Publishers 2003) word #3021, p. 417

be overcome by *any* set of circumstances! The promise is that they will keep putting on fresh strength.[54]

As I was working on this lesson God provided me with a wonderful illustration of how we can continue to run and not grow weary, how we can walk and not faint amid adversity. My car was having problems starting because the battery was no longer holding its charge the way it did when it was new. My husband was hoping against hope (the wishful thinking kind of hope) he could maintain enough charge to prolong the battery life and avoid purchasing a new one for as long as he could. So, in the evening he would often hook up the battery to a charger to rejuvenate it overnight. After being charged all night that old battery would start in the morning. This problem of not holding its charge continued for several weeks until one day I put the key in the ignition and it wouldn't start at all. Unfortunately, the car was not parked in our garage. I had driven my mom to a medical appointment about 25 minutes away. The plan was to meet up with my husband for breakfast when we finished. Instead of going straight to breakfast, however, my husband had to drive to the place where we were stranded, use the jumper cables and jump-start my car. He followed us to the breakfast place and we all enjoyed a nice breakfast after a trying experience. However, when we finished breakfast – you guessed it – my car wouldn't start. So out came the jumper cables and my car once again received a jolt of fresh power so it could start again. My husband's wishful kind of hope came to a dead end and he replaced the battery in my car that afternoon. That new battery now holds a charge and my car starts as soon as I turn the key in the ignition.

The promise of God to His covenant people is this: when the circumstances are such that our hoping heart needs to be recharged (like my old car battery) we can come to Him. When we do, He won't just put jumper cables on our weary, fainting heart. He will exchange *His* "unwearying, unfainting strength" for our weariness and fainting strength. In other words, He will give us a fresh new

---

54 Motyer, J. Alec, *The Prophecy of Isaiah: An Introduction & Commentary* (InterVarsity Press 1993) Isaiah 40:30, p. 308

hope-battery full of *His* strength. As He does, He provides us with sufficient inner resources to maintain hope and that hope ensures we do not become sick at heart no matter what life demands.[55]

Jim Cymbala, the pastor of the Brooklyn Tabernacle, describes an "evening, when [he] was at [his] lowest, confounded by obstacles, bewildered by the darkness that surrounded [them], unable even to continue preaching." He writes, "I discovered an astonishing truth: God is attracted to weakness. He can't resist those who humbly and honestly admit how desperately they need him. Our weakness, in fact, makes room for his power."[56] Here's the point: when God doesn't change the circumstances, He chooses to change us. Thus, our path to overcoming victory "lies not in liberating ourselves from oppressive circumstances; it lies in waiting for the Lord. In that way the Lord enables us to transcend our circumstances."[57]

Hear What The Spirit is Saying to the Church: *My Kingdom advancement relies on hope in this now-but-not-yet season. The enemy is without power to defeat hope. His only option in the face of hope is to try to encourage hope to be forfeited for when it is laid down then his power is restored. Because hope functions in this way it will always be required of my people in the darkest days. Great Kingdom advancement can occur in those seasons when the enemy's power is defeated.*

---

55 Motyer, J. Alec, *The Prophecy of Isaiah: An Introduction & Commentary* (InterVarsity Press 1993) Isaiah 40:31, p. 308
56 *Isaiah 40:31 Commentary*, Precept Austin, citing Jim Cymbala, *Fresh Wind, Fresh Fire*. Retrieved from https://www.preceptaustin.org /isaiah_4031_commentary (last accessed August 8, 2021)
57 *Isaiah 40:31 Commentary*, Precept Austin. Retrieved from https://www.preceptaustin.org/isaiah_4031_commentary (last accessed August 8, 2021)

Lesson 7:

The Hope of Every Christ-Follower

"Therefore remember that formerly you, the Gentiles in the flesh, who are called 'Uncircumcision' by the so-called 'Circumcision,'... *remember* that you were at that time separate from Christ, excluded from the commonwealth of Israel, and strangers to the covenants of promise, having no hope and without God in the world." Ephesians 2:11-12, italics in original

THE FIRST VERSE of the letter to the church at Ephesus identifies the Apostle Paul as the author of the biblical book we call Ephesians. Among the New Testament authors, Paul used *elpizo* and *elpis* more than anyone else. We first encountered those two words in Lesson 2 where we learned that *elpis* is the Greek noun for hope and *elpizo* is the verb meaning hope in action. Given Paul's frequent references to hope I think it is fitting to dub him the "Apostle of Hope." When he writes to Titus, Paul refers to this hope as "blessed hope (Titus 2:13)." When he writes to the church at Thessalonica he urges them to be comforted by this hope (1 Thessalonians 4:13-18). In Colossians, Paul references "the hope of glory" and says this hope is "reserved in heaven" for Christ-followers (Colossians 1:5, 27).[1]

---

[1] These are not all of the references Paul makes to hope in his epistles. I have been selective and chosen only those which in one way or another label hope in a unique way.

While Paul refers to hope more often than other New Testament authors, he is not exclusive in his references. We also find, for example, the author of Hebrews refers to "the hope of which we boast" "the hope set before us" a hope that is "both sure and reliable" and a hope which serves "as an anchor of the soul (Hebrews 3:6; 6:19)." Peter calls this hope a "living hope" in 1 Peter 1:3. John testifies to a "purifying hope" asserting that "everyone who has this hope set on God purifies himself, just as God is pure (1 John 3:3)."

In this lesson, we want to identify with clarity the hope that is to fill the heart of every Christ-follower. Whether you are a Jewish *talmid* (disciple)[2] or a Gentile *talmid* (disciple)[3] our journey to comprehend that biblical truth must begin with understanding the "Hope of Israel." Acts 23 – 28 narrates Paul's imprisonment and several trials all related to the same charges against Paul. His accusers were fellow Jews who claimed that as the ringleader of the sect of the Nazarenes Paul had tried to desecrate the Temple and was teaching everyone everywhere to disregard the laws of Moses. As we look at Paul's testimony in these various trials, as well as his witness to the Jewish leaders in Rome, we will see a common thread of hope.

> [Paul's testimony before the Sanhedrin in Jerusalem when he was in custody of Roman soldiers]: "… 'Brethren, I am a Pharisee, a son of Pharisees; **I am on trial for the hope and resurrection of the dead**!'" Acts 23:6, bold added

> [Paul's testimony before Roman Governor Felix in Caesarea]: "But this I admit to you, that according to

---

2   Hebrew word for "disciple" – See Preface to this study for explanation
3   As noted in Lesson 2, footnote 8, from the New Testament perspective, the world was divided into two groups: Jews and non-Jews (Gentiles). Gentiles who became Christ-followers remained Gentiles and were not required to become Jews. They became Gentile members of the people of God. On this point, see Tucker, Brian J., *Reading 1 Corinthians* (Cascade Books 2017) p. 84, interpreting Paul's statement that, "Each one should remain in the condition in which he was called (1 Corinthians 7:20 ESV)."

the Way which they call a sect I do serve the God of our fathers, believing everything that is in accordance with the Law and that is written in the Prophets; **having a hope in God**, which these men cherish themselves, that there shall certainly be a resurrection of both the righteous and the wicked." Acts 24:14-15, bold added

[Paul's testimony before King Agrippa in Caesarea]: "And now **I am standing trial for the hope of the promise made by God to our fathers**; *the promise* to which our twelve tribes **hope to attain**, as they earnestly serve *God* night and day. And for **this hope**, O King, I am being accused by Jews." Acts 26:6-7, italics in original, bold added

[Paul's witness to the Jewish leaders while in custody in Rome] "… I am wearing this chain for the sake of **the hope of Israel**." Acts 28:20, bold added

Paul said he was bound in chains because his testimony to his Jewish brothers, as well as across the known Gentile world, was that God had fulfilled His covenant promises.[4] Paul recognized that when God raised Jesus it was His decisive public announcement that Jesus was indeed the promised Messiah.[5] Paul was convinced that God's covenantal faithfulness meant those hope-filled ancient promises had been realized in Christ.

---

[4] Paul uses the phrase "the Jew first and also the Greek" three times in his letter to the Romans. "'To the Jew first' is Paul's shorthand for God's continued prioritization of Israel in his plans and purposes, leading to the establishment of God's kingdom on earth with the son of David on the throne (Rom 1:3)." Rudolph, David J., "*To the Jew First" Paul's Vision for the Priority of Israel in the Life of the Church*, July 22, 2020, *Kesher: A Journal of Messianic Judaism*, Issue 37 Summer/Fall 2020. Retrieved from https://www.kesherjournal.com/article/to-the-jew-first-pauls-vision-for-the-priority-of-israel-in-the-life-of-the-church/ (last accessed September 23, 2021)

[5] Blackwell, Goodrich, and Maston, editors, *Reading Romans in Context: Paul and Second Temple Judaism* (Zondervan 2015) p. 34

> For I say that Christ has become a servant to the [Jews] on behalf of the truth of God [to manifest God's faithfulness],[6] to confirm[7] the promises *given* to the fathers. Romans 15:8, italics in original

> For all of God's promises have been fulfilled in Christ with a resounding "Yes!" And through Christ, our "Amen" (which means "Yes") ascends to God for his glory. 2 Corinthians 1:20 NLT

Generally speaking, Israel had hope in God because throughout her history God had faithfully acted as her savior in times of trouble and distress.[8] As a result, He was considered to be the "Hope of Israel." For example, when the people called on Yahweh to rescue them from drought in the days of Jeremiah, they referred to Him as: "Hope of Israel, its Savior in time of distress."[9] Even the enemies of Israel were figuratively viewed as referring to Israel's God as "the LORD [Yahweh], the hope of their ancestors."[10] The Psalms are notable for their promise of blessings to those who put their hope in Yahweh.[11]

However, beyond this general hope of rescue from physical distress and calamity (which is the core biblical definition of salvation) Paul is clear that there were specific promises made to Israel which were then fulfilled in Christ. Down through the centuries, Israel had placed her hope in those promises (revelations from God which had found a home in their collective hearts). Paul does not

---

6   Keck, Leander E., *Romans*, Abingdon New Testament Commentaries (Abingdon Press 2005) The Grand Horizon ([Romans] 15:7-13), p. 355
7   In Romans 15:8, the word *confirm* "is a legal term, denoting the certainty with which the promises would be fulfilled." Schreiner, Thomas R., *Romans*, 2nd edition, Baker Exegetical Commentary on the New Testament (Baker Academic 1998, 2018) Romans 15:8, p. 729
8   Thompson, J. A., *The Book of Jeremiah*, The New International Commentary on The Old Testament (Eerdmans 1980) Jeremiah 14:8-9, p. 380
9   Jeremiah 14:8
10 Jeremiah 50:7 NIV
11 See for example: Psalm 31:23; 37:9; 38:15

delineate these promises one by one. He knew they were well-rehearsed in Israel's history. When we turn to the Hebrew Scriptures Paul read, we find three clusters of promises God made to Israel – all of which were fulfilled in Christ.

1. Promises Yahweh made to Abraham, Isaac and Jacob
2. Promises Yahweh made to King David
3. Promises Yahweh made to Israel about a new covenant

Before we look at these promises, it will be instructive for us to consider why God provides this type of advanced revelation. We have taken notice before, as in the case of God's promise to Abraham for a son, that hope essentially provides "a present perspective based upon a future expectation."[12] God alone knows that the way for His covenant people to *look through* and therefore *look beyond* distressing situations is to give them a point of reference that extends far into the future. He then uses *that* distant point of reference as an invitation to hope for the fulfillment of *that* revelation. Rather than fixing their eyes on the immediate distress or trouble, He invites them into His *Hope Waiting Room* where they can fully submit to Him. It is in that waiting period they can confidently trust in Him and focus on "the furthest point of revelation He has given."[13] This divine strategy works because, as we have already learned, hope is based on *who God is*. Because He alone knows the future, He can make the promise and then bring

---

12　Lane, Hal, *'Hope' in Paul's Letters*, Lifeway article, January 01, 2014. Retrieved from www.lifeway.com/en/articles/biblical-illustrator-hope-paul-letters-epistles-faith (last accessed August 8, 2021). This article originally appeared in *Biblical Illustrator*.
13　I credit Chuck Pierce for the concept of looking at your present circumstances through the furthest point of revelation that God has given. Pierce, Chuck, *Gaining Perspective! "Look Through" to See Your Future! How Are You Viewing Your Situation in the Midst of Great Change?* Glory of Zion. Received via E-mail February 22, 2021

to pass what He has promised. It is because of who God is that "hope attains unparalleled assurance in the realm of revelation."[14]

As we have seen, biblical hope is neither wishful thinking nor blind optimism. British New Testament scholar N. T. Wright describes hope well when he refers to hope as "a mode of knowing."[15] Hope for the Christ-follower is a manner, a means, a type and a way of having knowledge that those who lack hope do not have. Looking out beyond the circumstances of the moment to gaze on the furthest point that God has revealed to us, enables us to capture the faith dynamic He releases to help us see the circumstances in front of us from a heavenly perspective.[16] Even when everything that can be seen in the present runs counter to that heavenly perspective, we can make the choice to hope. When we do, we are trusting that God will be faithful for His Name's sake "not to disappoint the hope He has awakened through His word.... [And as a result] [t]hrough confidence and humility hope becomes a patient, persevering waiting which can endure anxiety."[17]

Somewhat surprisingly the treatment of motion sickness actually provides a good analogy for our consideration. I am not usually prone to motion sickness to any great degree. However, there was a season in my life when I was in a corporate management position that required me to board the corporate jet every so often to fly

---

14 Wenstrom, William E., Jr., *Greek Word Studies* (Wenstrom.org 2016) entry for *Elpis*, quoting Colin Brown, *New International Dictionary of New Testament Theology*, Volume 2, p. 240. Retrieved from https://www.wenstrom.org/downloads/written/word_studies/greek/elpis.pdf (last accessed August 8, 2021)

15 Wright, Tom, *Surprised by HOPE* (Society for Promoting Christian Knowledge 2007, reissued 2011) p. 83

16 Pierce, Chuck, *Gaining Perspective! "Look Through" to See Your Future! How Are You Viewing Your Situation in the Midst of Great Change?* Glory of Zion. Received via E-mail February 22, 2021

17 Wenstrom, William E., Jr., *Greek Word Studies* (Wenstrom.org 2016) entry for *Elpis*, quoting Colin Brown, *New International Dictionary of New Testament Theology*, Volume 2, p. 240. Retrieved from https://www.wenstrom.org/downloads/written/word_studies/greek/elpis.pdf (last accessed August 8, 2021)

to a meeting. Normally that was not a problem and was much more convenient than driving to the day-long meeting. That all changed when I was pregnant and motion sickness hit me like a ton of bricks! The normally comfortable and convenient ride on that small plane was turned into sheer misery.

Basically, motion sickness occurs when your brain can't make sense of information that is being sent from your eyes, ears and body. Your brain's confused reaction makes you feel physically sick. Instruction to maintain your balance and avoid, or at least reduce, the feelings of motion sickness centers on something known as "distant gaze."[18] The conventional medical advice is to:

- Relax and find a stable distant object to focus on.
- In a car, sit in the front seat and look at *the distant scenery*.
- On a boat, go up on the deck and *gaze at the horizon*.
- In an airplane, sit by the window, preferably in a seat over the wing and *look outside*.

In short, experts advise you to keep your eyes off your immediate surroundings and focus them on something in the distance. What works in the natural, works in the spiritual realm. When we find ourselves in circumstances that upset our emotional and spiritual equilibrium, God provides us with long-distance promises to help us get our eyes off of the immediate and engage in "distant gaze." He invites us to focus on His distant promises.

As a biblical case in point, we only need to read as far as the third chapter of Genesis. Adam and Eve had disobeyed God and were subject to the consequences He had warned in the event of their disobedience. However, in almost the same breath God pro-

---

18 *Motion Sickness,* Cleveland Clinic. Retrieved from https://my.clevelandclinic.org/health/articles/12782-motion-sickness (lasts accessed August 8, 2021). See also: *What's to know about motion sickness?* MedicalNewsToday. Retrieved from https://www.medicalnewstoday.com/articles/176198 (last accessed August 8, 2021); *Why Do I Get Motion Sickness?* WebMD. Retrieved from https://www.webmd.com/cold-and-flu/ear-infection/motion-sickness (last accessed August 8, 2021)

vided a point of revelation way out into the future which was the very first proclamation of the gospel.

> "... And I [God] will cause hostility between you [the serpent in the garden who deceived Eve] and the woman, and between your offspring and her offspring. He will strike your head, and you will strike his heel." Genesis 3:15 NLT

We know from the record of the New Testament that this is descriptive of the mission and the work of Christ.[19] In His amazing grace, God had set a point of revelation thousands of years into the future to provide every generation between Adam and Christ the opportunity to have a hope-infused distant gaze.

Now that we understand how hope works through God's promises, let's consider the three clusters of promises God made to Israel and how each was fulfilled in Christ thus forming the basis of the gospel message itself. To reiterate, those promises are ones Yahweh made to:

1. Abraham, Isaac and Jacob
2. King David
3. Israel (about a new covenant)

The first cluster involves the long-range promises God made to Abraham, which He confirmed to Isaac and Jacob.

> "... in you [Abraham] all the families of the earth will be blessed." Genesis 12:3

> [B]y your descendants [Isaac] all the nations of the earth shall be blessed. Genesis 26:4

---

19 Revelation 12:17 is viewed as being related to this promise. Beale and Carson, editors, *Commentary on the New Testament Use of the Old Testament* (Baker Academic 2007) Revelation 12:17, p. 1126

> Your descendants [Jacob] will also be like the dust of the earth, and ... in your descendants shall all the families of the earth be blessed. Genesis 28:14

God made essentially the same promise to each of the three patriarchs of Israel. Each time the promise was made it related to a period that extended way out into the future. We know from Scripture that God's plan was for Jesus (the eventual *seed* of Abraham)[20] to be the one through whom the promised blessing would be fulfilled. In Galatians, Paul makes clear that when we put our trust in Christ we become recipients of the redemptive blessings God promised to Abraham.

> And if you belong to Christ, then you are Abraham's descendants, heirs according to promise. Galatians 3:29

So, we see that the Bible makes clear that the cluster of promises God gave the patriarchs Abraham, Isaac and Jacob were fulfilled. During the days of King David's reign, God added further details to those promises speaking of the coming Messiah and the establishment of His kingdom.

> "... When your days [referring to King David's life] are complete and you lie down with your fathers [speaking of David's death], I will raise up your descendant [literally *seed*] after you, who will come forth from you, and I will establish his kingdom. He shall build a house [dwelling or habitation, could also refer to family] for My name, and I will establish the throne of his kingdom forever. I will be a father to him and he will be a son to Me .... My lovingkindness shall not depart from him .... Your house and your kingdom shall endure before Me forever; your throne shall be established forever." 2 Samuel 7:12-16[21]

---

20 The opening chapter of Matthew provides a genealogy that traces the birth of Jesus back to Abraham.
21 These promises were repeated throughout Israel's history. See for example: Isaiah 7:14; 9:6-7; Jeremiah 23:5-6; 33:14-16; Daniel 2:44-45; Micah 5:2

This prophecy most likely formed the basis of the second promise cluster Paul referenced in his self-defense. In 63 B.C. Roman General Pompey conquered Jerusalem and the cities and villages which surrounded it. That began Rome's dominance over the Jewish people and served to escalate Israel's hope for the promised Messiah. So, by the time of Paul almost a century later, Judaism had a firmly held Messianic expectation. Even though Messianic hope was diversified,[22] there were some common elements: The Messiah would be in the line of David, become the sovereign ruler over all Israel, gather the scattered Jews from every place where they had been dispersed, restore the full observance of the Torah and usher in *shalom* (well-being) to the whole world.[23] For example, a document written by Pharisees in the century just prior to Jesus entreats Yahweh to "raise up his Messiah, the Son of David, to rule over Israel, to destroy her enemies, and to establish a glorious and righteous kingdom."[24]

The significance of God's Messianic promise is reflected in Matthew's Gospel,[25] Mark's Gospel,[26] John's Gospel,[27] the book of Romans[28] and even in Revelation.[29] Let's look at how Luke underscores this promise as he records the announcement of Jesus' birth to Mary:

---

22 Strauss, Mark, "Luke," in *Zondervan Illustrated Bible Backgrounds Commentary*, Vol. 1, edited by Clinton E. Arnold (Zondervan 2002) *Messianic Expectations in Jesus' Day*, p. 333
23 Telushkin, Joseph, Rabbi, *Jewish Literacy: The Most Important Things To Know About the Jewish Religion, Its People, and Its History* (William Morrow and Co. 1991) p. 545
24 Strauss, Mark, "Luke," in *Zondervan Illustrated Bible Backgrounds Commentary*, Vol. 1, edited by Clinton E. Arnold (Zondervan 2002) Luke 17:20 under *When the kingdom of God would come*, p. 455, citing *Psalms of Solomon*, 17:21-46; 18:5-9 which was written in first-century B.C.
25 Matthew 1:1-17; 22:41-42
26 Mark 12:35-36
27 John 7:42
28 Romans 1:3
29 Revelation 22:16

> Now in the sixth month the angel Gabriel was sent from God to a city in Galilee called Nazareth, to a virgin engaged to a man whose name was Joseph, of the descendants of David; and the virgin's name was Mary. And coming in, he said to her, "Greetings, favored one! The Lord *is* with you." Luke 1:26-28, italics in original

> The angel said to her, "Do not be afraid, Mary; for you have found favor with God. And behold, you will conceive in your womb and bear a son, and you shall name Him Jesus. He will be great and will be called the Son of the Most High; and the Lord God will give Him the throne of His father David and He will reign over the house of Jacob forever, and His kingdom will have no end." Luke 1:30-33

The angels were the first to announce the birth of the promised Messiah:

> This very day, in the town of David, there was born for you a Deliverer who is the Messiah, the Lord. Luke 2:11 CJB

God, the Father, confirmed His true Identity:

> After being baptized, Jesus came up immediately from the water; and behold, the heavens were opened, and he saw the Spirit of God descending as a dove *and* lighting on Him, and behold, a voice out of the heavens said, "**This is My beloved Son**, in whom I am well-pleased." Matthew 3:16-17, italics in original, bold added

The phrase "This is my beloved Son" which has been highlighted in bold, echoes Psalm 2:7. That portion of Psalm 2 is understood as referring to a king in the line of David and the establishment of God's earthly Kingdom.[30]

Clearly, the disciples of Jesus understood Him to be the promised Messiah:

> [Peter] answered, "You are the *Mashiach* [Hebrew for Messiah], the Son of the living God." Matthew 16:16 CJB

> [Martha] said to [Jesus], "Yes, Lord; I believe that you are the Messiah, the Son of God, the one coming into the world." John 11:27 CJB

Jesus Himself confessed His identity to the Samaritan woman and thereafter many other Samaritans recognized who He was:

> The [Samaritan] woman [at the well] said to [Jesus], "I know that Messiah is coming (He who is called Christ); when that One comes, He will declare all things to us." Jesus said to her, "I who speak to you am *He*." John 4:25-26, italics in original

> [A]nd [the Samaritans] were saying to the woman [at the well], "It is no longer because of what you said that we believe, for we have heard for ourselves and know that this One is indeed the Savior of the world." John 4:42

When Jesus appeared to His disciples after His resurrection (before His ascension), their expectation that the promised Messiah would be the one to restore Israel led them to ask Him whether

---

30 Gundry, Robert H., *Commentary on the New Testament* (Hendrickson Publishers 2010) Matthew 3:16-17, p. 11. Psalm 2 gives understanding to "God's covenant with David and properly extends David's rule to the ends of the earth." Longman III and Garland, general editors, *The Expositor's Bible Commentary: Psalms*, Vol. 5, Revised Edition (Zondervan 2008) Psalm 2:7, p. 95

it was at that time that He was "reestablishing the kingdom and restoring it to Israel?"[31]

We have consistently noted throughout this study that God is faithful in fulfilling what He promises. Thus far in this lesson, we have tracked the fulfillment of the first two clusters of ancient promises which were likely included in Paul's testimony. Let's turn our attention to the third and final cluster. Following His promises to King David, God continued His pattern of providing long-range promises during the days of evil Kings in Israel and Judah. He repeatedly sent His prophets who engaged in "hope-telling"[32] encouraging His covenant people to employ distant gazing so they could *see* a better future. He promised a coming day when He would initiate a new covenant with them. There are prophetic passages in the Old Testament where the concept of a new covenant is present without using that specific terminology.[33] However, there is one place in prophetic literature where the precise phrase "new covenant" is used. It is found in the book of Jeremiah. We concluded Lesson 3 with this promise from Jeremiah 31, but it is worth restating it here.

> "Behold, days are coming," declares the LORD, "when I will make a **new covenant** with the house of Israel and the house of Judah, not like the covenant which I made with their fathers in the day I took them by the hand to bring them out of the land of Egypt, My covenant which they broke, although I was a husband to them," declares the LORD. "But this is the covenant which I will make with the house of Israel after those days," declares the LORD, "I will put My law within them and on their heart I will write it; and I will be their God, and they shall be My people...." Jeremiah 31:31-33, bold added

---

31   Acts 1:6 AMP, italics omitted
32   Brueggemann, Walter, *Truth & Hope: Essays For a Perilous Age* (Westminster John Knox Press 2020) p. 126
33   See for example: Isaiah 42:6; 49:8; 54:10; 55:3; 56:5-6; 61:8; Ezekiel 36:26-27

When Jesus celebrated the Passover with His disciples before His crucifixion, He told them clearly that through His shed blood He was inaugurating the promised "new covenant."

> He did the same with the cup after the meal, saying, "This cup is **the New Covenant**, ratified by my blood, which is being poured out for you...." Luke 22:20 CJB, bold added

The fact that all three promise clusters can be traced through Scripture from initial promise to literal fulfillment is a reverberating testimony to God's faithfulness. All of the promises we have been discussing were unique to Israel. That's the reason Paul, in our Key Scripture for this lesson, told the Gentile Christ-followers in Ephesus that *before* they became disciples of Christ they were "without hope [*elpis*]." As we have noted, our relationship with God as *talmidim* (disciples)[34] falls under the terms of the new covenant. Although the promises were made to Israel and Jesus came as a Jewish Messiah to fulfill them, the Bible is very clear that Gentile *talmidim* are grafted into this covenant with its promised blessings (Romans 11:24).

Our goal in this lesson is to identify the hope that should fill the heart of every Christ-follower – both Jew and Gentile. The promises that have already been fulfilled in Christ should fuel our hope, as it did for Paul, that our Promise Keeper will be faithful to do *all* He has promised. In fact, in Romans 15:8 when Paul says through Christ the promises made to Israel's patriarchs have been "confirmed," he used the Greek word *bebaioo* {beb-ah-yo'-o}. It is a legal term that reflects the absolute certainty that those promises would be fully realized.[35]

---

34 Hebrew word for disciples – See Preface to this study for explanation
35 Schreiner, Thomas R., *Romans*, Baker Exegetical Commentary on the New Testament, 2nd edition (Baker Academic 1998, 2018) Romans 15:8, p. 729; Keck, Leander E., *Romans*, Abingdon New Testament Commentaries (Abingdon Press 2005) The Grand Horizon ([Romans] 15:7-13) p. 355

The Power of Hope

Up to this point in our lesson we've conducted a pretty thorough review of the promises Paul was most likely referring to in his self-defense. The remaining promise we want to address is found in Paul's testimony before the Sanhedrin in Jerusalem that he was on "trial for the hope and resurrection of the dead (Acts 23:6)!" As *Zondervan Illustrated Bible Backgrounds Commentary* points out, "[I]t is of paramount importance to recognize that this is the central issue for which [Paul] is being persecuted and tried."[36] Paul founded his preaching about the hope of resurrection for every *talmid* on the evidence of Christ's resurrection. The entirety of the New Testament witnesses to the fact of that glorious resurrection.

> The Gospels contain abundant testimony to the resurrection of Christ .... In addition to these detailed narratives in the four gospels, the book of Acts is a story of the apostles' proclamation of the resurrection of Christ and of continued prayer to Christ and trust in him as the one who is alive and reigning in heaven. The Epistles depend entirely on the assumption that Jesus is a living, reigning Savior who is now the exalted head of the church, who is to be trusted, worshiped, and adored, and who will some day return in power and great glory to reign as King over the earth. The book of Revelation repeatedly shows the risen Christ reigning in heaven and predicts his return to conquer his enemies and reign in glory.[37]

Paul was of the opinion that if Christ was not really resurrected then those who have believed in Him are to be pitied above all men (1 Corinthians 15:19), the Apostles had been false witnesses and their preaching amounts to nothing (1 Corinthians 15:14,15).

---

36 Arnold, Clinton E., "Acts" in *Zondervan Illustrated Bible Backgrounds Commentary*, Vol. 2, edited by Clinton E. Arnold (Zondervan 2002) I stand on trial because of my hope in the resurrection of the dead ([Acts] 23:6), p. 445

37 Grudem, Wayne, *Systematic Theology: An Introduction to Biblical Doctrine* (InterVarsity Press 1994) p. 608

Moreover, the faith of Christ-followers is also "unfounded [being] devoid of value and benefit (1 Corinthians 15:14 AMP)." But he knew beyond doubt that those who became the *doulos* (slaves) of Christ did *not* live in a false hope. Paul had seen the resurrected Christ and so had every other Apostle along with many other witnesses. The resurrection of Christ took center stage in the record of the New Testament because it is the centerpiece of the gospel message. It is central to every twist and turn of what we believe and hope for as followers of Christ. So essential was the fact of resurrection to the early church that, "For Paul, without a belief in the resurrection of Christ and its accompanying hope in their own resurrection through God's grace, there is no reason for the Christ-groups [the *ekklesia*] to continue."[38]

The resurrection of Christ demonstrates God's faithfulness to fulfill His promises: We have already noted Paul's defense in his various trials centered on Christ who had been resurrected and was exalted by God to be Savior, King and Judge according to the promises made to Israel. That was also what Paul preached (Acts 13:33).

The resurrection of Jesus proves God was satisfied with His sacrifice: For Paul, the death of Jesus on the cross and the fact of His resurrection cannot be separated from each other.[39] In 1 Timothy 3:16 he succinctly explained the joint importance of the cross and the resurrection like this, "He who was revealed in the flesh, Was **vindicated** in the Spirit [and] … Taken up in glory." The Greek word translated as "vindicated" (highlighted in bold) is *dikaioo* {dik-ah-yo'-o}. In this context, Paul used it to say the resurrection demonstrates God's approval that Jesus' death on the cross sufficiently paid for sin. The cross was the payment for sin,

---

38 Tucker, J. Brian, *Reading 1 Corinthians* (Cascade Books 2017) p. 127
39 Schreiner, Thomas R., *Romans*, Baker Exegetical Commentary on the New Testament, 2nd edition (Baker Academic 1998, 2018) Romans 4:25, p. 251, citing McNeil 1975:104-5

The Power of Hope

but the resurrection was proof positive that the payment was satisfactory to the Father.[40]

The resurrection of Jesus reorients Messianic expectation from a present earthly kingdom to the hope of a future eternal kingdom. At the time of Jesus, the Jewish people were looking for a political solution to a spiritual problem. When Jesus entered Jerusalem on what we now call "Palm Sunday" the people were waving palm branches. It was their way of saying, "Free us from Roman rule the way the Maccabees freed us from Assyrian oppression." They had misinterpreted the prophecies about the Messiah and limited them to what God would do to relieve their suffering on earth. God had so much more in mind! He understood that the greatest need of men isn't relief from political oppression and suffering, it is relief from spiritual oppression and suffering.

Paul taught that God's great power was "worked in Christ when he raised him from the dead and seated him at his right hand in the heavenly places, far above all rule and authority and power and dominion, and above every name that is named, not only in this age but also in the one to come (Ephesians 1:19-20 ESV)." In similar fashion, Peter declared that the resurrected Christ is now "at the right hand of God, having gone into heaven, after angels and authorities and powers had been subjected to Him (1 Peter 3:22)."

Christ's resurrection ushered in the eternal kingdom of God that advances as His followers obey the commands they have received from their King. In this way God's kingdom advances on earth as it is in heaven. In the fullness of time, the present earth will give way to the new heaven and earth which will be the eternal home of all those who have submitted their lives to the Lordship of King Jesus.

---

40 *ESV Study Bible* (Crossway Books 2008) study note 1 Corinthians 15:17 under *still in your sins*, p. 2214; Schreiner, Thomas R., *Romans*, Baker Exegetical Commentary on the New Testament, 2nd edition (Baker Academic 1998, 2018) Romans 4:25, pp. 251-252; Keck, Leander E., *Romans*, Abingdon New Testament Commentaries (Abingdon Press 2005) Abraham's Faith and Christian Faith ([Romans] 4:23-25), p. 132

The resurrection of Jesus is proof that God had launched the new creation He had promised: As one Easter sermon proclaimed, "Never since the creation of the world had a day dawned with so much power and newness! The third day began the first day of the new creation."[41] Paul, like the other Apostles, understood that the empty grave was proof positive that death was defeated and God's new creation had begun. By His death and resurrection Jesus was established as Lord and King over that new creation.[42] The Apostles preached what they understood, the "power of resurrection has [already] penetrated this evil age."[43]

Through the power of the Holy Spirit, every Christ-follower has present-day resurrection power to overcome sin and live a new born again (or born from above) life as a part of the new creation.[44] Even though Christ-followers are not yet physically raised from the dead, they "have begun to experience truly, not metaphorically, the beginning form of end-time resurrection life."[45] Said another way, the fact that we have "already participated in the power of Christ's resurrection and life" means we have the present "ability to live a new life."[46] That means this life is *not* the waiting room for eternal

---

41 Biggs, Charles R., *An Easter Sermon: Resurrection and the New Creation*, reprinted in Reformed Perspectives Magazine, Volume 6, Number 12, April 14 to April 20, 2004. Retrieved from https://thirdmill.org/magazine/article.asp/link/cr_biggs%5ENT.Biggs.Easter.Luke_24_4.14.04.html/at/Resurrection%20and%20the%20New%20Creation (last accessed August 2, 2022)

42 Wright, Tom, *Surprised by HOPE* (Society for Promoting Christian Knowledge 2007, reissued 2011) p. 259

43 Schreiner, Thomas R., *Romans*, Baker Exegetical Commentary on the New Testament, 2nd edition (Baker Academic 1998, 2018) Romans 6:9, p. 321

44 Schreiner, Thomas R., *Romans*, Baker Exegetical Commentary on the New Testament, 2nd edition (Baker Academic 1998, 2018) Romans 6:13, p. 325; "[Eternal life] refers to life from the Holy Spirit (Rm 6:22)." *Holman Christian Standard Bible*, Study Bible edition (Holman Bible Publishers 2010) study note Galatians 6:8 under *eternal life*, p. 2022

45 Beale, G. K., *A New Testament Biblical Theology: The Unfolding Of The Old Testament In The New* (Baker Academic 2011) p. 255

46 Schreiner, Thomas R., *Romans*, Baker Exegetical Commentary on the New Testament, 2nd edition (Baker Academic 1998, 2018) Romans 6:13, p. 325

life. Eternal life has already begun![47] "Therefore if anyone is in Christ, he is a new creation. The old has passed away; behold, the new has come (2 Corinthians 5:17 ESV)."

The resurrection of Jesus fuels the hope of every Christ-follower: One of the most definitive statements of this truth is found in Paul's letter to the Corinthians. He asserted that because Christ had "*in fact* been raised from the dead" and was the "first fruits" then they too would "be resurrected with an incorruptible, immortal body (1 Corinthians 15:20 AMP, italics in original)." Paul's mention of "first fruits" refers to a familiar agricultural image. The first of the ripening crop to be harvested was a type of guarantee for a full harvest. In this way, Paul affirmed that the resurrection of those who die in Christ "is absolutely inevitable; it has been guaranteed by God himself."[48] In fact, Paul's testimony to the church in Rome was exactly that, "For if we have been united with him in a death like his, we shall certainly be united with him in a resurrection like his (Romans 6:5 ESV)."

Recall in Lesson 3 we discussed the fact that the gospel message is like a seed that becomes implanted in our hearts. That seed, as we recognized, contains resurrection life! In the fullness of time, God will birth the life in that seed into its fully mature state. The result will be a new resurrected body that will live with Him for all of eternity. And that's the hope that should fill the heart of every Christ-follower.

---

[47] The expression "eternal life" "describes not only a life that endures forever but, primarily, the highest quality of living that one can experience (cf. Ps 51:12; Jn 10:10; Ep. 1:3,18)." MacArthur, John, *The MacArthur Study Bible* (Thomas Nelson 2006) study note Galatians 6:8 under *eternal life*, p. 1769; "Eternal life refers not only to eternal quality but divine quality of life. It means lit. 'life of the age to come' and refers therefore to resurrection and heavenly existence in perfect glory and holiness. This life for believers in the Lord Jesus is experienced before heaven is reached." Ibid., study note John 3:15 under *eternal life*, pp. 1547-1548

[48] Fee, Gordon D., *The First Epistle To The Corinthians*, New International Commentary on the New Testament (Eerdmans 1987) 1 Corinthians 15:20, p. 749

Before we close our lesson, I want to tie up one loose end. I mentioned at the outset of this lesson that Paul referred to hope more than any other New Testament author. When we consider the uncertainty that permeated the pagan culture he was sent to evangelize his frequent use of the word "hope" makes perfect sense. To the ancient Greeks, the future was so indefinite that any attempt to have confidence in the future invited disappointment.[49] "In [ordinary] Greek thought, hope consisted merely of a consoling dream of the imagination designed to forget present troubles, but yet leaving one with many uncertainties."[50]

Because the pagan gods were unable to provide assurance or security in the world,[51] imagine the amazement of those pagan Gentiles who became Christ-followers. They would have been stunned to learn that Paul, who based his understanding of hope on his Old Covenant Scriptures,[52] firmly believed hope was anything but uncertain. For Paul hope is based on who God is and confident trust in what He will do. While the Greek gods were capricious and not at all predictable and certain,[53] Paul understood that those who are in covenant relationship with Yahweh could count on Him. He was

---

49 Wenstrom, William E., Jr., *Greek Word Studies* (Wenstrom.org 2016) entry for *Elpis*. Retrieved from https://www.wenstrom.org /downloads/written/word_studies/greek/elpis.pdf (last accessed August 8, 2021)
50 Hoehner, Harold W., "Romans," in *The Bible Knowledge Word Study, Acts-Ephesians*, edited by Darrell L. Bock (Victor 2006) Romans 4:18 under *Hope (elpis)*, pp. 150-151
51 Sarna, Nahum M., *Understanding Genesis Through Rabbinic Tradition and Modern Scholarship* (The Jewish Theological Seminary 2015) p. 17
52 "Old Covenant" is another way to refer to the Old Testament
53 The Bible does not expressly deny the existence of other gods. Nelson, Richard D., *Deuteronomy*, The Old Testament Library (Westminster John Knox Press 2002) Deuteronomy 6:4-5, p. 91. While verses like Exodus 9:14; Deuteronomy 4:35, 32:39; Psalm 18:31 and Isaiah 43:10, 45:5 seem, on their face, to deny the existence of any other "god" except Yahweh, these are in reality "statements of incomparability." Heiser, Michael S., *The Unseen Realm: Recovering the Supernatural Worldview of the Bible* (Lexham Press 2015) pp. 34-35. In other words, what we may think of as "denial statements" are in fact declarations that compared to Yahweh other gods are nothing. Ibid, pp. 34-35; McConville, J. G., *Deuteronomy*,

certain that Yahweh is eternally faithful and trustworthy. According to the Scriptures Paul read, Yahweh is "the faithful God who keeps His covenant (Deuteronomy 7:9)," the "God of faithfulness (Deuteronomy 32:4)" whose "work is done in faithfulness (Psalm 33:4 ESV)." Paul knew Yahweh's "faithfulness will be a protective shield" to His covenant people (Psalm 91:4 HCSB), causing Jeremiah to exclaim even in the midst of misery, "Great is Your faithfulness (Lamentations 3:23)."

Hear What The Spirit is Saying to the Church: *Behold I am coming soon.*

Apollos Old Testament Commentary 5 (IVP Academic 2002) Deuteronomy 4:35, pp. 112-113

Lesson 8:

What's Love Got To Do With It?

"But now faith, hope, and love abide, these three; but the greatest of these is love."
1 Corinthians 13:13

IN 1984 ROCK STAR Tina Turner released a Grammy award-winning song entitled, *What's Love Got to Do With It* in which the refrain asks the question what does love have to do with life?[1] The answer is implied in the lyrics when love is dismissed as nothing but a "second-hand emotion." The song then leaves the listener with this self-confident conclusion, "Certainly no one needs that!"

Paul would beg to differ. He understood the supremacy of love. According to Paul love is central to the gospel message and the life of discipleship.[2] It is Paul's biblical view of love and its connection to faith and hope that we will be exploring in this lesson. Paul's faith in Christ led to an entirely different worldview than that which is expressed in Turner's popular 80's song – one succinctly expressed by our Key Scripture for this lesson.

As to the format of the verse itself, Paul is of course thinking like a Jew. The combination of *three great things* is common in

---

1   According to Songfacts, the song composers were Terry Britten and Graham Lyle. The song won the 1985 Grammy for Song of the Year. That same year Turner's album, Private Dancer, won Record of the Year and she was awarded the Grammy as Best Female Vocal Performance. Retrieved from https://www.songfacts.com/facts/tina-turner/whats-love-got-to-do-with-it (last accessed April 13, 2022)
2   Beale and Carson, editors, *Commentary on the New Testament Use of the Old Testament* (Baker Academic 2007) 1 Corinthians 12:31, p. 738

Jewish literature.³ One of the more famous sayings attributed to early Judaism is: "There are three crowns: the crown of Torah; the crown of priesthood and the crown of royalty. However, the crown of a good name is greater than all of them."⁴ A similar pattern is found in Jewish writing identifying humility as the greater of the *three great things* named: "wisdom, fear, humility, they are alike, 'but humility is greater than them all.'"⁵

As to the meaning of our Key Scripture, I'll spoil the surprise right up front. Together these three virtues ~ *faith * hope * love* ~ "encompass the totality of the Christian life."⁶ Therefore, evidence suggests this triad of terms was a favorite way to summarize teaching in the early church. Love sets in place the starting and ending point of response to the gospel. Love both initiates the *talmid's* relation-

---

3   Stern, David, H., *Jewish New Testament Commentary* (Jewish New Testament Publications, Inc. 1992) 1 Corinthians 13:13 under *Three things last: trust, hope, love*, p. 482. We see a type of threesome reference in Micah, "He has told you, O man, what is good; And what does the Lord require of you But to **do justice**, to **love kindness**, And to **walk humbly** with your God (Micah 6:8, bold added)?"
4   *Pirkei Avot Ethics of the Ancestors*, ReformJudaism.org. Retrieved from https://reformjudaism.org/pirkei-avot /learning/sacred-texts/pirkei-avot (last accessed August 8, 2021). The saying is attributed to Rabbi Shimon and recorded in *Pirkei Avot 4:13*. The *Pirkei Avot* citation refers to the most popular tractate of the Mishnah which is often called "Chapter of the Fathers." Even though it was not compiled until the early third century C.E., it contains the "sayings" of the first "fathers" of Judaism.
5   Gill, John, *The New John Gill Exposition of the Entire Bible*, 1 Corinthians 13:13, quoting Piske Toseph in *T. Bab. Yebamot*, art. 196. Retrieved from https://www.studylight.org/commentaries /eng/geb/1-corinthians-13.html (last accessed August 8, 2021). T. Bab. is an abbreviation for the *Babylonian Talmud* which is the culmination of oral teachings from the scribes and Pharisees completed in the 6th century A.D. While that postdates Paul by some 5 centuries, since it is a collection of rabbinic wisdom over the ages it is possible that the saying could have existed even at the time of Paul.
6   *Spirit Filled Life Bible* (Thomas Nelson 1991) study note 1 Thessalonians 1:3, p. 1826; Cockerill, Gareth Lee, *The Epistle to the Hebrews*, New International Commentary on the New Testament (Eerdmans 2012) Hebrews 10:19-25, p. 465

ship with Christ and is the expected outcome of that relationship with Him. We are a people of faith called to endure through hope as we impact the world around us by expressing God's love. That's the gospel in a nutshell: it is *faith* that saves us, *hope* that sustains us and *love* that distinguishes us – all by God's amazing grace! Notably, the one who does *not* follow Christ, experiences "more or less of the three opposites—unbelief, despair, hatred."[7]

If it is true that the combination of faith and hope and love was a favorite way to succinctly summarize early church discipleship then we would expect to find it with some frequency in the New Testament. As a matter of fact, the triad is found in other epistles authored by Paul. See for example:

> Through him we have also obtained access by **faith** [*pistis*] into this grace in which we stand, and we rejoice in **hope** [*elpis*] of the glory of God. Not only that, but we rejoice in our sufferings, knowing that suffering produces endurance, and endurance produces character, and character produces **hope** [*elpis*], and **hope** [*elpis*] does not put us to shame, because God's **love** [*agape*] has been poured into our hearts through the Holy Spirit who has been given to us. Romans 5:2-5 ESV, bold added

> For we, through the Spirit, by **faith** [*pistis*], are waiting for the **hope** [*elpis*] of righteousness. For in Christ Jesus neither circumcision nor uncircumcision means anything, but faith working through **love** [*agape*]. Galatians 5:5-6, bold added

> Therefore I … implore you to walk in a manner worthy of the calling with which you have been called … showing tolerance for one another in **love** [*agape*] …. *There is* one body and one Spirit, just as you also were

---

7   Jamieson, Fausset, and Brown, *Commentary Critical and Explanatory on the Whole Bible*, 1 Corinthians 13:13. Retrieved from Hill, Gary, *The Discovery Bible*, HELPS Ministries, Inc.

called in one **hope** [*elpis*] of your calling; one Lord, one **faith** [*pistis*], one baptism. Ephesians 4:1-5, italics in original, bold added

We give thanks to God, the Father of our Lord Jesus Christ, praying always for you, since we heard of your **faith** [*pistis*] in Christ Jesus and the **love** [*agape*] which you have for all the saints; because of the **hope** [*elpis*] laid up for you in heaven, of which you previously heard in the word of truth, the gospel. Colossians 1:3-5, bold added

We give thanks to God always for all of you, making mention of *you* in our prayers; constantly bearing in mind your work of **faith** [*pistis*] and labor of **love** [*agape*] and steadfastness of **hope** [*elpis*] in our Lord Jesus Christ in the presence of our God and Father. 1 Thessalonians 1:2-3, italics in original, bold added

But since we are of *the* day, let us be sober, having put on the breastplate of **faith** [*pistis*] and **love** [*agape*], and as a helmet, the **hope** [*elpis*] of salvation. 1 Thessalonians 5:8, italics in original, bold added

The author of Hebrews also uses this ~ *faith* * *hope* * *love* ~ trio:

For God is not unjust so as to forget your work and the **love** [*agape*] which you have shown toward His name, in having ministered and in still ministering to the saints. And we desire that each one of you show the same diligence so as to realize the full assurance of **hope** [*elpis*] until the end, so that you will not be sluggish, but imitators of those who through **faith** [*pistis*] and patience inherit the promises. Hebrews 6:10-12, bold added

> [L]et us draw near with a sincere heart in full assurance of **faith** [*pistis*], having our hearts sprinkled *clean* from an evil conscience and our bodies washed with pure water. Let us hold fast the confession of our **hope** [*elpis*] without wavering, for He who promised is faithful; and let us consider how to stimulate one another to **love** [*agape*] and good deeds. Hebrews 10:22-24, italics in original, bold added

Peter likewise uses the triad:

> Blessed be the God and Father of our Lord Jesus Christ, who according to His great mercy has caused us to be born again to a living **hope** [*elpis*] through the resurrection of Jesus Christ from the dead, to *obtain* an inheritance *which is* imperishable, undefiled, and will not fade away, reserved in heaven for you, who are protected by the power of God through **faith** [*pistis*] for a salvation ready to be revealed in the last time. In this you greatly rejoice, even though now for a little while, if necessary, you have been distressed by various trials, so that the proof of your **faith** [*pistis*], *being* more precious than gold which is perishable, even though tested by fire, may be found to result in praise and glory and honor at the revelation of Jesus Christ; and though you have not seen Him, you **love** [*agapao*] Him, and though you do not see Him now, but **believe** [*pisteuo*] in Him, you greatly rejoice with joy inexpressible and full of glory. 1 Peter 1:3-8, italics in original, bold added

Notice that I have put the Greek words in brackets in each of the triad quotes. We have already studied *pisteuo/pistis* (Lessons 1 & 3 respectively) and *elpis* (Lesson 2). As you can see, the Greek word translated as "love" is either the noun *agape* or the verb *agapao*. These words are so central to the message of the New Testament that it is worthwhile to do a Word Study before we proceed.

WORD STUDY

Both the Greek verb agapao *{ag-ap-ah'-o} and its derivative noun* agape *{ag-ah'-pay} are translated as* **love** *in our triad Scripture quotes. The starting point for defining these words is that when they refer to human love they indicate willful love rooted in God's love.[8] The agapao "word group refers to willed love, an act of willed self-sacrifice for the good of another. [Agape love] has no necessary emotional component ...."[9] In other words, agapao primarily denotes something that we do not something that we feel.*

Agape is expressed in deeds that seek to benefit the one loved rather than seeking benefit for self. Agape compels one "to shower love upon" the recipient without regard to how they respond.[10]

This type of love is a "deep, genuine, selfless love, a love characteristic of God, a divine love."[11] When referring to God's love, agape denotes God's willful direction toward mankind resulting in what is best for him, not necessarily what he desires.[12] John 3:16 is the premiere example of God's agapao love.

---

8   Zodhiates, Spiros, *The Complete Word Study Dictionary: New Testament* (AMG Publishers 1992) word #25, p. 64; Mounce, William D., editor, *Complete Expository Dictionary of Old & New Testament Words* (Zondervan 2006) entry for *Love*, pp. 427-429

9   Carson, D. A., *Difficult Doctrine Of The Love Of God* (Crossway Books 2000) p. 26

10 Renner, Rick, *Sparkling Gems from the Greek* (Harrison House Publishers 2003) July 23, p. 526

11 Smith, Jay E., "1 Corinthians," in *The Bible Knowledge Word Study Acts-Ephesians*, edited by Darrell L. Bock (Victor 2006) 1 Corinthians 13:4-7 under *Love*, p. 295

12 Zodhiates, Spiros, *The Complete Word Study Dictionary: New Testament* (AMG Publishers 1992) word #26, p. 66

> *In the Greek translation of the Old Testament, "agapao describes the Lord's virtue-love for Israel (Hosea 11:1), and how Israel was to reciprocate with virtue-love (Deut. 6:5; 11:1, 13)."*[13]

If we look collectively at those Scriptures I quoted which use the ~ *faith* * *hope* * *love* ~ trio, we can conclude that the use of love in the triad almost always refers to one of the two greatest commands: love for God and love for others. This instruction comes directly from the teachings of Jesus.

> One of [the Pharisees], a lawyer, asked [Jesus] *a question*, testing Him, "Teacher, which is the great commandment in the Law?" And He said to him, "'YOU SHALL LOVE THE LORD YOUR GOD WITH ALL YOUR HEART, AND WITH ALL YOUR SOUL, AND WITH ALL YOUR MIND.' This is the great and foremost commandment. The second is like it, 'YOU SHALL LOVE YOUR NEIGHBOR AS YOURSELF.' On these two commandments depend the whole Law and the Prophets." Matthew 22:35-40, italics and uppercase text in original

What is commanded is an ongoing love relationship reaching upwards and a continual love relationship reaching outwards. We know from our Word Study of *agape/agapao* that both love relationships must be demonstrated by willful actions which seek to benefit the love recipient.

Jesus placed such a high level of importance on these two commandments that He concluded, "The entire law and all the demands of the prophets are based on these two commandments."[14] In other words, love is "'the primary ... principle for interpreting

---

13 Wenstrom, William E., Jr., *Greek Word Studies* (Wenstrom.org 2016) entry for *Agapao*. Retrieved from https://www.wenstrom.org/downloads/written/word_studies/greek/agapao.pdf (last accessed October 29, 2021)

14 Matthew 22:40 NLT

and applying the [instruction and commandments of God].'"[15] With this understanding, we are beginning to have meaningful insight into why "love" would be named as one of the three character traits that summarizes the life of a Christ-follower!

As we continue to explore Paul's biblical view of love and its connection to faith and hope our next step is to put our Key Scripture into the larger context of Paul's first epistle to the Corinthians.

At the time of Paul's ministry, Corinth was a Roman Colony[16] meaning it was an entirely pagan city until Paul founded the church there. First Corinthians suggests those initial Christ-followers were quite immature *talmidim*. Even though they were disciples of Christ, they were still acting very much like the pagan culture around them. As scholar Gordon Fee says, "[A]n inordinate amount of Corinth was yet in them, emerging in a number of attitudes and behaviors that required radical surgery without killing the patient. This is what 1 Corinthians attempts to do."[17]

We find our Key Scripture as the closing verse of Chapter 13. What precedes it is Paul's corrective admonition regarding spiritual gifts beginning in Chapter 12. He starts his instruction by clarifying what true spirituality means to the Christ-follower. The Corinthians had apparently been boasting that they were highly spiritual because of certain practices they were doing. The biggest issue seemed to be an over-emphasis on the gift of tongues. In his commentary on First Corinthians, Gordon Fee suggests that the Corinthian disciples may have considered themselves to already be like angels and therefore truly spiritual. Their over-emphasis on speaking in tongues, which they seemed to believe was the language

---

15 France, R. T., *The Gospel of Matthew*, New International Commentary on the New Testament (Eerdmans 2007) Matthew 22:40, p. 847, quoting R. Mohrlang, *Matthew*, 95

16 A colony in the Roman Empire was a Roman settlement in a conquered territory. A core group of Roman citizens from Rome were moved to that settlement to be living examples of Rome's culture and influence. In this way, a colony became a miniature type of Rome.

17 Fee, Gordon D., *The First Epistle To The Corinthians*, New International Commentary on the New Testament (Eerdmans 1987) Introduction, p. 4

The Power of Hope

of angels, provided them with all the evidence they needed that they had already "arrived" in terms of spirituality.[18] Paul had a different perspective. He understood true Spiritual life for a Christ-follower means Holy Spirit is operating full throttle *in* you so that Christ can work *through* you! Paul knew from his own experience that the Spirit is the key to *everything* in the life of the *talmid*.

> For Paul the reception of the Spirit is the *sine qua non* of [essential condition of; that which is absolutely necessary for] Christian life. The Spirit is what essentially distinguishes the believer from the nonbeliever ([1 Cor.] 2:10-14); the Spirit is what especially marks the beginning of Christian life (Gal. 3:2-3); the Spirit above all is what makes a person a child of God (Rom. 8:14-17).[19]

Because "the genuine Christian life is 'supernatural' (i.e., divinely empowered) from start to finish, a life by God's own Spirit,"[20] Paul refused to accept their litmus test for true spirituality. Paul says the true test of spirituality is for one to declare Jesus is Lord of their life!

> So I want you to know that no one speaking by the Spirit of God will curse Jesus, and no one can say Jesus is Lord, except by the Holy Spirit. 1 Corinthians 12:3 NLT

Paul assures the Corinthians this declaration of Lordship is reliable evidence that provides undeniable proof that the Holy Spirit is active in someone's life. Of course, he is referring to more than lip service. He is in essence saying, "I'm giving you a distinguishing

---

18 Fee, Gordon D., *The First Epistle To The Corinthians*, The New International Commentary on the New Testament (Eerdmans 1987) 1 Corinthians 12:1-14:40, pp. 570-573
19 Fee, Gordon D., *The First Epistle To The Corinthians*, The New International Commentary on the New Testament (Eerdmans 1987) 1 Corinthians 12:13, p. 603, italics in original
20 Keener, Craig S., *Romans*, New Covenant Commentary (Cascade Books 2009) Fusing the Horizons: Faith and Righteousness, p. 104

rule by which you may know with certainty which influences and operations are from God: only those who abandon every other 'god' are led by the Spirit of God."[21]

To put Paul's litmus test into proper perspective we need to place ourselves in the shoes of those first-century Christ-followers living as citizens in the Roman Empire. To say "Jesus is Lord" would have been a radical and even life-threatening confession. The Greek word for "Lord" is *kurios* {koo'-ree-os}. A *kurios* was a person who exercised absolute ownership rights.[22] The derivative word *kuriakos* means "belonging to the Lord."[23] Jesus is recognized as the true *Kurios* because:

> … God highly exalted Him, and bestowed on Him the name which is above every name, so that at the name of Jesus EVERY KNEE WILL BOW, of those who are in heaven and on earth and under the earth, and that every tongue will confess that Jesus Christ is Lord [*Kurios*], to the glory of God the Father. Philippians 2:9-11, uppercase text in original

To confess "Jesus is Lord" in this way was a declaration of absolute allegiance to Jesus as your *only* "God" and Master to the exclusion of all others.[24] The challenge came from the fact that in Paul's culture, the Greek word *kurios* was a title applied to the

---

21 Barnes, Albert, *Barnes' Notes On The Old And New Testaments*, 1 Corinthians 12:3. Retrieved from Hill, Gary, *The Discovery Bible*, HELPS Ministries, Inc.
22 Hill, Gary, *The Discovery Bible*, HELPS Ministries, Inc., [G]2962 *kýrios*
23 Zodhiates, Spiros, *The Complete Word Study Dictionary: New Testament* (AMG Publishers 1992) word #2960, p. 899
24 Fee, Gordon D., *The First Epistle To The Corinthians*, The New International Commentary on the New Testament (Eerdmans 1987) 1 Corinthians 12:3, p. 581. In contrast, Nero, who was Emperor at the time Paul wrote his letter to the church at Corinth, was one of the Roman Emperors who accepted worship as a "god" during his lifetime. Burton, Henry Fairfield, *The Worship of the Roman Emperors*, The Biblical World 40, no. 2 (1912): 80-91, at p. 83. Retrieved from http://www.jstor.org/stable/3141986 (last accessed June 11, 2021). Nero reigned as

Roman Emperor. As a result, confessing that "Jesus is *Kurios/ Lord*" would have set you noticeably and dangerously apart from your fellow citizens. At that time in the Roman Empire, every person's allegiance was owed first and foremost to the Roman Emperor (*Kurios*) and secondarily to the pantheon of Roman gods![25] Your declaration of faith in Jesus would have been treason against Rome's most foundational ideologies.[26] Only by the testimony of God's Spirit could you recognize the truth of Jesus and only by the courageous power of His Spirit could you openly confess this truth with your mouth and then proclaim it with your lifestyle.

Having established that foundational truth, Paul goes on to consider the proper role of spiritual gifts. Although there are diverse gifts Paul acknowledges that the source, enablement and empowerment of *every* gift is the Holy Spirit. The primary purpose of these manifestations of the Spirit's presence is to build up the entire body of Christ in a diverse type of unity.

> For to one is given the word of wisdom through the Spirit, and to another the word of knowledge according to the same Spirit; to another faith by the same Spirit, and to another gifts of healing by the one Spirit, and to another the effecting of miracles, and to another prophecy, and

---

Emperor from 54 A.D. to 68 A.D., Paul's first letter to the church at Corinth is dated about 55 A.D.

25 "... religion was a function of the state, and the worship of the gods which were recognized by the state was part of the duty of the citizen." Burton, Henry Fairfield, *The Worship of the Roman Emperors*, The Biblical World 40, no. 2 (1912): 80-91, at p. 86. Retrieved from http://www.jstor.org/stable/3141986 (last accessed June 11, 2021)

26 Those who followed Christ honored the Emperor as ruler, but refused to acknowledge that he was a god. The Roman authorities "insisted that the worship of the national gods—and the Emperor in particular—was the duty of every citizen and that to refuse was an act of disloyalty. Hence the mere profession of Christianity was regarded as a crime against the state." Burton, Henry Fairfield, *The Worship of the Roman Emperors*, The Biblical World 40, no. 2 (1912): 80-91, at p. 90. Retrieved from http://www.jstor.org/stable/3141986 (last accessed June 11, 2021)

to another the distinguishing of spirits, to another *various* kinds of tongues, and to another the interpretation of tongues. But one and the same Spirit works all these things, distributing to each one individually just as He wills. 1 Corinthians 12:8-11, italics in original

To better understand why grace gifts are given to every *talmid* it will be helpful to consider them in the context of the mission of the church. The church is designed by God to be a "functional outpost of God's Kingdom.... By its very existence the church is called and equipped to be [a theater displaying God, a picture window allowing the world to see Him, a lighthouse letting His light shine, legal proof that God exists all] for the benefit of the world."[27] In short, "the church is an instrument through which [God] reveals himself."[28] Thus when Paul says the gifts are given by God for the common good, he is indicating that those gifts in proper operation permit the church to function in unity like one body (which would otherwise be impossible) so she can present the truth of the gospel as both the messenger and the message. In doing so, she will correctly display God's character and glory to the watching world who doesn't yet know Him. This is descriptive of the type of work we do while we are in God's *Hope Waiting Room*.

After establishing that there are many more gifts than speaking in tongues, Paul proceeds to highlight how the gifts function in the church emphasizing both the need and the value of diversity. He again underscores their divine source. Paul then transitions into his reminder that everything is to be done in love which he calls "a more excellent way."[29] For Paul, love is the only way in which the gifts can properly function in the body of Christ. "Love is primary for him … Love is not an idea … [nor is it] a 'motivating factor'

---

[27] Barth, Markus, *Ephesians: Introduction, Translation, and Commentary on Chapters 1-3*, The Anchor Bible Vol 34 (Doubleday 1974) Ephesians 3:1-13 under *Comment IV*, p. 364, italics in original, citations omitted
[28] Barth, Markus, *Ephesians: Introduction, Translation, and Commentary on Chapters 1-3*, The Anchor Bible Vol 34 (Doubleday 1974) Ephesians 3:1-13 under *Comment IV*, p. 364, italics in original, citations omitted
[29] 1 Corinthians 12:31

The Power of Hope

for behavior. It *is* behavior. To love is to act; anything short of action is not love at all."[30] Paul uses all of Chapter 13 to prove his point mentioning love no less than nine times. In each reference, he used the Greek word *agape* {ag-ah'-pay} which as we learned in our Word Study is a selfless type of love that originates with God.

Paul concluded Chapter 13 with our Key Scripture for this lesson. Why would he conclude a section on spiritual gifts with the ~ *faith * hope * love* ~ triad? Remember we learned earlier in our lesson that the use of this particular trio was thought to be a succinct way to summarize instruction on the Christian life. If that was Paul's intention here, then I believe Paul may have intended Chapters 12 and 13 in this letter to be a single unit of thought with two bookends. The unit begins in Chapter 12 with the first bookend. Paul describes the essence of the gospel message, the truth that Jesus is Lord. The second bookend which ends Paul's thought in this unit is our Key Scripture 1 Corinthians 13:13. Paul closes the unit with a reminder that the Lordship of Christ is about much more than spiritual gifts. He might well have been saying, "Spiritual gifts are good, but don't ever lose sight that we are saved by *faith*, endure through *hope* and are known by our *love*."

As we continue to explore Paul's biblical view of love and its connection to faith and hope, we need to note that while all three are critical elements in the life of the Christ-follower, Paul does not view faith, hope and love as of equal importance. He points to love as being the *greatest* of the three. In our Key Scripture, the word "greatest" is the Greek word *meizon* {mide'-zone}. In this particular context, it denotes a comparison of greater importance.[31] Paul declares faith is important, hope is important, but love is comparatively more important than either faith or hope.

In previous lessons, we have examined the requirements of "faith" and "hope" in the life of a *talmid*. We will use the remain-

---

30 Fee, Gordon D., *The First Epistle To The Corinthians*, New International Commentary on the New Testament (Eerdmans 1987) 1 Corinthians 13:1-13, p. 628
31 Zodhiates, Spiros, *The Complete Word Study Dictionary: New Testament* (AMG Publishers 1992) word #3173, p. 952, referring to *meizon* (3187)

der of this lesson to focus on "love" and explore how love fits into the life of the Christ-follower while we are in God's *Hope Waiting Room*.

Matthew, Mark, Luke and John tell the story of how Jesus, the Jewish Messiah, *"ushered in a new world order* within which a new way of life was not only possible, but mandatory for" everyone who follows Him.[32] At the time the gospels were written "any man or woman who was persuaded of a particular philosophy or religious claim expected at the same time to follow that group's way of life; they became a member of a community. Identification with a group included behavioral commitments ...."[33] The New Testament firmly establishes the identification of a Christ-follower as one characterized by love.

> ... [T]he in-Christ identity has only come into existence as a result of God's acts of love: the gospel itself and God's love that has been poured out though the Spirit. So, love has become a defining characteristic of this alternative community which should then reflect a distinct [character] that contrasts the broader civic community.[34]

Jesus said it best, "By this all men will know that you are My disciples, if you have love [*agape*] for one another."[35] When Jesus said His *talmidim* would be known by their love for each other He meant that those who learn to love as He loved are His true *talmid*. Jesus modeled love not as an emotion but as an observable action. This new community, whether Jew or Gentile, would be recognizable to the rest of the world because they act like Jesus. A century after Jesus gave His disciples the love command that's exactly how

---

32 Wright, N.T., *How God Became King: The Forgotten Story of the Gospels* (HarperOne 2012) p. 118, italics in original
33 Cohick, Linn H., *The Letter To The Ephesians*, The New International Commentary on the New Testament (Eerdmans 2020) Excursus: *"In Christ,"* p. 98
34 Tucker, J. Brian, *Reading 1 Corinthians* (Cascade Books 2017) p. 117, citations omitted
35 John 13:35

they were recognized! Aristides was an Athenian philosopher in the second century A.D. He was also one of the earliest Christian apologists. Aristides is quoted as describing Christ-followers to the Roman Emperor Hadrian in terms of their love for one another.[36]

> Here follows the defence which Aristides the philosopher made before Hadrian the King on behalf of reverence for God…. All-powerful Caesar Titus Hadrianus Antoninus, venerable and merciful, from Marcianus Aristides, an Athenian philosopher…. XV…. [Christians] do not worship strange gods, and they go their way in all modesty and cheerfulness. Falsehood is not found among them; and **they love one another**, and from widows they do not turn away their esteem; and they deliver the orphan from him who treats him harshly. And he, who has, gives to him who has not, without boasting. And when they see a stranger, they take him in to their homes and rejoice over him as a very brother; for they do not call them brethren after the flesh, but brethren after the spirit and in God. And whenever one of their poor passes from the world, each one of them according to his ability gives heed to him and carefully sees to his burial. And if they hear that one of their number is imprisoned or afflicted on account of the name of their Messiah, all of them anxiously minister to his necessity, and if it is possible to redeem him they set him free. And if there is among them any that is poor and needy, and if they have no spare food, they fast two or three days in order to supply to the needy their lack of food. They observe the precepts of

---

36 Aristides, *The Apology of Aristides* (125 - 145 A.D.) translated from the Syriac, bold added. Retrieved from https://www.tertullian.org/fathers/aristides_02_trans.htm#1 (last accessed February 20, 2022). The date the Apology was written is attributed to: *The Apology of Aristides the Philosopher*, earlychristianwritings.com. Retrieved from https://www.earlychristianwritings.com/info/aristides.html (last accessed February 20, 2022)

their Messiah with much care, living justly and soberly as the Lord their God commanded them.... XVI. Such, O King, is the commandment of the law of the Christians, and such is their manner of life....

What Aristides was describing is the kingdom of God which was being made visible by the actions of those who had chosen to follow Christ. Notice the first point he made is that "they love one another." Then the rest of Aristides' description documents the evidence of their service to one another, their observable *love* in action. Writing about 50 years later, another early church apologist by the name of Tertullian wrote his own apology for Christians.[37] Like Aristides, Tertullian emphasized the love Christ-followers had for one another.[38]

When Jesus gave His disciples the command to love one another He identified the *one commandment* that will most readily define His disciples.[39] Those early *talmidim* were recognizable by that *one* action. From the beginning, "Love for other believers

---

37 "*The Apologeticus* [*The Apology Of Tertullian For The Christians*], which in the 3rd century was translated [from Latin] into Greek, is the weightiest work in defense of Christianity of the first two centuries. It disposes of the charges brought against Christians for secret crimes (incest, etc.) and public offenses (contempt of the State religion and high treason), and asserts the absolute superiority of Christianity as a revealed religion beyond the rivalry of all human systems." *Tertullian*, NNDB (Soylent Communications 2019). Retrieved from https://www.nndb.com/people/741/000071528/ (last accessed February 20, 2022)

38 In *The Apology Of Tertullian For The Christians*, "Tertullian records the heathens' observation on the Christians, 'See, they say, how they love one another' (*Apol.* 39)." Mounce, Robert H., *Revelation*, The New International Commentary on the New Testament (Eerdmans 1998) Revelation 2:4, footnote 16, p. 70, citing Tertullian, *The Apology Of Tertullian For The Christians* (197 A.D.) translated by T. Herbert Bindley (Parker and Co. 1890). The date the Apology was written is attributed to: Tertullian.org. Retrieved from https://www.tertullian.org/articles/bindley_apol/bindley_apol.htm (last accessed February 20, 2022)

39 Keener, Craig S., *The Gospel Of John: A Commentary*, Volume Two (Hendrickson Publishers 2003) 3. Following Jesus' Model ([John] 13:34-35), p. 925

The Power of Hope

was the distinctive badge for Christian discipleship ...."[40] Nothing else has the same capacity to maintain our unique and distinctive identity in the world than expressing God's love. While Satan is a master counterfeiter, the world over which he presently has dominion cannot replicate the love of God.

To explain how the love of God works, I need to share a testimony. In 1999 I knew God was calling me out of my profession as a practicing attorney and by the summer of 2000, I was beginning to regularly enter a men's medium-security prison in Ohio as a volunteer. As I began that Kingdom assignment, I was keenly aware that I did not *love* those men. I was certain there wasn't *hate* in my heart. The best description of my heart condition at that time was a sort of apathetic uncaring. I knew that would never do. The realization that I could not do the work God had called me to do unless His love was in my heart drove me to my knees in earnest prayer.[41] God heard and He answered. He poured out such incredible love into my heart that it was overwhelming. About two years later, I received a very public invitation from the Governor-appointed Director of the Ohio prisons to expand my work in one prison into every prison in Ohio. When it came time to begin in Ohio's correctional institution for women, I cried out once again for God's love to be poured into my heart for those women. He answered in abundance. And then a third time when the re-entry work I was doing expanded into youth correctional facilities I asked for that same love and God once again poured out love seemingly without measure into my heart. I learned firsthand that I could not manufacture the love I needed to do that work. It was *His* love that created the desire to serve others. It was a love

---

40 Mounce, Robert H., *Revelation*, The New International Commentary on the New Testament (Eerdmans 1998) Revelation 2:4, p. 70
41 Looking back on that acknowledgment, I realize that it was the Holy Spirit leading me. He led me to recognize that void and then led me to ask for God's love to be poured out into my own receptive heart. I'm confident that at the time I did not have the spiritual maturity to have made that prayerful request on my own. Praise God for the work of Holy Spirit who always leads us into truth (John 16:13).

that only God could supply. I made myself an available vessel, He released His love into my willing heart then I became a willing conduit. I simply let *His* love flow through me so I could distribute it according to His leading.

As Jewish New Testament scholar David Stern concludes, "Such love goes beyond what one can generate of oneself, because it has its origin in God. When such love is experienced by one person from another, the experience is of God's love channeled through that other."[42] What an amazing partnership! This is the love I believe Paul knew from his own experience and considered so vital to the life of every Christ-follower.

Let's continue to pursue our understanding of how this love fits into the ~ faith * hope * love ~ trio at the end of 1 Corinthians 13. In the last verse of Chapter 13, our Key Scripture for this lesson, Paul wraps up his discussion. Earlier in this same epistle Paul told the church at Corinth God had prepared unimaginable blessings *for those who love Him* (1 Corinthians 2:9). The phrase "those who love God" was not coined by Paul. Its roots run deep in the Old Testament long before its use in the New Testament. The well-established meaning is that it describes the ones who continually submit to God, are receptive to His instruction, faithful to His covenant and obey His commands.[43] A Christ-follower who keeps God's commands, especially His commands related to love, makes his "permanent dwelling in God's love, internalizing the principle of love."[44]

In 1 Corinthians 13 Paul continues to make his point that love is most important in the life of the Christ-follower:

---

42 Stern, David, H., *Jewish New Testament Commentary* (Jewish New Testament Publications, Inc. 1992) 1 Corinthians 13:1-14:1a, p. 481

43 Durham, John I., *Word Biblical Commentary: Exodus*, Volume 3 (Word Books 1987) Exodus 20:6 under *Comment*, p. 287; McConville, J. G., *Deuteronomy*, Apollos Old Testament Commentary 5 (IVP Academic 2002) Deuteronomy 5:8-10, p. 127; Deuteronomy 7:9-10, pp. 157-158

44 Keener, Craig S., *The Gospel Of John: A Commentary*, Volume Two (Hendrickson Publishers 2003) 4. Perseverance or Apostasy ([John] 15:6) under *4A. The Johannine Meaning of "Abiding,"* p. 999, citations omitted

> A true disciple of Christ demonstrates love by never ceasing to have faith (*pisteuo*) and never losing hope (*elpizo*). 1 Corinthians 13:7 NLT, my paraphrase

Faith and hope originate in God's love and are ways we express our reciprocal love for Him. Faith and hope outwardly demonstrate loyalty (covenantal love) to what God said. Once our feet have been placed in the starter blocks of discipleship, persisting in faith and growing in hope keeps us in the race. Paul knows that *the love of God* at work in our hearts has a staying power in the present and supplies absolute confidence in the future. Those two truths work together to enable every Christ-follower to walk out his faith during every kind of circumstance while always directing his love upwards and outwards.[45] Paul's own life and ministry were proof positive of these very truths!

A quick review of what we've learned in this study will pull it all together. Love initiates a relationship with God[46] and faith accepts His invitation. That faith produces faithfulness which is the fertile soil in which hope thrives. Hope enables and equips us to stay the course and maintain our relationship with God. The end result is true discipleship.

What's love got to do with it? Everything in every way! Love permeates everything we do as a Christ-follower in this present age while we wait with confident expectation for God to keep His promises about the age to come. In other words, for the one who follows Christ, ~ faith * hope * love ~ sums up true discipleship. Of the three, love is the greatest, the most important, because it is the starting point of faith and thereafter every command God has given us is connected in one way or another to loving God and loving others.

---

45 Fee, Gordon D., *The First Epistle To The Corinthians*, New International Commentary on the New Testament (Eerdmans 1987) 1 Corinthians 13:7, p. 640

46 John 6:44, 1 John 4:7-10

Hear What The Spirit is Saying to the Church: *If the question is: "What's love got to do with it?" – the answer is that for the one who follows me, love is everything! It is the beginning of all things, the end of all things and everything in between.*

Lesson 9:

Adversity Strengthens Hope

 "... we rejoice in our sufferings, knowing that suffering produces endurance, and endurance produces character, and character produces hope." Romans 5:3–4 ESV

IF TRUTH BE TOLD there are more verses in the New Testament about suffering and adversity than many of us wish were there. Quite obviously, God thought it important to alert His new covenant community that there would be nothing unusual about their experience of adversity as they lived out their lives in obedience to Him. "The new life [we have in Christ] does not yet remove us from the old life of the fallen world; rather, it places us at the center of the battle between the two orders."[1]

Jesus never hid the true cost of discipleship from His followers. He spoke plainly of continued suffering in this present age for those who would choose to be His *talmidim*:[2]

> You will be hated by all because of My name, but it is the one who has **endured** [*hypomone*] to the end who will be saved. Matthew 10:22, bold added

---

1 Beale and Carson, editors, *Commentary on the New Testament Use of the Old Testament* (Baker Academic 2007) The Love of God In Christ And Hope In Tribulation ([Romans] 5:1-8:39), p. 628
2 Remember this is the Hebrew word for true "disciples" (plural); a single disciple is a *talmid*

"Then they will deliver you to **tribulation** [*thlipsis*] and kill you, and you will be hated by all nations because of My name...." Matthew 24:9, bold added [see following Word Study of *thlipsis*]

They will make you outcasts from the synagogue, but an hour is coming for everyone who kills you to think that he is offering service to God. John 16:2

Our first task in this lesson is to define "adversity/suffering." Our Key Scripture for this lesson is from Paul's letter to the Christ-followers in Rome. In Romans 5:3, the word "suffering" is a translation of the Greek word *thlipsis*. As I pointed out in the quote from Matthew 24:9, this same word is used when Jesus refers to persecution. Throughout much of the New Testament persecution is the predominant form of suffering for the *talmidim*. However, as we will see from a Word Study, the use of the word *thlipsis* in the New Testament includes a much broader catalog of adversity.

WORD STUDY

The word translated as **suffering** *in Romans 5:3 is the Greek noun thlipsis {thlip'-sis} which "originally expressed sheer, physical pressure on a man."*[3] *This definition is easy to see when we understand that thlipsis was used to refer to squeezing olives in a press to extract the oil or squeezing grapes to remove the juice. Thlipsis actually describes an ancient torture where a person was stretched out on his back and one-by-one weights were put on his chest to crush him.*[4]

---

3   *2 Corinthians 4:17 Commentary*, Precept Austin. Retrieved from http://preceptaustin.org/2corinthians_417_commentary.htm (last accessed November 9, 2021)

4   *2 Corinthians 4:17 Commentary*, Precept Austin. Retrieved from http://preceptaustin.org/2corinthians_417_commentary.htm (last accessed November 9, 2021)

> *In general, thlipsis conveys the idea of being squeezed or placed under pressure or crushed beneath a heavy weight.*

The *Theological Dictionary of the New Testament* (*TDNT*) recognizes a broad meaning of *thlipsis* relating it to afflictions that include both internal and external suffering. The Greek translation of the Old Testament used the noun *thlipsis* (or the related verb *thlibo*) for: distress, anxiety, afflictions experienced by slaves and foreigners, oppression by an enemy, illness, desert wandering and being shipwrecked.[5] Similarly, in addition to persecution, the *TDNT* lists other specific New Testament references as including prison and hardship, contemptuous ridicule or mockery, poverty, inner distress and anxiety, conflict and fear and possibly sickness as well.[6] New Testament scholar, Thomas R. Schreiner, concludes that Paul's use of *thlipsis* in Romans 5:3 "is a general term … denoting the pressures and troubles that annoy believers in this present evil age."[7]

Elisabeth Elliot, who was no stranger to suffering, defined suffering very broadly as, "having what you don't want or wanting what you don't have."[8] Based on her experience, Elliot maintained that suffering *always* has a purpose, "Suffering is never for noth-

---

5   Bromiley, Geoffrey W., *Theological Dictionary of the New Testament*, Abridged in One Volume (Eerdmans 1985) entry for *thlibo* under B. *thlibo, thlipsis in the LXX*, p. 334
6   Bromiley, Geoffrey W., *Theological Dictionary of the New Testament*, Abridged in One Volume (Eerdmans 1985) entry for *thlibo* under C. *thlibo, thlipsis in the NT*, p. 335, citations omitted
7   Schreiner, Thomas R., *Romans*, Baker Exegetical Commentary on the New Testament, 2nd edition (Baker Academic 1998, 2018) Romans 5:3-4, p. 263, citations omitted
8   Elliot, Elisabeth, *Suffering Is Never For Nothing* (B & H Publishing Group 2019) p. 9. Elisabeth's first husband, Jim, was speared to death in 1956 by the Auca Indians he wanted to evangelize. She and her ten-month old daughter remained in Ecuador and lived among the same Indians who murdered her husband. She later remarried and her second husband, Addison, died of cancer less than four years later.

ing."[9] While our most natural response to adversity and suffering is to get out of it as fast as we can, Elliot advocated the best starting point in suffering is to *accept it*.[10] She was quick to point out that acceptance is a voluntary act of the will.

In Romans 5:2 Paul reassures Christ-followers to "rejoice in hope," and then in Romans 5:3 he encourages that "we also rejoice in suffering." Both times he used the Greek word *kauchaomai* {kow-khah'-om-ahee} which refers to *experiencing* joy as an emotion as well as *expressing* that feeling, especially in words.[11]

The biblical view is that the suffering of Christ-followers is a normal and expected part of advancing God's Kingdom. According to British scholar N. T. Wright:[12]

> ... the suffering and death of Jesus's people is not simply the dark path they must tread because of the world's continuing hostility toward Jesus and his message. It somehow has the more positive effect of carrying forward the redemptive effect of Jesus's own death, not by adding to it, but by sharing in it.... Jesus has constituted his followers as those who share his work of kingdom inauguration .... But if they are to bring his kingdom in his way, they will be people who share his suffering.... The slaughtered and enthroned lamb of Revelation 5 is not

---

9   Elliot, Elisabeth, *Suffering Is Not For Nothing*, Session 3. Acceptance, A teaching series by Elisabeth Elliot (Ligonier Ministries, originally released 1989). Retrieved from https://www.ligonier.org/learn/series/suffering-is-not-for-nothing (last accessed December 1, 2021). The book published by B & H Publishing in 2019 under the title, *Suffering Is Never For Nothing*, is essentially a transcript of this teaching series.

10 Elliot, Elisabeth, *Suffering Is Not For Nothing*, Session 3. Acceptance, A teaching series by Elisabeth Elliot (Ligonier Ministries, originally released 1989). Retrieved from https://www.ligonier.org/learn/series/suffering-is-not-for-nothing (last accessed December 1, 2021)

11 *Romans 5:3 Commentary*, Precept Austin. Retrieved from https://www.preceptaustin.org/romans_53-5 (last accessed February 21, 2023)

12 Wright, N.T., *How God Became King: The Forgotten Story of the Gospels* (HarperOne 2012) pp. 201-203

only the shepherd of his people; he is also their template. Sharing his suffering is the way in which they are to extend his kingdom in the world.

Suffering is *not* an entrance requirement to God's Kingdom. When a Christ-follower today has the same attitude of suffering that Jesus and His first *talmidim* had, it is evidence they have *already entered* God's Kingdom! When Jesus suffered He trusted His Father.[13] Suffering in this way demonstrates faithfulness along with the reality of the hope that empowers suffering for His name's sake. So, we find in Hebrews 10, this exhortation:

> But remember the former days, when, after being enlightened, you endured a great conflict of sufferings, partly by being made a public spectacle through reproaches and tribulations, and partly by becoming sharers with those who were so treated. For you showed sympathy to the prisoners and accepted joyfully the seizure of your property, knowing that you have for yourselves a better possession and a lasting one. Therefore, do not throw away your confidence, which has a great reward. For you have need of endurance, so that when you have done the will of God, you may receive what was promised. FOR YET IN A VERY LITTLE WHILE, HE WHO IS COMING WILL COME, AND WILL NOT DELAY. BUT MY RIGHTEOUS ONE SHALL LIVE BY FAITH; AND IF HE SHRINKS BACK, MY SOUL HAS NO PLEASURE IN HIM. Hebrew 10:32-38, uppercase text in original

Returning to our Key Scripture for this lesson we can see that after identifying the proper response to suffering Paul then speaks of endurance. He goes a step further and connects endurance directly to hope.

---

[13] 1 Peter 2:20-23

> ... we rejoice in our sufferings, knowing that suffering produces endurance, and endurance produces character, and character produces hope. Romans 5:3-4 ESV

One scholar points out that Paul simply states that tested character produces hope. In other words, Paul is asserting a fact that he believes stands on its own merits. He does not provide supportive details which would help verify his claim and convince his audience.[14] Paul can boldly state that tested character produces hope in a way in which only someone who has suffered for Christ can!

After the resurrected Christ met Paul on the road to Damascus, He sent Ananias to open Paul's blind eyes. Jesus overruled the objections of Ananias by informing him that Paul was a chosen instrument to testify before the Gentiles, kings and the sons of Israel. Jesus assured Ananias that Paul would be shown *how much he must suffer* on behalf of the name of Christ.[15] Paul's autobiography is not one many people would aspire to claim for themselves. He lists one distressing hardship after another: expended great labor, endured several imprisonments, beaten times without number, often in danger of death, five different times he received thirty-nine lashes from the Jews, beaten with rods three times, stoned once, shipwrecked three times, and he spent a full night and a day floating in the sea.[16]

Christ-followers ever since the first century have been living between two Kingdom events: "D-day," what God has already done, and "V-day," what God has yet to do.[17] D-day was realized in the first coming of Christ when He decisively defeated the ruler of this world. V-day will become a historical marker on God's Kingdom when Christ comes again signaling the end of our adversary's

---

14 Keck, Leander E., *Romans*, Abingdon New Testament Commentaries (Abingdon Press 2005) Beyond Rectification: Rescued and Reconciled ([Romans] 5:1-11), p. 138
15 Acts 9:15-16
16 2 Corinthians 11:23-25
17 Beale, G. K., *A New Testament Biblical Theology: The Unfolding Of The Old Testament In The New* (Baker Academic 2011) p. 162

The Power of Hope

rule on earth.[18] Scholars commonly refer to this present age as "the already" and "the not yet." In other words, we presently live in the gap in between. If you have ever traveled on the London Underground subway system you are familiar with the saying, "mind the gap." You hear it or read it when exiting the train onto the platform. It is the way passengers are warned about the spatial gap that exists between the train and the station platform. It is fitting for us to say that living in the present *foretaste*, but not yet in the *full taste* of God's eternal Kingdom[19] demands every Christ-follower to "mind the gap." We are to become proficient in endurance and hope! So, it behooves us to learn from the experience-based wisdom and counsel of Paul.

Endurance "does not derive from bravery or insensitivity but from faith and hope."[20] Notice that Paul speaks of endurance as being a product of trial/suffering. Endurance is not the end goal, but a means *to the goal* God has in mind. Paul's word choice here is the Greek word *hypomone* {hoop-om-on-ay'}, translated in our Key Scripture as "endurance." Notice the same word was also used by Jesus in Matthew 10:22, quoted at the beginning of this lesson, translated there as "endured." You might find it helpful to refer back to our Word Study of *hypomone* in Lesson 5.

From what we have already learned, *hypomone* means more than passively sitting still, gritting our teeth and holding on for dear life. It denotes being resolute, persistent and untiring in every trial and hardship so that God can bring good out of evil. *Hypomone* pictures us putting on blinders so that nothing distracts us from reaching the goal God has set for us.[21] The result is that we hold on

---

18 Beale, G. K., *A New Testament Biblical Theology: The Unfolding Of The Old Testament In The New* (Baker Academic 2011) p. 162
19 My research mentor Henri Louis Goulet suggests a more accurate phrase for this present age is "between the foretaste and the full taste."
20 Bromiley, Geoffrey W., *Theological Dictionary of the New Testament*, Abridged in One Volume (Eerdmans 1985) entry for *meno* under *C. The NT*, p. 583, citing Romans 8:2
21 As I was teaching this lesson one morning the Holy Spirit provided me with the illustration of a race horse wearing blinders. Blinders are used to

to faith and hope in a way that honors and glorifies our heavenly Father. Only when we endure by standing up under the weight of the trial do we reach that goal.

The Holy Spirit will enable, equip and empower *hypomone* in the life of every Christ-follower to "remain (endure) under" the challenges God permits. But here's the truth of the matter, our flesh demands to be relieved of the resulting pressure and discomfort as quickly as possible. Therefore, our natural tendency is to try to get out from under a trial as soon as we can. To choose to remain under a trial in a God-honoring way until we reach the goal He has set for us is utterly impossible to do in our natural self. It demands our mature determination to bear up under suffering with a heart attitude that pleases God. That choice permits Holy Spirit to do what only He can do.

In *Sparkling Gems From The Greek* Rick Renner highlights the connection between Paul's choices and his ability to endure trials and suffering. Renner points out the reason we never read about Paul being defeated by all that he endured was that Paul had the resolute determination that he would not resign from his God-given assignment until he had crossed the finish line God had set (Philippians 3:12).[22] For Holy Spirit to do His job, we must be wide open to His work in us and through us. His power works in those who resolve to stay the course so that He can finish the work He was sent to do. Renner highlights this truth when he writes that the power of the Holy Spirit:[23]

> ... works proficiently through people who have decided they will never turn back until the assignment is finished. God delights in using people who are steadfast and unmoving in their conviction, tenacious and diehard

---

reduce distractions and keep horses focused on what is in front of them. In that regard, blinders help them concentrate on the task at hand.

22   Renner, Rick, *Sparkling Gems from the Greek* (Harrison House Publishers 2003) August 17, pp. 600-602

23   Renner, Rick, *Sparkling Gems from the Greek* (Harrison House Publishers 2003) August 17, pp. 601-602, italics in original

The Power of Hope 167

in their commitment. He takes pleasure in those who have stamina, spunk, and a dogged determination to hold on to the vision He put in their hearts.... *Satan can't make us quit.* That choice lies in our hands alone.

When we have the same unyielding determination that Paul had, we will be able to withstand all of Satan's attacks and not quit until we have successfully completed the Kingdom assignment we have been given. The Bible makes it clear that it is those who demonstrate *hypomone* in this life who receive the eternal promises guaranteed by the cross.[24]

We see this type of endurance in Paul and Silas who were stripped and beaten with rods by order of the magistrate in Philippi. After being severely flogged, they were thrown into prison with their feet fastened in stocks. Even so, about midnight, Paul and Silas were praying and singing hymns to God and the other prisoners listened to them singing.[25] That's Spirit-empowered *hypomone* in action!

Returning to our Key Scripture Paul asserts that *hypomone* produces *dokime* {dok-ee-may'} which can be translated as "proven character" or "tested character."[26] In other words, endurance results in "tested genuineness"[27] and "tested value."[28] Paul is drawing from the secular Greek usage of *dokime* which describes metals that had been determined to be pure through a process of testing. The testing of the metal proved it to be authentic. Similarly, "a process

---

24 See for example: Hebrews 10:36; James 1:4; Revelation 2:7,11,17,26-28; 3:5,12,21; 21:1-22
25 Acts 16:25
26 Keck, Leander E., *Romans*, Abingdon New Testament Commentaries (Abingdon Press 2005) Beyond Rectification: Rescued and Reconciled ([Romans] 5:1-11), p. 138
27 Keck, Leander E., *Romans*, Abingdon New Testament Commentaries (Abingdon Press 2005) Beyond Rectification: Rescued and Reconciled ([Romans] 5:1-11), p. 138
28 Harrison and Hagner, "Romans," in *The Expositor's Bible Commentary: Romans ~ Galatians*, Vol. 11, Revised Edition, edited by Longman III and Garland (Zondervan Academic 2008) Romans 5:4, p. 89

of enduring something amounts to a test that promotes and validates the character of the one undergoing it."[29] Paul then concludes that this type of tested genuineness in the life of a Christ-follower strengthens hope. However, he does not explain why this is so, he merely asserts it as fact. That places the responsibility on the reader to infer what Paul means.[30] I believe it is reasonable to conclude that there are likely three interconnected aspects of this truth that Paul may have in mind.

First, character shaped by God's test receives His approval. Approved character assures us of eternal fellowship with God – such "character finds its ultimate resting place in the [eternal] presence of God, not in the grave."[31] Knowing God's approval is resting on us in this life increases and fortifies our hope.[32] Right relationship with Him encourages us to remain in His *Hope Waiting Room* no matter what the present circumstances are.

Second, experience-based confidence is convinced that having fought through past trials with God's help, all future trials can also be overcome.[33] A calm hope rises in the heart that has been tested and approved believing that the future will be like the past. Our

---

29 Bauer-Danker, *Greek-English Lexicon of the NT* (BDAG) entry for *2067 δοκιμή*. Retrieved from BibleWorks 9.0 software
30 Keck, Leander E., *Romans*, Abingdon New Testament Commentaries (Abingdon Press 2005) Beyond Rectification: Rescued and Reconciled ([Romans] 5:1-11), p. 138
31 Harrison and Hagner, "Romans," in *The Expositor's Bible Commentary: Romans ~ Galatians*, Vol. 11, Revised Edition, edited by Longman III and Garland (Zondervan Academic 2008) Romans 5:4, p. 90
32 *Romans 5:4-5 Commentary*, Precept Austin, citing Hendriksen & Kistemaker, *NT Commentary Set* (Baker Book). Retrieved from https://www.preceptaustin.org/romans_54-5 (last accessed August 8, 2021)
33 Alexander MacLaren, a Scottish Baptist minister (1826-1910) viewed the hope of Christ-followers as resulting equally from life's trials and life's blessings. "The one spark is struck from the hard flint by the cold steel, and the other is kindled by the sun itself, but they are both fire." MacLaren, Alexander, *Expositions of Holy Scripture*, The Sources of Hope (Romans 5:2-4). Retrieved from https://www.blueletterbible.org/comm/maclaren_alexander/expositions-of-holy-scripture/romans/the-sources-of-hope.cfm (last accessed February 21, 2023)

The Power of Hope

endurance in a time of suffering allows God to prove His faithfulness. Since the quality of our hope is directly related to our trust in God's faithfulness, character that has proven God's faithfulness through testing results in experience-based hope. Every experience we have of God's faithfulness becomes mounting evidence of His continued faithfulness. King David knew this truth and wrote: "Trust in the LORD, and do good ... and *feed on His faithfulness*."[34] Experience-based hope is saturated with confident assurance that has been well fed!

It seems to me that the third and most important truth underlying Paul's assertion is plain and simple. It is through the *law of use*[35] that adversity strengthens hope. Hope becomes stronger as we *need* to exercise hope. After all, "it is only when everything is hopeless that hope begins to be a strength."[36] Amid suffering the author of Hebrews advises us to "hold [*katecho* {kat-ekh'-o}] firmly to the confession of our hope without wavering, for He who promised is faithful."[37] *Katecho* pictures embracing something with ownership.[38] To hold firmly to our hope requires us to securely wrap our arms around God's promises.

Satan is not able to steal God's promises or our hope from us. However, he most certainly will work hard to convince us to forfeit those promises and surrender that hope by laying it down. Every time we face adversity we have a choice: we can either abandon our hope or we can persevere by securely hugging our promise(s) while pressing in more tightly to God. If we choose to cling firmly to

---

34 Psalm 37:3 NKJV, italics added
35 It is a biblical principle that if you use what you have been given you will gain more. On the other hand, if you fail to use what you already have, that which you had will be taken away. This is the "law of use" taught in the parable of the talents (Matthew 25:14-30).
36 *1 Peter 3:13-22 Commentary*, Precept Austin, quoting G. K. Chesterton. Retrieved from https://www.preceptaustin.org/1peter verse by verse __313-22 (last accessed August 8, 2021)
37 Hebrews 10:23
38 Renner, Rick, *Sparkling Gems from the Greek* (Harrison House Publishers 2003) March 20, pp. 170-171

our hope, we *will* endure through the trial and come out the other side victorious. On the other hand, when we lay hope down, hope loses its effective power.

When we are forced to face adversity, Holy Spirit will encourage us to tightly wrap our arms around the promise God gave us and embrace it with all our might. Every time we choose to press in more tightly we receive grace to exercise hope. As we do, we grow in our bold resolve to overcome the persistent determination of the enemy who works to convince us to give up and surrender our hope! In other words, *because of the struggle,* we learn out of necessity to "hold fast" [*katecho*] to the promise(s). In the process, we discover the more we exercise hope, the more hope we have to exercise!

Paul thoroughly understood that hope is not an afterthought for the one who is devoted to Christ – it is not just an extra something tacked onto our belief. Hope is the very essence of the gospel itself (the good news) which had the power to establish the first-century church. Hope is what defined those early Christ-followers as well as every other true disciple of Christ since then. It is hope that distinguishes us from those who are despairing (the unredeemed of this world).[39]

Like Paul, Peter seems to assume that during suffering Christ-followers will choose to hold on to hope. As a result, he exhorts us to be ready to explain that hope to anyone who asks.

> But even if you should suffer for what is right, you are blessed. "Do not fear their threats; do not be frightened." But in your hearts revere Christ as Lord. Always be prepared to give an answer to everyone who asks you to give the reason for the hope that you have. But do this with gentleness and respect. 1 Peter 3:14-15 NIV

---

39 *God's Word of Hope, The Believer's Blessed Hope Part 1*, Precept Austin, citing C. E. Sherman. Retrieved from https://www.preceptaustin.org/gods_word_of_hope (last accessed August 26, 2021)

The Power of Hope

We will begin by putting Peter's exhortation in context. The first epistle written by Peter was intended to be a circular letter primarily to Jewish Christ-followers who were living outside the land of Israel. Peter desired these fellow disciples to live faithfully as God's chosen people amid a culture that was inherently opposed to God.[40] Before he instructs them on suffering, he first reminds them they have been born anew (or born from above) into a "living hope" which he refers to as their inheritance (1 Peter 1:3-4). By this he means they have a hope that is *actively alive*.[41] The eternal life of every *talmid* has been firmly established. Although purchased and adequately paid for by the death and resurrection of Christ this rich inheritance is still invisible to the eye which is why it is yet something hoped for. However, because it "is grounded in a completed act, our hope is sure and living (1 Pet. 1:3)."[42] Said another way, "The hope of the final victory is so much more vivid because of the unshakably firm conviction that the battle that decides the victory has already taken place."[43] Given this certainty of outcome, the fear of the future which grips much of the world has no place in the life of a Christ-follower. Instead living (actively alive) hope should be *normal* for every disciple of Christ.[44] In turn this type of hope has the power to change how we live.[45]

In his first epistle Peter was reminding his readers that they possess (have in them) a hope that is full of effective working pow-

---

40   Ryken, Wilhoit, and Longman III, editors, *Dictionary of Biblical Imagery* (Intervarsity Press 1998) entry for *Peter, First Letter Of*, p. 638
41   Hill, Gary, *The Discovery Bible*, HELPS Ministries, Inc., Cognate: [G]2198 *záō*, quoting K. Wuest, italics in original
42   Bromiley, Geoffrey W., *Theological Dictionary of the New Testament*, Abridged in One Volume (Eerdmans 1985) entry for *zao* under *E. The Concept of Life in the NT*, p. 294
43   Beale, G. K., *A New Testament Biblical Theology: The Unfolding Of The Old Testament In The New* (Baker Academic 2011) p. 162
44   Hill, Gary, *The Discovery Bible*, HELPS Ministries, Inc., Cognate: [G]2198 *záō*, quoting *3, Treasures*, 21,22, italics in original
45   Piper, John, *The Power of Hope*, Sermon Bethlehem Baptist Church, Easter Sunday, April 19, 1981. Retrieved from https://www.desiringgod.org/messages/the-power-of-hope (last accessed November 11, 2021)

er. They were already experiencing abuse from harsh slave masters (1 Peter 2:18), threats from unbelieving spouses (1 Peter 3:1,6) as well as disdainful mockery and insults from skeptical neighbors and associates (1 Peter 4:14).[46] To add to that suffering, Peter anticipates they will likely experience additional persecution. The construction of the original Greek language in 1 Peter 3:14 "implies that such suffering was not [yet] the norm, even though it could happen, and in fact may well have happened to some of the readers."[47] Life for the fellow *talmidim* he is writing to is about to take a turn for the worse! Peter understands that "adversity is the soil in which the gospel thrives"[48] so he counsels his readers to always be prepared to explain the source and the nature of the hope that is living within them. This power-filled hope that is alive in their hearts "is dynamic, energizing and capable of stimulating a strong confidence in God." [49] Peter knows that living hope, when kept alive through use, has more than sufficient power to influence their day-to-day thoughts and behavior.

Before we proceed with understanding our Key Scripture I want to take a short detour here so we can consider the early church model of suffering for the sake of the gospel. This detoured consideration is particularly important for those of us in the Western church who have for the most part so far escaped the persecution and suffering that is the norm for our brothers and sisters in Christ in many parts of the world today. A thoughtful approach begins in the book of Acts as the church itself is being birthed.

---

46 Piper, John, *The Power of Hope*, Sermon Bethlehem Baptist Church, Easter Sunday, April 19, 1981. Retrieved from https://www.desiringgod.org/messages/the-power-of-hope (last accessed November 11, 2021)

47 *Net Bible Notes*, study note 20, 1 Peter 3:14. The first Roman Emperor credited with persecution of Christians is Nero. Scholars believe 1 Peter was probably written in the early 60's during the reign of Nero.

48 Deffinbaugh, Bob, *18. A New Slant on Suffering (1 Peter 3:13-4:6)*, Bible.org. Retrieved from https://bible.org/seriespage/new-slant-suffering-1-peter-313-46 (last accessed August 8, 2021)

49 *God's Word of Hope*, Precept Austin, quoting John Piper. Retrieved from https://www.preceptaustin.org/gods_word_of_hope (last accessed August 8, 2021)

In Acts 4 we read of Peter and John being arrested by the Jewish religious authorities. Their crime was that they had permitted the healing power of Christ to flow through them to a man who had been lame from birth. They were also *guilty* of teaching the people and preaching that Jesus had been resurrected (Acts 3:1-8; 4:2). When Peter and John were freed by the authorities they joined fellow Believers and prayed with one accord for *more boldness*. Notice they didn't pray for the persecution to end, instead, they asked that the Holy Spirit embolden them to become even more outspoken![50] There is a subtle point worth making here that is too important to miss before we move on. Those prayers for boldness rather than for avoiding suffering were in perfect alignment with the promise Jesus had made to them.

We made the point earlier in this lesson that Jesus spoke plainly to His disciples about the hostility and suffering they would encounter. Jesus promised they did not need to prepare or plan ahead for those expected times of persecution.[51] He told them at their exact time of need they could trust Holy Spirit to give them the right words to speak. Here is the point I don't want us to brush past too quickly. Jesus did not promise them a way out, they were assured they would be given words that would be a "testimony" (*marturion* {mar-too'-ree-on}) about Him. That means whatever words Holy Spirit gave them to speak might actually make matters worse from a suffering point of view! In fact, some time after the first century *marturion* became synonymous with martyrdom – those whose testimony for Jesus led to their death.[52]

In Acts 5 the Jewish religious authorities were once again determined to stop the work of the Apostles in Jerusalem so they apparently imprisoned all of the Apostles in the common prison.[53] At night an angel came and opened the prison door and instructed

---

50 Acts 4:23-31
51 Matthew 10:17-20
52 *Mark 13 Commentary*, Precept Austin, citing *Eerdman's Dictionary of the Bible*. Retrieved from https://www.preceptaustin.org/mark-13-commentary (last accessed April 14, 2022)
53 Acts 5:18

them, "Go, stand and speak to the people in the temple area the whole message of this Life."⁵⁴ They obeyed and early the next morning that is exactly where the Jewish religious officials found them! After they were arrested again and beaten, Luke tells us in Acts 5:

> So they went on their way from the presence of the Council, rejoicing that they had been considered worthy to suffer shame for *His* name. And every day, in the temple and from house to house, they kept right on teaching and preaching Jesus *as* the Christ. Acts 5:41-42, italics in original

Despite the punishment and the public shame, the Apostles reacted in joy! Later Peter would write:

> For what credit is there if, when you sin and are harshly treated, you endure it with patience? But if when you do what is right and suffer *for it* you patiently endure it, this *finds* favor with God. 1 Peter 2:20, italics in original

> [B]ut if *anyone suffers* as a Christian, he is not to be ashamed, but is to glorify God in this name. 1 Peter 4:16, italics in original

> After you have suffered for a little while, the God of all grace ... will Himself perfect, confirm, strengthen *and* establish you. 1 Peter 5:10, italics in original

Peter was following the template for discipleship Jesus had modeled for him. In that culture, persecution of various forms was calculated to bring shame in an attempt to force noncompliant behavior to become compliant with public norms.⁵⁵ The exclusivity of belief in one God and worship of Him alone was viewed

---

54 Acts 5:20
55 deSilva, David A., *Hope of Glory: Honor Discourse and New Testament Interpretation* (Wipf & Stock 1999). See for example: pp. 7, 63, 103

The Power of Hope 175

by those outside the growing church as deviant behavior in need of change. The New Testament authors, Peter included, turn the paradigm upside down. They encourage Christ-followers to be willing to suffer in order to advance the gospel in the same way in which Jesus was motivated by "the joy [of accomplishing the goal] set before Him [and] endured the cross, disregarding the shame."[56]

Now let's return to our study of Peter's counsel in 1 Peter 3. I'll restate it here.

> But even if you should suffer for what is right, you are blessed. "Do not fear their threats; do not be frightened." But in your hearts revere Christ as Lord. Always be prepared to give an **answer** to everyone who asks you to give the reason for the hope that you have. But do this with gentleness and respect. 1 Peter 3:14-15 NIV, bold added

When Peter advised his readers to be prepared to give an "answer" to anyone who asks about their hope he used the Greek word *apologia* {ap-ol-og-ee'-ah}. *Apologia* sounds like our English word apology but it does not mean to apologize in our modern understanding of the word. *Apologia* was the term used for making a legal defense in an ancient court.[57] Peter used the word to refer to the well-reasoned, compelling reply that should be given by anyone who is accused of wrong beliefs and inappropriate hope. Peter urged their answer to present sufficiently persuasive evidence to convince someone else that what they believe and what they hope for is really true.[58] Peter was not advising them to present a

---

56   Hebrews 12:2 AMP
57   Hill, Gary, *The Discovery Bible*, HELPS Ministries, Inc., [G]627 *apología*
58   Hill, Gary, *The Discovery Bible*, HELPS Ministries, Inc., [G]627 *apología*; Ellicott, Charles John, *Ellicott's Commentary for English Readers*, 1 Peter 3:15. Retrieved from Hill, Gary, *The Discovery Bible*, HELPS Ministries, Inc.; Barnes, Albert, *Barnes' Notes on the New Testament*, 1 Peter 3:15. Retrieved from Hill, Gary, *The Discovery Bible*, HELPS Ministries, Inc.

good defense on their own behalf. He was telling them to present a bold *testimony* to the reality of Christ and His power to save!

Living in a world that was largely hostile to Christ meant that these Christ-followers were at risk of accusation from the Roman courts of law. However, perhaps even more often, they were at risk of accusation or worse in the courts of public opinion. Peter wanted to help them develop a strong spiritual backbone.[59] Peter did not dream up a new set of instructions when he wrote, "… DO NOT BE AFRAID OF THEIR INTIMIDATING THREATS, NOR BE TROUBLED *or* DISTURBED [by their opposition]. But in your hearts set Christ apart [as holy—acknowledging Him, giving Him first place in your lives] as Lord…."[60] Peter was repeating history. He turned to the counsel God gave the prophet Isaiah during challenging circumstances. His background came from Isaiah 8:12-13.[61]

> "… you are not to fear what they fear nor be in dread of it. It is the LORD of hosts whom you are to regard as holy *and* awesome. He shall be your [source of] fear, He shall be your [source of] dread [not man]…." Isaiah 8:12-13 AMP, italics in original

It is commonly thought that Peter was quoting from the LXX, the Greek version, of Isaiah 8:13, which translates into English as follows:

---

59 Beale and Carson, editors, *Commentary on the New Testament Use of the Old Testament* (Baker Academic 2007) 1 Peter 3:14-15 under F. *Theological Use*, p. 1038
60 1 Peter 3:14-15 AMP, italics in original, uppercase text in original indicating a quotation from the Old Testament
61 Peter uses the Greek version of Isaiah 8:12-13 in his letter. By changing two words found in the original Greek text of Isaiah 8:12-13, Peter is able to shift the quote from Yahweh to Christ. Davids, Peter, "1 Peter," in *Zondervan Illustrated Bible Backgrounds Commentary*, Vol. 4, edited by Clinton E. Arnold (Zondervan 2002) 1 Peter 3:14 under *"Do not fear what they fear; do not be frightened,"* p. 138

> Consecrate the Lord himself and he will be your fear.
> Isaiah 8:13 LXX[62]

In other words, in a time when fear and dread were normal in Israel Yahweh advised Isaiah to live a conspicuously different lifestyle. Isaiah was to have no part in fearing what his fellow Jews feared. He was to remain calm in the middle of the social and cultural storm swirling around him. Isaiah was instructed to set God apart in his heart so that *He* was the only one Isaiah feared. In Old Testament language, the fear of God "decisively affects human conduct."[63] It acts as a restraint against unfaithfulness and motivates obedience to God's divine will. To rightly "consecrate the LORD himself (Isaiah 8:13 LXX)" would require Isaiah to definitively set Yahweh apart in his heart as Lord of his life. As he did, Isaiah's life would be a walking testimony that the *only* fear capturing him was the fear (reverential awe) of the Lord God Almighty.[64] Yahweh knew that if Isaiah walked in *that* type of fear he would have the power necessary to overcome *every other kind* of fear![65]

Peter was certain God had not changed and that the counsel Yahweh gave Isaiah was equally applicable to those who were following Christ in his day. He was instructing his fellow Christ-followers to "sanctify Christ as Lord in your hearts."[66] Sanctify is the word *hagiazo* (the root word is *hagios* meaning holy, set apart from the

---

62 Beale and Carson, editors, *Commentary on the New Testament Use of the Old Testament* (Baker Academic 2007) 1 Peter 3:14-15 under *D. Textual Matters*, p. 1038

63 Sarna, Nahum M., *Exploring Exodus: The Origins of Biblical Israel* (Schocken Books 1996) p. 120

64 Motyer, J. Alec, *The Prophecy of Isaiah: An Introduction & Commentary* (InterVarsity Press 1993) Isaiah 8:12, p. 95. In the thought world of the Old Testament, a person who was said to "fear the Lord" did not fear anything else! Brown, Michael L., *Compassionate Father or Consuming Fire: Engaging The God of The Old Testament* (AWKNG Press 2021) p. 14

65 Christensen, Duane L., *Word Biblical Commentary: Deuteronomy 1 - 21:9*, Volume 6A, Second Edition (Zondervan 2014) Deuteronomy 10:12-11:9 under *Explanation*, p. 205

66 1 Peter 3:15a

world unto God). Peter knew from his Old Testament heritage, as well as his own experience, when Jesus is properly-revered in their hearts they will fear nothing but Him[67] and confidently hope for everything He promised. Their hope will lead the way to "active, transformative conduct"[68] and that's the whole point!

Hear What The Spirit is Saying to the Church: *If only my disciples would learn that in every instance of adversity there is strength waiting to be had. I am ever willing and able to provide more than sufficient grace in every circumstance for anyone who trusts me and my ways.*

---

[67] Beale and Carson, editors, *Commentary on the New Testament Use of the Old Testament* (Baker Academic 2007) 1 Peter 3:14-15 under *D. Textual Matters*, p. 1038

[68] Brueggemann, Walter, *Truth & Hope: Essays For a Perilous Age* (Westminster John Knox Press 2020) p. 127

LESSON 10:

OVERFLOWING WITH HOPE

> "May God, the source of hope, fill you completely with joy and shalom as you continue **trusting**, so that by the power of the *Ruach HaKodesh* [Holy Spirit] you may overflow with hope." Romans 15:13 CJB, italics in original

DOWN THROUGH THE CENTURIES Christ-followers have commonly found themselves in an unavoidable conflict between challenge and privilege.[1] Those who chose Christ as Lord and Savior are no longer at home in this world and are urged "to keep away from worldly desires that wage war against [our] very souls."[2] Enjoying the hope of eternal citizenship demands that we relinquish some of the benefits enjoyed by those who make this present world their home.[3]

We are encouraged to see ourselves by faith as members of a community whose true home is neither of this age nor of this world.[4] The New Testament pictures us as foreigners and exiles in this lifetime as we await our true heavenly home.[5] The Greek word

---

1 Beale and Carson, editors, *Commentary on the New Testament Use of the Old Testament* (Baker Academic 2007) 1 Peter 2:9-10, p. 1033
2 1 Peter 2:11 NLT; Hebrews 13:14
3 Cockerill, Gareth Lee, *The Epistle to the Hebrews*, New International Commentary on the New Testament (Eerdmans 2012) Hebrews 11:13, p. 551
4 See for example: Philippians 3:20; Hebrews 12:22–24; Revelation 21:2-4
5 Exile can refer to the condition of someone who is forced to live away from their native country or home. In such cases, the idea of punishment is predominant. However, exile can also be voluntary and self-imposed.

parepidemos {par-ep-id'-ay-mos} refers to "a foreigner who has settled down, however briefly, next to or among the native people."[6] The word is used for Abraham in the Greek translation of the Old Testament when he is described as a sojourner, a temporary resident (*parepidemos*) in the land of Canaan.[7] Peter employed *parepidemos* to reference those who obediently follow Christ and "reside as temporary residents [*parepidemos*] and foreigners."[8] Calling early *talmidim* temporary residents and foreigners identified them as those who lacked the normal rights and privileges associated with first-century Roman citizenship.[9] For example, they no longer supported the Roman form of theater, the popular sport of gladiator combat[10] or the Roman style races. They were known to neglect family or civic duty if pagan worship was inseparably intertwined with that duty.[11] That meant they withdrew from participation in religious festivals or feasts that ascribed worth to gods other than the one true God. Their distinctive identity made them sufficiently different from first-century Roman society that it didn't take long

---

Merriam-Webster.com Dictionary, entry for *exile*. Retrieved from https://www.merriam-webster.com/dictionary/exile (last accessed April 14, 2022)

6 Zodhiates, Spiros, *The Complete Word Study Dictionary: New Testament* (AMG Publishers 1992) word #3927, p. 1118

7 Genesis 23:4

8 1 Peter 1:1-2; 2:11

9 Davids, Peter, "1 Peter," in *Zondervan Illustrated Bible Backgrounds Commentary*, Vol. 4, edited by Clinton E. Arnold (Zondervan 2002) 1 Peter 2:11 under *Aliens and strangers*, p. 134

10 A gladiator is defined as, "A person, usually a professional combatant, a captive, or a slave, trained to entertain the public by engaging in mortal combat [to the death] with another person or a wild animal in the ancient Roman arena." *American Heritage® Dictionary of the English Language*, Fifth Edition (Houghton Mifflin Harcourt Publishing Company Copyright © 2016) entry for *gladiator*. Retrieved from https://www.thefreedictionary.com/Gladiatorial+combat (last accessed April 15, 2022)

11 Beale and Carson, editors, *Commentary on the New Testament Use of the Old Testament* (Baker Academic 2007) 1 Peter 2:9-10, p. 1033, citing Colwell 1939; Judge 1960; Davids, Peter, "1 Peter," in *Zondervan Illustrated Bible Backgrounds Commentary*, Vol. 4, edited by Clinton E. Arnold (Zondervan 2002) 1 Peter under *A Portrait of the Situation*, pp. 122-123

before they were feeling the effects of ostracism and persecution.[12] They were surrounded by a culture that routinely used shame to encourage people to engage in deviant behavior in order to realign themselves with cultural norms. Consequently, the lifestyle they chose made them social outcasts and earned them labels such as "unpatriotic," "disloyal," "atheists" and "haters of their family and humankind."[13] As scholar Gareth Lee Cockerill points out those who are by born again nature citizens "of the world to come, and thus only temporary aliens in this world.... should not be surprised if they lack the protection of citizens [of this world] and are persecuted by those who consider here and now their home."[14]

Because *talmidim* of Christ view themselves as part of an eternal Kingdom under the Lordship of Jesus, it is necessary in every era and culture to work out in practical ways how to follow in the footsteps of King Jesus. Every Christ-follower is called to live out their heavenly life here on earth.[15] That means each one must resolve how to "[r]ender therefore to Caesar the things that are

---

12   As a result of following Christ, they became subject to "insults, abuse, rejection, shame, and likely economic persecution with the resulting loss of property.... rejection, abuse, punishment by family leaders ... and perhaps mob violence had certainly taken their toll. (Official persecution would come in the time of Pliny [as documented by Pliny's letter to Emperor Trajan in 112 A.D. asking for instruction as to how to interrogate, persecute and put Christians to death].) Their fellow citizens thought that these believers in Jesus no longer belonged in their city or family and were communicating the message loud and clear." Davids, Peter, "1 Peter," in *Zondervan Illustrated Bible Backgrounds Commentary*, Vol. 4, edited by Clinton E. Arnold (Zondervan 2002) 1 Peter under *A Portrait of the Situation*, p. 123

13   Davids, Peter, "1 Peter," in *Zondervan Illustrated Bible Backgrounds Commentary*, Vol. 4, edited by Clinton E. Arnold (Zondervan 2002) 1 Peter under *A Portrait of the Situation*, pp. 122-123

14   Cockerill, Gareth Lee, *The Epistle to the Hebrews*, New International Commentary on the New Testament (Eerdmans 2012) Hebrews 11:13, pp. 550-551

15   Ingram, Chip, *I Choose Peace: How To Quiet Your Heart In An Anxious World* (Baker Books 2021) Introduction & Chapter 1: Choose Peace in Relational Conflict, p. 22

Caesar's, and to God the things that are God's."[16] In a nutshell, it is that tension I want to explore in this lesson. As we will see, the Bible contains very clear instruction on the matter. Our starting place is the biblical starting place – Jeremiah's instruction to the Jewish people living in Babylonian exile.

Over a long season of time, Israel as a nation had been disobedient to God's commands. As a result, prophets were sent by Yahweh to give His covenant people fair warning of His judgment if they persisted in their covenant violations. When repentance did not result, God carried out His promised judgment.

The majority of Jewish people were forcibly removed from the land and found themselves an underprivileged minority in a new land with a new culture steeped in the worship of pagan gods. Babylon was one of the most wicked and idolatrous cities in the ancient world. Some Jews responded to their captivity by forcibly resisting Babylon while others blended in by adopting the way of life and culture of Babylon.[17] These are, after all, what would seem to be the only two options available. However, the prophet Jeremiah, as Yahweh's messenger, presented a distinctively different third option that must have sounded radical.[18]

> "Thus says the LORD of hosts, the God of Israel, to all the exiles whom I have sent into exile from Jerusalem to Babylon, 'Build houses and live *in them*; and plant gardens and eat their produce.... multiply there and do

---

16 Luke 20:25 NKJV; Beale and Carson, editors, *Commentary on the New Testament Use of the Old Testament* (Baker Academic 2007) 1 Peter 2:9-10, p. 1033
17 Mackie and Collins, *Way of the Exile*, BibleProject Video. Retrieved from https://www.bing.com/search?q=The+Way+of+Exile+youtube.com&form=ANSNB1&refig=62fcd9a2c4984840b1d315873d4bac-7d&pc=U531&ntref=1 (last accessed March 20, 2022). The BibleProject website begins with this description, "BibleProject is a nonprofit, crowd-funded organization that produces 100% free Bible videos, podcasts, blogs, classes, and educational Bible resources to help make the biblical story accessible to everyone everywhere."
18 Thompson, J. A., *The Book of Jeremiah*, The New International Commentary on The Old Testament (Eerdmans 1980) Jeremiah 29:5-6,7, p. 546

not decrease. Seek the welfare of the city where I have sent you into exile, and pray to the LORD on its behalf; for in its welfare [*shalom*] you will have welfare [*shalom*].' ..."
Jeremiah 29:4-7, italics in original

Jeremiah told those in exile to settle into a new life by doing those things they would normally do – build houses, plant gardens and expand their families. But they were also told to seek Babylon's welfare and pray to the Lord on behalf of their Babylonian captors. A quick Word Study will help us see how astonishing this instruction must have been.

WORD STUDY

In Jeremiah 29:7 the word **welfare** *is a translation of the Hebrew word shalom {shaw-lome'}. It is commonly rendered "peace," however the Hebrew idea of shalom is a much broader concept. It can be described as "wholeness, completeness, soundness, sufficiency, satisfaction, harmony, peace, or holistic wellbeing."*[19]

Notice that in their captivity the *only* way the Hebrew exiles would be able to experience *shalom* is if they lived according to Yahweh's instruction and prayed for Yahweh to provide *shalom* to their captors! In other words, they needed to personally invest themselves in seeking the well-being of those who violently overthrew their nation and forcibly removed them from their land.

---

19   Goulet, Henri, Louis, *Persevering Through the Very Long Period of Groaning and Suffering*, The Weekly Messianic Taste of Hidden Manna #43. Received via E-mail July 24, 2020

Most certainly, obeying this command would have "required an almost superhuman patience."[20]

The book of Daniel teaches us that the way envisioned by Jeremiah for the exiles is an appropriate blend of faithful service and nonviolent noncompliance.[21] Daniel highlights a number of clear examples of what it looks like in practice to follow the counsel of Jeremiah that promoted neither compromise nor incited revolt. Daniel and his Hebrew friends faithfully served the King of Babylon. However, they did it in a way that did not cause them to concede their unique identity as worshippers of Yahweh. When pagan worship was intertwined with Babylonian civic duty, they nonviolently refused to engage in that civic duty[22] and in some cases suffered the natural consequences. In this way, they demonstrated that the ultimate source of their loyalty was to Yahweh. With that background, we'll pick up our study in Daniel Chapter 1:

> In the third year of the reign of Jehoiakim king of Judah, Nebuchadnezzar king of Babylon came to Jerusalem and besieged it. The Lord gave Jehoiakim king of Judah into his hand, along with some of the vessels of the house of God; and he brought them to the land of Shinar, to the house of his god, and he brought the vessels into the treasury of his god. Daniel 1:1-2

---

20   Ellicott, Charles John, *Ellicott's Commentary for English Readers*, Jeremiah 29:7. Retrieved from Hill, Gary, *The Discovery Bible*, HELPS Ministries, Inc.

21   I credit BibleProject with the understanding that Jeremiah's instruction is applicable to Daniel. Mackie and Collins, *Way of the Exile*, BibleProject Video. Retrieved from https://www.bing.com/search?q=The+Way+of+Exile+youtube.com&form=ANSNB1&refig=62fcd9a2c4984840b1d315873d4bac7d&pc=U531&ntref=1 (last accessed March 20, 2022)

22   The BibleProject uses the term "subversion" for such refusal. Subversion refers to the undermining of the power and authority of an established system or institution; literally the turning over of something. I think a more appropriate phrase is "nonviolent noncompliance."

These opening verses of Daniel provide a succinct historical account of the first Babylonian siege against Jerusalem which occurred "in the third year of the reign of Jehoiakim king of Judah."[23] In the culture of the ancient Near East, removing temple vessels from Jerusalem and placing them in a Babylonian temple would normally be a public declaration that the gods of Babylon were thought to be superior over the God of Israel.[24] Notice however that in Daniel 1 the reader is informed otherwise. It was Yahweh who permitted those vessels to be taken to Babylon.

At that time, Yahweh also permitted some of the Jewish people to be taken to Babylon. In those days it was customary for a conquering nation to identify the brightest captives and put them through cultural indoctrination so their talents and skills could benefit their captors.[25] That's exactly what we'll see in the story of Daniel.

> Then the king ordered Ashpenaz, the chief of his officials, to bring in some of the sons of Israel, including some of the royal family and of the nobles, youths in whom was no defect, who were good-looking, showing intelligence in every *branch of* wisdom, endowed with understanding and discerning knowledge, and who had ability for serving in the king's court; and *he ordered him* to teach them **the literature and language of the Chaldeans**. The king ... *appointed* that they should be educated three years, at the end of which they were to

---

23 Parallel accounts are found in 2 Kings 24:1-2 and 2 Chronicles 36:5-7
24 Lucas, Ernest C., "Daniel," in *Zondervan Illustrated Bible Backgrounds Commentary*, Vol. 4, edited by John H. Walton (Zondervan 2009) Daniel 1:2 under *Articles from the temple*, p. 527. When one nation conquered another, it was assumed that the god of the conquering nation was more powerful than the god of the conquered nation.
25 Lucas, Ernest C., "Daniel," in *Zondervan Illustrated Bible Backgrounds Commentary*, Vol. 4, edited by John H. Walton (Zondervan 2009) Daniel 1:4 under *The language and literature of the Babylonians*, p. 528

enter the king's personal service. Daniel 1:3-5, italics in original, **bold** added

Scripture tells us that Daniel, Hananiah, Mishael and Azariah (all descendants of Judah) were among those who met the qualifications and were placed in the King's training program (Daniel 1:6). In the verses just quoted I have highlighted in bold the phrase "the literature and language of the Chaldeans." It refers to an ancient university-style education in the Sumerian, Akkadian and Aramaic languages.[26] This education was designed to thoroughly assimilate a foreign captive into Babylonian life. Students were required to learn hundreds of language symbols as well as the precise rules for the proper use of each symbol.[27] They learned by copying books in the original language, including many with religious content. These assignments methodically trained them in the worldview and the culture of Babylon. At the end of three years those who passed the test would be given royal positions in the service of King Nebuchadnezzar.[28]

As a part of their cultural re-orientation, the Bible points out that Daniel and the other three young men were given new Babylonian names (Daniel 1:7). Changing a person's name was one way in which a conqueror asserted his authority over the one taken captive.[29] However, there is more than assertion of power going on

---

26 *Holman Christian Standard Bible*, Study Bible edition (Holman Bible Publishers 2010) study note Daniel 1:4, p. 1433
27 Lucas, Ernest C., "Daniel," in *Zondervan Illustrated Bible Backgrounds Commentary*, Vol. 4, edited by John H. Walton (Zondervan 2009) Daniel 1:4 under *The language and literature of the Babylonians*, p. 528
28 Daniel 1:5. Historians believe the three years identified in the biblical account of Daniel's training equated to the typical length of time to train a competent scribe. Lucas, Ernest C., "Daniel," in *Zondervan Illustrated Bible Backgrounds Commentary*, Vol. 4, edited by John H. Walton (Zondervan 2009) Daniel 1:5 under *Trained for three years*, p. 529
29 Lucas, Ernest C., "Daniel," in *Zondervan Illustrated Bible Backgrounds Commentary*, Vol. 4, edited by John H. Walton (Zondervan 2009) Daniel 1:7 under *New names*, p. 529. In the ancient world the right to give a person a name communicated superiority and power over the recipi-

when Daniel and the other three Jewish young men are renamed. In each case, their Hebrew birth names which honored Yahweh were changed to Babylonian names that either honored the Babylonian king or the Babylonian gods.[30]

Hebrew Birth Name & Meaning	New Babylonian Name & Meaning
Daniel – God is my judge or God has judged	Belteshazzar – Bel protect the king
Hananiah – Yahweh has been gracious	Shadrach – Command of Aku (a Babylonian god)
Mishael – Who is what God is? (Who is like the Lord?)	Meshach – Who is what Aku is? (Who is like Aku?)
Azariah – Yahweh is my helper	Abed-nego – Servant of Nego (another Babylonian god)

In our culture, we might not think a name change is such a big deal. However, in the Babylonian culture, changing their names was an attempt to transfer the core identity of these young Hebrews from Yahweh to the King and the gods of Babylon. The next aspect of the cultural integration program for the Hebrew youths involved the food they were served.

> The king appointed for them a daily ration from the king's choice food and from the wine which he drank ....
> Daniel 1:5

---

ent. Sarna, Nahum M., *Exploring Exodus: The Origins Of Biblical Israel* (Schocken Books 1986, 1996) p. 52

30 Lucas, Ernest C., "Daniel," in *Zondervan Illustrated Bible Backgrounds Commentary*, Vol. 4, edited by John H. Walton (Zondervan 2009) Daniel 1:7 under *New names*, p. 529; MacArthur, John, *The MacArthur Study Bible* (Thomas Nelson 2006) study note Daniel 1:7 under *new names*, p. 1201

This was another common practice in the ancient Near East. Those given daily rations by the king were *expected* to show reciprocal loyalty to the king.[31] However, as we will see, Daniel and the other youths drew a line in the sand at this point!

> But **Daniel made up his mind** that he would not **defile** himself with the king's choice food or with the wine which he drank; so he sought *permission* from the commander of the officials that he might not **defile** himself. Daniel 1:8, italics in original, bold added

> But Daniel said to the overseer whom the commander of the officials had appointed over Daniel, Hananiah, Mishael and Azariah, "Please test your servants for ten days, and let us be given some vegetables to eat and water to drink. Then let our appearance be observed in your presence and the appearance of the youths who are eating the king's choice food; and deal with your servants according to what you see." Daniel 1:11-13

In Daniel 1:8, the phrase "Daniel made up his mind" has been highlighted in bold. In other translations that same text is rendered "Daniel resolved."[32] In other words, Daniel had a strong inner determination. He "set it upon his heart"[33] not to do this particular thing which the king had ordered.

By using the word "defile" (emphasized by bold text in the Daniel 1:8-13 quote) the author gives us an important clue to explain *why* Daniel and his friends asked to be treated differently. The reader is put on notice that Daniel's objection was a matter of

---

31 Lucas, Ernest C., "Daniel," in *Zondervan Illustrated Bible Backgrounds Commentary*, Vol. 4, edited by John H. Walton (Zondervan 2009) Daniel 1:5 under *A daily amount of food and wine from the king's table*, p. 529

32 Daniel 1:8 NIV, ESV, CJB

33 The word "determined" literally means "set upon his heart." *Holman Christian Standard Bible*, Study Bible edition (Holman Bible Publishers 2010) study note Daniel 1:8, p. 1433

The Power of Hope 189

personal integrity related to his unwavering loyalty to Yahweh.³⁴ The Hebrew word is *ga'al* {gaw-al'}. Its use in the Old Testament refers to uncleanness, being polluted, defiled, or disqualified in some manner for service to Yahweh.³⁵ In this context *ga'al* could be properly understood as Daniel refused to "make himself ceremonially [or ritually] unclean."³⁶ The author doesn't find it necessary to tell us specifically what it was about the King's food and wine that was objectionable. The important detail is that in Daniel's mind there was something about the offered food and wine that would make him unacceptable in his service to Yahweh and for *that reason*, he chose vegetables and water instead.

In case you missed it, I want to call your attention to an interesting and informative fact in the Daniel 1:11-13 Scripture which I have quoted. At this point, although we are about midway through this narrative, the author used the *Jewish birth names* for Daniel, Hananiah, Mishael and Azariah rather than their newly assigned Babylonian names. Old Testament scholar Walter Brueggemann suggests this is quite intentional and should alert us to the fact that these young men are *still Jews*. Their true identity has *not* been completely assimilated into the Babylonian way of life!³⁷

As we will see, these young men were tested for *ten* days using the alternative diet. Ten could refer to a literal number of days or

---

34 Lucas, Ernest C., "Daniel," in *Zondervan Illustrated Bible Backgrounds Commentary*, Vol. 4, edited by John H. Walton (Zondervan 2009) Daniel 1:8 under *Daniel resolved not to defile himself with the royal food and wine*, pp. 529-530

35 Ezra 2:62; Nehemiah 7:64; Isaiah 59:3, 63:3; Lamentations 4:14; Zephaniah 3:1

36 *NET Bible Notes*, translator's note 36, Daniel 1:8. Simply stated, the Old Testament contrasted that which was holy from that which was common. The holy, uncommon things were then further subdivided into that which was clean and that which was unclean. God Himself is holy. Only that which was clean could come in contact with that which was holy. When something clean was defiled, it required cleansing in the ways prescribed by the law of Moses so that it could become clean again.

37 Brueggemann, Walter, *Truth & Hope: Essays For a Perilous Age* (Westminster John Knox Press 2020) p. 12

it could be a symbolic reference point. In biblical terms, *ten* is a perfect number and it signifies the perfection of Divine order.

> So [the overseer whom the commander of the officials had appointed] listened to them in this matter and tested them for ten days. At the end of ten days their appearance seemed better and they were fatter than all the youths who had been eating the king's choice food. So the overseer continued to withhold their choice food and the wine they were to drink, and kept giving them vegetables. Daniel 1:14-16

The fact of *ten* days "implies that nothing is wanting … that the whole cycle is complete."[38] Mission accomplished! Daniel and his friends remain fit for Yahweh's service and at the same time still qualify to serve the King of Babylon.

As we continue to review the book of Daniel for examples of how one esteems God while living in exile we find two more well-known incidents where these Hebrew men drew a line in the sand. In both cases, they stood their ground against civic duties ordered by the King because what was required was inseparably intertwined with pagan worship. In order to maintain their loyalty to Yahweh these men respectfully refused to comply and suffered the natural consequences.

The first incident is found in Daniel Chapter 3. King Nebuchadnezzar made a huge image of gold and then decreed that every person in his empire bow down in worship to that statute. When Hananiah, Mishael and Azariah (the Jewish birth names for Shadrach, Meshach and Abed-nego) refused, they were reported to the King. The infuriated King confronted their disobedience and gave them another opportunity to bow before the statute. Standing before the King they respectfully refused to worship that idol even if it meant they would be thrown into a burning furnace. Their

---

38 Bullinger, E. W., *Number in Scripture: Its Supernatural Design and Spiritual Significance*, Part II Its Spiritual Significance, entry for *Ten*. Retrieved from http://www.biblebelievers.org.au/number14.htm (last accessed August 8, 2021)

worship belonged exclusively to Yahweh and their confidence was in Him alone.

> [They] replied to the king, "O Nebuchadnezzar, we do not need to give you an answer concerning this matter. If it be *so*, our God whom we serve is able to deliver us from the furnace of blazing fire; and He will deliver us out of your hand, O king. But *even* if *He does* not, let it be known to you, O king, that we are not going to serve your gods or worship the golden image that you have set up." Daniel 3:16-18, italics in original

The enraged King ordered them to be bound and thrown into the furnace. When God demonstrated His divine protection of these men, the King commanded them to come out of the furnace acknowledging that he had never seen such a miraculous rescue by any god. Daniel 3:30 reports, "Then the king caused Shadrach, Meshach and Abed-nego to prosper in the province of Babylon."

The second example of nonviolent noncompliance involves Daniel individually. After the Medo-Persian Empire conquered Babylon, Daniel remained in service to the King. As he continued to distinguish himself by his loyal service, envious men set a trap for him. They convinced the King to issue a decree that any person in the Empire who petitioned any god other than the King himself would be thrown into the lion's den. Even though Daniel knew of the decree, he did not change his habit of praying to Yahweh three times a day. His refusal to comply with the King's order was anticipated and eagerly reported by his adversaries. Even though the King had great respect for Daniel he could not go back on his word and ordered Daniel to be thrown into the lion's den. When the King rushed to check on Daniel early the next morning he was relieved to learn that Daniel was safe. Because Daniel had honored Yahweh, protective angels had stood guard to keep the mouth of every lion closed! Daniel was removed unharmed from the den and Daniel 6:28 concludes, "So this Daniel enjoyed success in the reign of Darius and in the reign of Cyrus the Persian."[39]

The prophet Jeremiah provided the counsel, the book of Daniel records the lives of four Hebrew men who walked it out, demonstrating for us how to live lives that honor God while in exile. Their stories offer wisdom for navigating the tension that naturally occurs when in exile. But we also learn from Daniel's example the importance of maintaining a strong sense of God-ordained identity. Those in the community who maintain that identity can be confident in the things that God has promised to that community – the things for which they hope. In other words, there is a vital connection between holiness (remaining set apart from the world's ways) and hope. So, it is not at all surprising that Daniel steps forward onto the pages of Israel's history as the now much older prophet standing in the gap for Israel. He prays with confident expectation for the end of the 70-year Babylonian captivity! When he did, he was praying according to the promise Yahweh had made even before the captivity began (Jeremiah 29:10-14). We find the story in Daniel 9.

> In the first year of Darius ... who was made king over the kingdom of the Chaldeans [Babylonians] ... I, Daniel, observed in the books the number of the years which was *revealed as* the word of the LORD to Jeremiah the prophet for the completion of the desolations of Jerusalem, *namely*, seventy years. So I gave my attention to the Lord God, to seek *Him by* prayer and pleading, with fasting, sackcloth, and ashes. Daniel 9:1-3, italics in original

---

[39] It was common in the ancient Near East for a king to have more than one throne name. The original language of Daniel 6:28 can be translated to read "the reign of Darius, that is, the reign of Cyrus." In other words, it is thought that the two names reference the same King. Lucas, Ernest C., "Daniel," in *Zondervan Illustrated Bible Backgrounds Commentary*, Vol. 4, edited by John H. Walton (Zondervan 2009) Daniel 6:28 under *The reign of Darius and the reign of Cyrus*, p. 547

The Power of Hope

By this time Daniel, still captive, had been faithfully serving wicked kings for 67 years. For almost seven decades he patiently remained in God's *Hope Waiting Room* maintaining the strong *set apart* identity of his Jewish heritage. As a result, he could take personally the message of hope found in the age-old prophecies of Jeremiah and that hope fueled his actions.

Jeremiah set a pattern for how those in covenant relationship with God are to live in exile. In the Old Testament exile was literal. God expelled Israel from the land and dispersed the vast majority of the people to live in Babylonian captivity for 70 years. In the New Testament, exile is metaphorical and figurative. The Jewish people were back in their own land, but they were no longer an independently sovereign nation. They were ruled by the Romans. Although not all scholars agree, N. T. Wright asserts that most Jewish people in the first century considered themselves to be living in an extended state of punitive exile.[40]

Through the centuries God never changed the life-style pattern He had established for His covenant people. Accordingly, the life and ministry of Jesus continued to be aligned with the instruction of Jeremiah. Jesus never advocated the overthrow of the pagan Roman government while at the same time making clear there is a distinct difference between what is owed to Caesar (another title for the Roman Emperor) and what is owed to God. His first-century disciples understood the pattern and followed His example – the way of Jeremiah. They taught their disciples to:

> Keep your behavior excellent among the Gentiles …. Submit yourselves for the Lord's sake to every human institution, whether to a king as the one in authority, or to governors …. For such is the will of God that by doing right you may silence the ignorance of foolish men. *Act* as free men, and do not use your freedom as a

---

40 Wright, N. T., *Exile: A Conversation with N. T. Wright* (IVP Academic 2017) edited by James M. Scott. The Publisher's book description itself notes that "critical responses [to Wright's characterization of exile] also abound."

covering for evil, but *use it* as bondslaves of God. Honor all people, love the brotherhood, fear God, honor the king. 1 Peter 2:12-17, italics in original

To gain some perspective of the difficulty Christ-followers might encounter obeying Peter's instruction, it will help to understand the Roman Empire in the first century. Beginning with Caesar Augustus (the ruling Emperor when Jesus was born) the Roman emperors were thought to be the "son of god." This belief in the divinity of the Emperor was promoted in various ways throughout the Roman Empire. It was common practice to use coins, statues, sculptures and festivals to indoctrinate the citizens of the empire with this ideology. Matthew, Mark and Luke all tell us that Jesus was asked the question about the lawfulness of paying tribute to Caesar, referring to a tax paid to Rome.[41] Jesus responded by asking for a denarius which was the silver coin used for payment of this tax. The coin handed to Jesus could have been issued by Tiberius, Roman Emperor during Jesus' ministry, or of his predecessor, Emperor Augustus.[42] Both emperors had issued denarii with their face on one side along with an inscription that would have in some way indicated their divinity. The image on

---

41 Matthew 22:15-22; Mark 12:13-17; Luke 20:20-26. The Roman Emperor imposed this annual tax on the Jewish people around 6 A.D. Patriotic Jews highly resented it. France, R. T., *The Gospel of Matthew*, New International Commentary on the New Testament (Eerdmans 2007) 1. The Question about the Poll Tax ([Matthew] 22:15-22) p. 829

42 Some scholars suggest it was likely the coin issued by Tiberius because he was the Emperor at the time of Jesus. See for example: Strauss, Mark, "Luke," in *Zondervan Illustrated Bible Backgrounds Commentary*, Vol. 1, edited by Clinton E. Arnold (Zondervan 2002) Luke 20:24 under *Show me a denarius. Whose portrait and inscription were on it?* p. 473; See also: Lewis, Peter, *The Denarius in Mark 12:15*, The Australian Numismatic Society Library. Retrieved from http://www.the-ans.com/library/2012PeterLewis.html (last accessed August 8, 2021). On the other hand, Dr. Grant Osborne believes the coin was the one issued by Augustus. Osborne, Grant, *Notes on the Gospel of Luke by Dr. Grant Osborne* (unpublished). Received via E-mail from Gary Hill, *The Discovery Bible*

the other side of these coins was thought to be that of a woman representing a female goddess with the inscription "High Priest."

There were few aspects of society from which first-century disciples could escape pressures of idolatry. Approval from these gods was not dependent on behavior, approval depended on accurately observing religious rituals. The ideology of the Roman Empire was inseparably linked to the religious, economic and social facets of culture.[43] Religion and worship of the various gods were evidence of loyalty and considered to be a *civic duty* of every citizen in the Roman Empire.[44] The actual forms of worship varied from place to place, but it was often incorporated into regular community life through public celebrations that involved the whole community in one way or another. Sacrifices to the gods and to the Emperor was commonplace during these celebrations.

Another unavoidable conflict occurred at the entrance of the *agora*, the chief marketplace in the city. Placing incense in the incense burner found there would have been mandatory before entering the marketplace. This act was a public demonstration that you recognized the Emperor as a "god."

Even practicing your trade posed serious problems for Christ-followers. To be commercially viable necessitated membership in the guild associated with their trade. Those guilds provided a setting for important social and business interactions.[45] However,

---

43 Beale, G. K., *The Book of Revelation*, The New International Greek Testament Commentary (Eerdmans 1999) p. 717

44 Burton, Henry Fairfield, *The Worship of the Roman Emperors*, The Biblical World 40, no. 2 (1912) pp. 80-91. Retrieved from http://www.jstor.org/stable/3141986 (last accessed August 9, 2021). In 197 A.D. Tertullian wrote an apology for Christ-followers which identified the two main charges brought against the Christians as being: sacrilege and disloyalty to the Emperor. Tertullian, *The Apology Of Tertullian For The Christians*, translated by T. Herbert Bindley (Parker and Co. 1890). Retrieved from https://www.tertullian.org/articles/bindley_apol/bindley_apol.htm#:~:text=The%20APOLOGY%20was%20written%20in%20the%20year%20197%2C,the%20subsequent%20lapse%20of%20its%20author%20into%20heresy (last accessed February 20, 2022)

45 Nelson, Kraybill J., *Imperial Cult and Commerce in John's Apocalypse* (Sheffield Academic Press 1996) pp. 111-113

every guild had its own form of *god* which would have been honored through regular feasts to gain the god's favor.⁴⁶

Anyone who would not pay respectful (or worshipful) tribute to the Roman gods or the altars set up to worship the Emperor was considered an "atheist."⁴⁷ The common thought was that failure to properly worship the gods could put the Empire at risk of that god's disfavor resulting in some type of disaster. What began as social harassment increased to physical persecution and over time the exclusivity of worshipping the one true God marked Christ-followers as those who deserved to be put to death.

Now that we understand something about the dominant culture of the Roman Empire, we can see that obeying Peter's instruction to Christ-followers in 1 Peter 2:12-17 would present challenges similar to those the Jewish people faced when living in exile in Babylon. Like Daniel and his Hebrew friends, identity maintenance would require first-century *talmidim* to draw a line in the sand whenever civic duty demanded worship of false gods.

Paul, living in the midst of the evil Roman world, reverenced the Lordship of Jesus and understood the potential of continuous lived-out-faith which leads to a distinct identity. Paul turned his knowledge into a powerful prayer of hope. That prayer is our Key Scripture for this lesson.

> May God, the source of hope, fill you completely with joy and *shalom* as you continue **trusting**, so that by the power of the *Ruach HaKodesh* [Holy Spirit] you may overflow with hope. Romans 15:13 CJB, italics in original, bold added

---

46 Paul addresses the issue of eating meat sacrificed to idols in Romans 14 and 1 Corinthians 8 and 10

47 Welma, Jeffrey A. D., "2 Thessalonians," in *Zondervan Illustrated Bible Backgrounds Commentary*, Vol. 3, edited by Clinton E. Arnold (Zondervan 2002) *Social Harassment of Christians in the Greco-Roman World*, p. 434; *ESV Study Bible* (Crossway Books 2008) *The Roman Empire And The Greco-Roman World At The Time of the New Testament, Religion and Magic*, p. 1796

In the original Greek version of Romans 15:13, the word translated as "trusting" (highlighted in bold) is in the present tense meaning it pictures ongoing, continual and habitual faith/trust/belief. Paul understood hope as inspired, generated and imparted by God to those who habitually believe.[48] Paul prays that as a result of continual, non-stop faith (living life day in and day out led by the Spirit) the Christ-followers in Rome will not merely have *some* hope they will *overflow* with the kind of hope which is generated by God and empowered by His Spirit. He knows, no doubt based on his own experience, that the only way to abound in hope is to habitually trust God.

> … believing [or trusting and acting on that trust/belief] is the real answer. It isn't Bible reading, or prayer or Christian fellowship that unlocks the power of the Holy Spirit. It is believing …. which means to act on what we know…. [I]t is when we believe and act that the power of the Holy Spirit begins to work through us and causes us to abound in hope …."[49]

Paul wants his readers to picture a superabundance of hope that God releases to them as they are faithful to keep His commands. That type of faithful living establishes a solid core identity which keeps hope alive and ready to be activated as the need arises.

Hear What The Spirit is Saying to the Church: *My Bride needs to lose her identity with the ways of the world and find her identity in Me alone. It is in her true identity as My*

---

48 Harrison and Hagner, "Romans," in *The Expositor's Bible Commentary: Romans ~ Galatians*, Vol. 11, Revised Edition, edited by Longman III and Garland (Zondervan Academic 2008) Romans 15:13, p. 216; *Romans 15:11-14 Commentary*, Precept Austin, quoting Kenneth Wuest. Retrieved from https://www.preceptaustin.org/romans_15_notes_pt2 (last accessed May 31, 2022)

49 Stedman, Ray C., *Power To Please*, RayStedman.org. Retrieved from https://www.raystedman.org/romans1/0029.html (last accessed May 31, 2022)

Bride she will be equipped with hope. The clearer her true identity the more power and hope she will walk in. Such is my way.[50]

LESSON 11:

LOSE YOUR IDENTITY ~ LOSE YOUR HOPE!

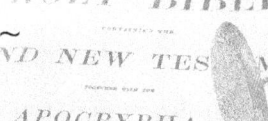

"And everyone who has this hope in Him purifies himself just as He is pure." 1 John 3:3 HCSB

WE HAVE BEEN LEARNING that those in covenant relationship with God are called to display a distinct identity in the world in which they live. In the last lesson we noted that identity maintenance is vitally connected to hope maintenance. In our Key Scripture for this lesson John makes clear that hope motivates holy living as an ongoing lifestyle.

In 1 John 3:3 the Apostle John uses the Greek noun *elpis* (translated "hope") in reference to the second coming of Christ.[1] Previously in the study we said *elpis* means confident expectation based on solid certainty. It is an absolute assurance of future good based on the character and nature of God. To place our Key Scripture in context let's zoom out a bit and begin reading at 1 John 2:28:

> And now, dear children, remain in fellowship with Christ so that when he returns, you will be full of courage

---

[1] The second coming of Christ is often referred to as the *Parousia*. "In the ancient world *parousia* has a pertinent twofold sense: (1) the coming of a hidden divinity who makes his presence felt by his power or miracles; (2) the visit of a king or emperor to a province." Brown, Raymond E., *The Epistles of John: A New Translation With Introduction and Commentary by Raymond E. Brown*, The Anchor Yale Bible (University Press 1982) 1 John 2:28c under *Notes*, pp. 381-382

and not shrink back from him in shame. Since we know that Christ is righteous, we also know that all who do what is right are God's children. See how very much our Father loves us, for he calls us his children, and that is what we are! But the people who belong to this world don't recognize that we are God's children because they don't know him. Dear friends, we are already God's children, but he has not yet shown us what we will be like when Christ appears. But we do know that we will be like him, for we will see him as he really is. And all who have this eager expectation [*elpis*] will keep themselves pure, just as he is pure. 1 John 2:28-3:3 NLT

John tells his readers that they already are God's children, His sons and daughters. He then tells them what they will be when Christ returns – they will be like Christ. Next, he informs them how they should live between now and then. John testifies that to live in the hopeful reality of Christ's return naturally impacts behavior. John, like the other New Testament authors, understands that believing the gospel necessitates allowing yourself to be shaped by its truth.[2] Therefore he urges Christ-followers toward ethical integrity that is wholly consistent with their spiritual identity.[3]

> And everyone who has this hope [*elpis*] in Him **purifies** himself just as He is pure. 1 John 3:3 HCSB, bold added

The verb "purifies" (highlighted in bold) is a translation of the Greek verb *hagnizo* {hag-nid'-zo}. Most often in the New Testament it refers to cleansing from ritual defilement as defined

---

[2] Keck, Leander E., *Romans*, Abingdon New Testament Commentaries (Abingdon Press 2005) Error as Disobedience ([Romans] 10:14-21), p. 259

[3] *ESV Study Bible* (Crossway Books 2008) study note 1 John 2:28-3:3, p. 2433

by the Mosaic law.[4] *Hagnizo* would be the proper Greek word to describe Daniel's need to purify himself if he had eaten the King's food (see Lesson 10 and footnote there).

In the Old Testament *hagnizo* referred to the Israelites' purification preparation when they were getting ready to be in the physical presence of Yahweh at Mt. Sinai.[5] While John is not referring to physical purification in our Key Scripture he likely wanted *that* picture to be in the minds of his listeners as he instructed them to be ready for the second coming of Christ.[6]

When John described Jesus as "pure" he used the Greek word *hagnos* {hag-nos'} which is the root word of *hagnizo*. *Hagnos* refers to being free from *all* moral or spiritual defilement.[7] Christ has set the pattern for every *talmid* to follow. He was "a perfect realization of human conformity to God."[8] When Jesus said He is the Truth (John 14:6), the Greek word *aletheia* {al-ay'-thi-a}

---

4   John 11:55, Acts 21:24,26; 24:18. Under the law of Moses there was a requirement of ritual purity. In the world of the Old Testament it was possible for a person or thing to become ritually unclean (or impure) "by skin diseases, discharges of bodily fluids, touching something dead (Numbers 5:2), or eating unclean foods (Leviticus 11; Deuteronomy 14)." As was noted in Lesson 10, an unclean person was obligated to take the necessary steps to become clean again. Elwell, Walter A., editor, *Baker's Evangelical Dictionary of Biblical Theology* (Baker Books 1996) entry for *Clean, Unclean*. Retrieved from https://www.studylight.org/dictionaries/eng/bed/c/clean-unclean.html (last accessed August 28, 2021)
5   Exodus 19:10-11; Brown, Raymond E., *The Epistles of John: A New Translation With Introduction and Commentary by Raymond E. Brown*, The Anchor Yale Bible (University Press 1982) 1 John 3:3b under *3b. makes himself pure even as Christ is pure*, p. 397; Olsson, Birger, *A Commentary on The Letters of John: An Intra-Jewish Approach* (Pickwick Publications 2013) 1 John 3:3 under *purifies himself ... pure*, p. 163
6   Brown, Raymond E., *The Epistles of John: A New Translation With Introduction and Commentary by Raymond E. Brown*, The Anchor Yale Bible (University Press 1982) 1 John 3:3b under *3b. makes himself pure even as Christ is pure*, pp. 397-398
7   Hill, Gary, *The Discovery Bible*, HELPS Ministries, Inc., [G]53 *hagnós*
8   Spence and Exell, general editors, *The Pulpit Commentary*, 1 John 3:3. Retrieved from Hill, Gary, *The Discovery Bible*, HELPS Ministries, Inc.

indicates that He walked in moral integrity, He was the accurate and trustworthy disclosure of His Father's nature and that He was entirely consistent with what He professed to be.[9]

Every Christ-follower is to *hagnizo* (purify) himself just as Christ is *hagnos* (pure).[10] The gospel has "no room for [someone] claiming to be redeemed while providing no evidence of practical transformation."[11] For Christ-followers to walk in truth means that we too must be an accurate and trustworthy disclosure of our Father's nature and live entirely consistent with what we profess to be!

John is counseling every Christ-follower that the hope they have in Christ should provide strong motivation. True disciples reject blind conformity to the norms of the world's way. Instead, they imitate the character of Christ. An alternative counter-cultural community obedient to Christ amid an empire that did not fear God is what enabled those early disciples to remain set apart as holy.[12] Jesus called that community His *ekklesia*. In this lesson we want to explore the vital role that fellowship with other Christ-followers plays in identity maintenance and how the *ekklesia* is designed to fulfill that role.

Let's look at the first announcement of the *ekklesia* made by Jesus in Matthew 16. We'll begin by setting the context. Jesus and His disciples were standing on rocky ground at the foot of Mt. Hermon in the district of Caesarea Philippi. This area was

---

9   *2 Peter 2:2-3 Commentary*, Precept Austin, quoting Gilbrant, *Complete Biblical Library Greek-English Dictionary*. Retrieved from https://www.preceptaustin.org/2_peter_22-3 (last accessed May 24, 2022); *Colossians 1:6-8 Commentary*, Precept Austin. Retrieved from https://www.preceptaustin.org/colossians_16-10 (last accessed May 24, 2022)
10 As scholar Robert Gundry points out, John's use of the word "everyone" makes clear there are no exceptions to this rule! Gundry, Robert H., *Commentary on the New Testament* (Hendrickson Publishers 2010) 1 John 1:2-3, p. 975
11 *ESV Study Bible* (Crossway Books 2008) study note Titus 2:14, p. 2350
12 Brueggemann, Walter, *Truth & Hope: Essays For a Perilous Age* (Westminster John Knox Press 2020) p. 202

apparently dedicated to "the celestial gods" and hosted more than twenty pagan temples including a temple to Zeus.[13]

Jesus had just asked His disciples the question: "Who do you say that I am?" Peter answered, "You are the Christ, the Son of the living God."[14] In response, Jesus declared:

> I also say to you, that you are *Petros* [a stone], and upon this *petra* [a massive rock formation; bedrock] I will build **My** *ekklesia* [assembly, congregation, community], and the gates of Hades will not overpower it. Matthew 16:18 NASB 1995, my paraphrase with key Greek words and bold added

Let's first address the meaning of the Greek word *ekklesia* {ek-klay-see'-ah}, then we will consider what Jesus meant by His reference to building His *ekklesia* "on this rock." Most English translations render the word *ekklesia* as "church." Because our modern use of that word is much broader and includes meanings that were never a part of the first century understanding of *ekklesia* we need to go back in history and take a fresh look at this word. As a starting point, let's be clear that there is *no* instance in the New Testament where this word refers to a physical building or a religious organization. It more literally means "called out ones" and it is always a reference to a community or assembly of people.[15]

In the first century there were two commonly understood meanings of the Greek word *ekklesia*. Both are likely relevant for Jesus' choice of that particular word in His response to Peter. In its ordinary Greek use, *ekklesia* was the word for an assembly of free citizens (aliens and slaves were excluded) in a city who gathered "to carry out specific governmental functions as directed by the *boulē*

---

13 Heiser, Michael S., *The Unseen Realm: Recovering the Supernatural Worldview of the Bible* (Lexham Press 2015) p. 284
14 Scripture quotes are from Matthew 16:13,16
15 Korner, Ralph J., *Reading Revelation After Supersessionism: An Apocalyptic Journey of Socially Identifying John's Multi-Ethnic Ekklesiai with the Ekklesia of Israel* (Cascade Books 2020) p. 23

(civic councilors)."[16] The Jewish community of Christ-followers was also familiar with the use of the word *ekklesia* because it was used to designate a synagogue.[17] The Greek translation of the Hebrew Scripture uses the phrase "the *ekklēsia* of the LORD" when referring to the national identity of God's covenant people as they wandered through the desert.[18] It is plain to see that Jesus did not choose a new term when He called those who would follow Him *His ekklesia*. Rather He used a word that was already in use with common understanding by other Jews as well as by Greeks and Romans.

Bible teacher Ray Vander Laan who is most noted for his film series, *That The World May Know*, refers to the *ekklesia* challenge Jesus presents to His disciples as a "sort of 'graduation speech.'"[19] Jesus was preparing to leave them. His disciples would remain on earth and be commissioned as His Spirit-filled representatives. He encouraged them to go "build" an *ekklesia* that would advance His Kingdom on earth as it is in heaven. As we will see, contained within that instruction was a wealth of information about what the Kingdom of God was not! The word *ekklesia* revealed to the disciples that the promised Kingdom would be fulfilled in a society, an assembly of Christ-followers.[20]

While that is clear, there is intense scholarly debate over exactly what Jesus meant when He said, "you are Peter and on this rock I

---

16 Korner, Ralph J., *Reading Revelation After Supersessionism: An Apocalyptic Journey of Socially Identifying John's Multi-Ethnic Ekklesiai with the Ekklesia of Israel* (Cascade Books 2020) p. 23
17 Korner, Dr. Ralph J., *The Book of Revelation: An Apocalyptic Journey into an Eternal Jewish Identity*, MSI 2021 Visiting Scholar Symposium, Session #3, June 12, 2021
18 Korner, Dr. Ralph J., *The Book of Revelation: An Apocalyptic Journey into an Eternal Jewish Identity*, MSI 2021 Visiting Scholar Symposium, Session #1, June 11, 2021
19 Vander Laan, Ray, *That The World May Know with Ray Vander Laan*, Gates of Hell. Retrieved from https://www.thattheworldmayknow.com/gates-of-hell-article (last accessed August 18, 2021)
20 Ellicott, Charles John, *Ellicott's Commentary for English Readers*, Matthew 16:18. Retrieved from Hill, Gary, *The Discovery Bible*, HELPS Ministries, Inc.

will build my *ekklesia*." My research mentor, Henri Louis Goulet, asserts that the most plausible full meaning is that this passage involves a *double entendre*, meaning it has a double meaning.[21] Initially, it is thought that the location in which this discussion took place has a bearing on what Jesus meant. As we have already noted, Jesus and the disciples were at that time in "the district of Caesarea Philippi."[22] Because it was a pagan worship center, author Michael Heiser refers to it as "Ground Zero: The Gates of Hell."[23] To quote Heiser:[24]

> Peter confesses Jesus as the Christ, the Son of the living God, at "this rock" (this *mountain*—Mount Herman). Why? This place was considered the "gates of hell," the gateway to the realm of the dead, in the Old Testament times.

Certainly, Heiser's explanation adds new meaning to the promise that "the gates of Hades will not overpower [this *ekklesia*]."[25] The second meaning of Jesus' statement views Peter himself as the *petra*/rock upon which the Messiah "will build" His new covenant *ekklēsia*.[26] The background for this understanding is found in Isaiah 51.

---

21 Goulet, Henri Louis, Email to Deborah Roeger, August 18, 2021
22 Matthew 16:13
23 Heiser, Michael S., *The Unseen Realm: Recovering the Supernatural Worldview of the Bible* (Lexham Press 2015) p. 281
24 Heiser, Michael S., *The Unseen Realm: Recovering the Supernatural Worldview of the Bible* (Lexham Press 2015) p. 284, italics in original
25 Matthew 16:18b
26 Goulet, Henri Louis, *Was There a First Century Church? Ekklesia Restored*, MSI mini course February/March 2021. The fact that, on the one hand, the *disciples* are commissioned to build the *ekklesia* and, on the other hand, Jesus says *He* will build His *ekklesia* reflects biblical truth. There is a part of the building process that only God can do and there is an important part of the building process that He has assigned to every Christ-follower.

> "Listen to Me, you who pursue righteousness, Who seek the LORD: Look to the rock from which you were hewn And to the quarry from which you were dug. Look to Abraham your father And to Sarah who gave birth to you in pain; When *he was but* one I called him, Then I blessed him and multiplied him." Isaiah 51:1-2, italics in original

A thoroughly Hebraic way of looking at Isaiah 51:1-2 is found in ancient Jewish writing from the Middle Ages.[27]

> When the Holy One wanted to create the world he passed over the generation of Enoch and the Flood; but when he saw Abraham who was to arise, he said 'Behold, I have found a rock (*petra*) on which I can build and establish the world.' Therefore he called Abraham a rock, as it is said in (Isaiah 51:1), 'Look to the rock from which you were hewn.'

Through the prophet Isaiah God reminded Israel that Abraham was their founding father. Metaphorically Abraham was the *rock* from which Israel, as God's people, was carved. He had been without natural hope of becoming the father of a multitude of nations as God had promised.[28] Yet Abraham symbolized "the transforming power of God in the blessing and divine energizing whereby *one* without hope of increase became *many*."[29] Isaiah attributes this divine increase to something only God can do![30] With

---

27   Stern, David, H., *Jewish New Testament Commentary* (Jewish New Testament Publications 1992) Matthew 16:18 under *You are Kefa*, p. 54, noting that "*petra*" appears as a loanword here. Stern cites Yalkut 766, *Yalkut Shimoni*, written in the Middle Ages on Numbers 23:9. He points out that Yalkut 766 was quoting an even earlier source, *Tanchuma B, Yelamdenu*.
28   Genesis 17:4
29   Motyer, J. Alec, *The Prophecy of Isaiah: An Introduction & Commentary* (InterVarsity Press 1993) Isaiah 51:1-3, p. 404, italics in original
30   Motyer, J. Alec, *Isaiah*, Tyndale Old Testament Commentaries (IVP Academic 1999) Isaiah 51:1-3, p. 362

this background, it appears that Jesus was saying to Peter, "like Abraham was to my people Israel, you will be as a *founding father* of the new covenant community. As Abraham was the measure of what I can do – making one many, so too will you, Peter, be a measure of what I can do – once again making one many!"[31] In fact, the book of Acts records the truth that what Jesus had promised Peter was factually fulfilled.[32]

That fulfillment happened when Peter stood up on the day of Pentecost to preach the first sermon and 3,000 new disciples were added to the *ekklesia* (Acts 2:41). Acts 21:20 references many thousands (*muriades* meaning ten thousand; an innumerable multitude, an unlimited number) of Torah-observant Jewish Christ-followers in Jerusalem just six decades after Christ was crucified.[33] As one author notes, while we don't know actual numbers of new Christ-followers in the early church, the numbers which are reported in the Bible are "only 'meant to render impressive the marvel that here the Lord himself is at work.'"[34]

---

31 For a reference to Peter being a "founding father" to "the new covenant community, just as Abraham was for Israel," see: Beale and Carson, editors, *Commentary on the New Testament Use of the Old Testament* (Baker Academic 2007) Matthew 15:21-18:14, p. 55

32 When determining actual numbers of disciples added to the growing *ekklesia* it is important to keep in mind that in antiquity numbers were stated as a part of "rhetorical exercises." They "were not meant to be taken literally." Stark, Rodney, *The Rise of Christianity: How the Obscure, Marginal Jesus Movement Became the Dominant Religious Force in the Western World in a Few Centuries* (HarperSanFrancisco 1996) p. 5, citing Robert M. Grant

33 Stark, Rodney, *The Rise of Christianity: How the Obscure, Marginal Jesus Movement Became the Dominant Religious Force in the Western World in a Few Centuries* (HarperSanFrancisco 1996) p. 5

34 Stark, Rodney, *The Rise of Christianity: How the Obscure, Marginal Jesus Movement Became the Dominant Religious Force in the Western World in a Few Centuries* (HarperSanFrancisco 1996) p. 5, quoting Hans Conzelmann

What has been entrusted to those who are part of this continually growing *ekklesia* is the responsibility to boldly RE•present[35] Christ to the dominant culture that surrounds them. As we will see, the design and function of the *ekklesia* is perfectly suited to the task. To begin with it will be helpful to review our biblical instruction for living in exile. We learned in our last lesson that God set forth His directives through the prophet Jeremiah. I'll repeat that instruction here.

> "Thus says the LORD of hosts, the God of Israel, to all the exiles whom I have sent into exile from Jerusalem to Babylon, 'Build houses and live *in them*; and plant gardens and eat their produce.... multiply there and do not decrease. Seek the welfare of the city where I have sent you into exile, and pray to the LORD on its behalf; for in its welfare you will have welfare.' ..." Jeremiah 29:4-7, italics in original

We've also learned that Jesus followed Jeremiah's instruction.[36] It is well attested that most Jewish people expected the Messiah to lead a physical revolt against the Roman Empire to reestablish Israel as sovereign under the leadership of Yahweh. However, what we see from Scripture is that Jesus initiated a revolution of a different sort. He called for a revolution of lifestyle which "must begin at the level of personal transformation rather than with the change

---

35 I am intentionally repurposing the word "represent" at times in this study by making a clear separation between the prefix "re" and the remainder of the word "present." The prefix "re" indicates repetition and has an ordinary meaning of "again" or "back." My goal in showing the word in this unique form is to highlight the truth that one who is God's representative does not act on his own accord, that representative is actually commissioned by God to repeat what God has done, to show again who God is. I have placed the prefix "re" in all caps to indicate the emphasis on that syllable when pronouncing the word.

36 As we noted in Lesson 10, Jeremiah's instructions were restated to the first-century *talmidim* through the pen of the Apostle Peter. See 1 Peter 2:12-17

of social or political systems."[37] The message of repentance which began with John the Baptist[38] and continued into the mission and ministry of Jesus[39] is a message of transformation, reorientation and new beginning.[40] It is an invitation to spiritually transfer from the kingdom of darkness to the Kingdom of Light and begin to live life here and now under the authority of King Jesus.

Jesus did come as a rival King and He did come to overthrow a rival kingdom. However, His target was the spiritual kingdom of darkness which had been holding people captive to sin. As we read about His disciples advancing His Kingdom in the first century we witness the story of anointed influencers who take up the sword of the Spirit – the word of God.[41] The author of Hebrews notes that the penetrating power of God's word is able to "divide the indivisible."[42] It is able to go deep and judge even thoughts and intentions in the human heart.

Those *talmidim* permitted the gospel to reorient their life. Then they went forth and boldly discipled nations through teaching and instructing which was confirmed by demonstrations of God's power. By doing so they proclaimed the rule of King Jesus on earth and defeated the power of darkness. It is in this way that the New Testament tells the story of the Kingdom of God becoming progressively more visible on earth as it is in heaven. As individuals accept the invitation of the gospel, the cumulative result is:

---

37 France, R. T., *Divine Government: God's Kingship In The Gospel of Mark* (Regent College Publishing 1990) p. 61
38 See for example: Matthew 3:1-2
39 See for example: Matthew 4:17
40 Repent is a translation of the Greek word *metanoeo* {met-an-o-eh'-o}. "Repentance is an expression of faith in God that leads to living faithfully, expressed initially in baptism." Lowery, David K., "Matthew," in *The Bible Knowledge Word Study, The Gospels,* edited by Eugene H. Merrill (Victor 2006) Matthew 3:2 under *Repent*, p. 44
41 Ephesians 6:17
42 Cockerill, Gareth Lee, *The Epistle to the Hebrews*, New International Commentary on the New Testament (Eerdmans 2012) Hebrews 4:12, p. 216

> ... a transformed community, an alternative society in conscious contrast with the way of the world. In this topsy-turvy community, where the first are last and the last first, the new values of [God's] divine government can begin to take visible form. And when that happens, as a result of the inward transformation which God's kingship demands, there is the promise of a *truly* transformed society, not changed merely by a reordering of its structures, but by a reorientation of its values.[43]

As I was editing this lesson my husband and I watched the movie *Woodlawn*, the true story of football superstar Tony Nathan. In 1973 Nathan was one of several African American high school students who were the first to play on the football team for Birmingham's newly integrated Woodlawn High School. Racial tensions ran high until a sports chaplain challenged the team to make Christ number one in their life instead of football. As the team met together to study God's Word and then apply on the football field what they were learning, racial division was healed in the school. That transformation began to impact the city. Not just in the movie, but in real life Woodlawn became a transformed community, an alternative society in conscious contrast with the way of the world. The new values of God's divine government began to take visible form. Change took place as a result of the inward transformation that was happening in the player's lives. The chaplain's memorable line was, "This is what happens when God shows up."[44]

Now that we have a better understanding of our Kingdom identity, let's consider how culture affects behavior to form social identity. For purposes of our discussion we'll keep it simple and assume that society is basically divided into two different cultures – a dominant culture and an alternative subculture (the *ekklesia*). The social identity of the dominant culture is shaped by the ideology

---

[43] France, R. T., *Divine Government: God's Kingship In The Gospel of Mark* (Regent College Publishing 1990) p. 62, italics in original
[44] Quote by actor Sean Astin who played the role of Hank Erwin, the Woodlawn High School team chaplain

of those who are empowered and use their power and resources to advance their beliefs.[45] Whenever the ideology of the dominant culture does not fear God and align with biblical truth, God opens the path for an alternative subculture to develop. We see this pattern throughout the Bible. Under the old covenant, Israel was invited to develop an alternative subculture shaped by her covenant relationship with Yahweh. Obedience to the covenant was intended to result in Israel being settled in the Promised Land and living as a light to all the Gentile nations (the dominant culture of that day). Even in her captivity God made a way for Israel to retain her identity while living in the midst of the dominant culture of her pagan foreign rulers. At the time of the cross, the Roman culture was the dominant anti-God culture of the day. Jesus initiated a new covenant and opened the way for a new God-fearing alternative subculture which He called His *ekklesia*.

For the dominant culture to maintain its distinct identity it must continuously enforce its values on everyone else. Behavior that deviates from that "norm" must be addressed swiftly and decisively. The basic way in which that happens today is the same way it happened in the first century when the *ekklesia* was first being formed by the early disciples of Christ. Behavior is either met with honor or with shame. Honor is used to maintain the desired behavior and shaming tactics are used in an effort to force deviant behavior back into alignment with cultural norms.

Honor can include things such as public praise of various types, increased job opportunity or other opportunity to advance economically or in social standing. On the other hand, disapproval is often expressed through insult, shunning of various degrees, acts which serve to marginalize the person, loss of social status, loss of job and at its most serious form martyrdom. Based on what we've

---

45 Dr. David A. deSilva provides this definition of dominant culture – "the culture of the empowered: those who can maintain and propagate their culture through the exercise of power and other resources." deSilva, David A., *Hope of Glory: Honor Discourse and New Testament Interpretation* (Wipf & Stock 1999) p. 29, citing discussion with Dr. Vernon Robbins "concerning the precise definition of 'dominant' culture."

experienced in the United States in recent years we could add things like name calling, vilifying, defaming and canceling (denying access to social media as a communication tool) to the list of shaming strategies.

This type of social pressure carries great weight. Let's consider for example what happens when a public figure such as a sports personality or a well-known actor takes a biblical stand on an issue adverse to the beliefs of the dominant culture. That person will be instantly shamed in a very public way through social media and mainstream news media (tools the dominant culture uses to maintain its norms). At that point the individual has a choice to make. Will he suffer the social and economic consequences instigated by the dominant culture or will he retreat from his biblical stance with public apology?

Those men who wrote the New Testament understood this dynamic.[46] They understood that in an honor driven culture people are "oriented from birth toward seeking the approval of the significant others [because] this is how the culture maintains its essential identity and values across generational lines."[47] What the authors of the New Testament do is turn honor and shame on its head. Rather than seeking honor from dominant culture, Christ-followers are encouraged to seek honor from within the subculture of the *ekklesia*. They are to be motivated by what God says is honorable behavior and are warned to avoid what He says is shameful behavior.[48] We

---

46 In his book, *Hope of Glory: Honor Discourse and New Testament Interpretation* (Wipf & Stock 1999) seminary professor David deSilva discusses New Testament references to honor and shame making it clear Matthew, John, Paul and the author of Hebrews understood their importance in both the dominant culture of the day and in the growing *ekklesia*.

47 deSilva, David A., *Hope of Glory: Honor Discourse and New Testament Interpretation* (Wipf & Stock 1999) p. 3

48 In our modern-day Western culture, the emphasis is on the shamed person's inner attitude or state of mind. Harris, Archer, and Waltke, editors, *Theological Wordbook of the Old Testament* (Moody Press 1999) word #222, p. 97. On the other hand, the biblical emphasis on shame is primarily on failed trust (realizing trust was placed in something that proved to be false or unworthy), God's judgment and modifying unacceptable

see this reversal, for example in the Scripture quote from 1 John 2:28 – 3:3 at the beginning of this lesson. Notice John warned that a Christ-follower who fails to purify himself will be put to shame at the return of Christ. Behind that warning are the words of Jesus:

> "Therefore everyone who confesses Me before men, I will also confess him before My Father who is in heaven. But whoever **denies** Me before men, I will also **deny** him before My Father who is in heaven...." Matthew 10:32-33, bold added

> " ... For whoever is **ashamed** of Me and My words in this adulterous and sinful generation, the Son of Man will also be **ashamed** of him when He comes in the glory of His Father with the holy angels." Mark 8:38, bold added

The words highlighted in bold in these two quotes function in similar ways. Someone who is ashamed of Jesus refuses to publicly confess Him as Lord, they deny Him in words and actions. These are the ones who prefer honor before men in this lifetime rather than suffering and sacrifice that may be required to maintain their witness and receive honor from God. It's a costly tradeoff! In return, Jesus will reciprocally refuse to acknowledge them before His Father.

The New Testament authors not only recognized the honor-shame dynamic and its impact on identity formation and maintenance, they also recognized that God's ready-made answer for every Christ-follower is the *ekklesia*. The way in which new Christ-followers become equipped and empowered to take a bold

---

behavior. The difference is significant. Our modern understanding of shame relates to being flawed or unworthy as a person, in ancient culture shame applies exclusively to the wrongful action. Kranz, Rob, *Has the Cross Lost its Shame*? posted May 22, 2021 at 3:00 a.m., citing social anthropologist Unni Wikan. Retrieved from https://steppingintothejordan.com/2021/05/22/has-the-cross-lost-its-shame/ (last accessed March 25, 2022)

stand for Christ and withstand the pressure of dominant culture shame is found in their reorientation to seek honor from within the *ekklesia*. In other words, the *ekklesia* as a subculture defines what is honorable and what is shameful and teaches its members to ignore the appeals of honor from the dominant culture. Those who follow Christ are encouraged to follow in His footsteps and "despise" shame directed at them from the dominant culture. Like Jesus, by their obedience they render dominant culture shame of no effect. Jesus was able to endure the cross despising its shame because His motivation was inwardly driven by His desire to be obedient to His Father and glorify Him.[49] When the *ekklesia* forms a strong culture of its own and supports its members with strong fellowship and equally strong discipleship the members of that community will be empowered to boldly represent Christ. The shaming strategies of the dominant culture will have no effect on them. In fact, the *talmidim* in the first-century rejoiced when they experienced dishonor for the sake of Christ (Acts 5:41).

I want to point out a pattern God seems to use purposely to aid in identity formation. We see this pattern in the life of Israel under the old covenant and in the life of the *ekklesia* under the new covenant. It appears that God intentionally plants His covenant people in the middle of a culture that does *not* fear Him or follow His ways. We see that pattern when God places Israel in the Promised Land amid all the pagan cultures that surrounded them. It is repeated during the Babylonian exile where they are in a foreign land surrounded by pagans. We see it again when the *ekklesia* of Christ is given the commission to grow among the pagan Roman Empire. In the midst of those hostile environments He isn't "looking for people whose aim is to effect political change. He is not looking for those who merely want to [maintain] comfortable lifestyles. He is looking for those who are willing to go outside their comfort zones and obey [Him]."[50] Could it be that

---

49 Hebrews 12:1-3
50 Kendall, R.T., *We've Never Been This Way Before: Trusting God in Unprecedented Times* (Charisma House 2020) p. 106

God knows what we fail to recognize? In His Kingdom, worldly opposition becomes an invaluable tool to build a strong God-honoring identity.[51] Not only do God's covenant people provide light in the midst of darkness, as strange as it may sound to our ears, that struggle *against* the influence of dominant culture actually aids in character formation.[52] It may be helpful here to see what happens when God's people live in a culture-friendly environment.

In 1892 the United States Supreme Court determined that the historical record of America overwhelmingly demonstrated that the United States "is a Christian nation."[53] According to scholar Walter Brueggemann:

> So long as U.S. society was visibly "a Christian society," no special effort was required to maintain Christian

---

51 Cockerill, Gareth Lee, *The Epistle to the Hebrews*, New International Commentary on the New Testament (Eerdmans 2012) Hebrews 12:5-6, p. 621

52 Hebrews 12:5-13

53 A relevant portion of the written opinion states, "If we pass beyond these matters to a view of American life, as expressed by its laws, its business, its customs, and its society, we find every where [sic] a clear recognition of the same truth. Among other matters, note the following: the form of oath universally prevailing, concluding with an appeal to the Almighty; the custom of opening sessions of all deliberative bodies and most conventions with prayer; the prefatory words of all wills, 'In the name of God, amen;' the laws respecting the observance of the Sabbath, with the general cessation of all secular business, and the closing of courts, legislatures, and other similar public assemblies on that day; the churches and church organizations which abound in every city, town, and hamlet; the multitude of charitable organizations existing every where [sic] under Christian auspices; the gigantic missionary associations, with general support, and aiming to establish Christian missions in every quarter of the globe. These, and many other matters which might be noticed, add a volume of unofficial declarations to the mass of organic utterances that this is a Christian nation." Quote taken from Syllabus of *Church of the Holy Trinity v. United States*, 143 U.S. 457 (1892) page 143 U.S. 471. Retrieved from https://supreme.justia.com/cases/federal/us/143/457/ (last accessed May 31, 2022)

identity. All of the institutional supports and practices of society assumed and affirmed Christian claims ....[54]

As a case in point let me share a portion of a discussion I had with a fellow Christ-follower. This woman had moved to the southern Bible belt from just outside Washington D.C. She remarked at how stunned she was at the difference in the overall Christian community. She explained that living so close to D.C. routinely placed her in the cross-hairs of those who stand firmly against God and everything associated with the Kingdom of God. The Christ-followers she worshipped with were ones who lived out their convictions. She was referring to those who are being called "convictional Christians" to distinguish them from "nominal Christians."[55] In her experience, if you were going to be a follower of Christ you had to be willing to take a stand and withstand ridicule because of it. Your beliefs *were* going to cost you something in the public opinion polls in your community. That means that for those Christ-followers, as their faith was tested and strengthened, their

---

54 Brueggemann, Walter, *Truth & Hope: Essays For a Perilous Age* (Westminster John Knox Press 2020) pp. 201-202

55 R. T. Kendall defines a "nominal Christian" as one who "accept[s] certain Christian truths in [their] head but not [their] heart." Kendall, R.T., *We've Never Been This Way Before: Trusting God in Unprecedented Times* (Charisma House 2020) p. 20. I question whether biblically speaking there is such a thing as a "nominal Christian." However, for the use of the terms "convictional Christian" and "nominal Christianity," see: Stetzer, Ed, *Nominal Christians are becoming more secular, and that's creating a startling change for the U.S.*, The Washington Post, November 4, 2015. Retrieved from https://www.washingtonpost.com/news/acts-of-faith/wp/2015/11/04/nominal-christians-becoming-more-secular-and-thats-creating-a-startling-change-for-the-u-s/ (last accessed August 8, 2021); See also: *4 Trends in Christianity That Could Scare You, According to Ed Stetzer*, CharismaNews, June 4, 2014. Retrieved from https://www.charismanews.com/culture/44114-4-trends-in-christianity-that-could-scare-you-according-to-ed-stetzer (last accessed August 8, 2021); *Nominal vs. Convictional Christians*, blog by Servetus on May 27, 2016. Retrieved from https://approachingjustice.net/2016/05/27/nominal-vs-convictional-christians/ (last *accessed* August 8, 2021)

unique identity as a Christ-follower was being forged! However, in the Bible belt, she has been surprised to encounter many people whose primary reason for going to church is because that's what their family has always done. It's just the routine of what you do on Sunday mornings. For those people, there is no real distinction in identity between them and the community of non-believers.

This is precisely the difference Brueggemann was pointing out! As long as the community itself generally supports Judeo-Christian values, such as is still largely true in the southern Bible belt, there is *little to no need* to develop (let alone maintain) a strong identity that sets you apart from the others around you. In fact, there is *diminished opportunity* for identity development because as we noted they lack the worldly opposition that aids in forming a God-centered identity.[56] Said another way, the absence of need and opportunity to be different from the world robs the Christ-follower of the very environment essential to establishing their strong Christ-like identity! The result is a watered-down nominal and ineffective "Christian" without distinction and utterly devoid of testimony. In those cases, "Christian" is a label without substance. The nominal church doesn't seem to be aware of the fact that they were entrusted with the hope of the gospel so they could be walking billboards of life and light to a dark and dying world! It is problematic when the *talmidim* of Christ don't walk in hope because they are the *only ones* who are able to have hope in the midst of a world desperate for hope!

If it is true that opposition from the dominant culture becomes a formative element of *ekklesia* identity development, then Christ-followers in America have been served up increased opportunity on a silver platter! In 2009 it was publicly announced that Americans "do not consider ourselves a Christian nation ... but

---

56 Cockerill, Gareth Lee, *The Epistle to the Hebrews*, New International Commentary on the New Testament (Eerdmans 2012) Hebrews 12:5-6, p. 621

rather, a nation of citizens who are ... bound by a set of values."[57] Much of the church was vocally angered, frustrated and caught off guard by that statement. What the announcement did, however, was make more widely known the position of the dominant culture in America. According to Brueggeman that announcement should have been a clarion call to the *talmidim* in America. It should have precipitated a shift from status quo to determined intentionality.

> Now however, in a society gone publicly secular, that [Christian] social identity is no longer "automatic" but now requires *determined intentionality* to make a case for "evangelical identity" in the midst of an imperial environment [dominant culture] that has lost its way in money, power, and violence.[58]

Similar to the picture Brueggemann paints of the United States today, Christ-followers in the first century eventually found themselves in an imperial environment that was openly hostile to the worship of one true God. But remember it was in *that* context the Apostle John called for "determined intentionality" of identity maintenance in 1 John 3:3. John was envisioning a purified, set apart community who, because of their strong convictions, had a distinctive Christ-like character enabling them to be a living witness to the truth of the gospel.

In the narrative of the New Testament, Jesus is credited with forming an alternative community of faithful followers – *His ekklesia* – who are willing, like Daniel, to risk death to maintain their distinctive identity. The lifestyle Jesus modeled was an alternative to Rome and all it stood for.[59] When lived out, the values He taught and modeled resulted in the accusation that His disciples

---

57 Eidsmoe, John, *Obama: America Not a Christian Nation*, NewAmerican, April 15, 2009. Retrieved from https://thenewamerican.com/obama-america-not-a-christian-nation/ (last accessed June 1, 2022)

58 Brueggemann, Walter, *Truth & Hope: Essays For a Perilous Age* (Westminster John Knox Press 2020) p. 202, italics added

59 Brueggemann, Walter, *Truth & Hope: Essays For a Perilous Age* (Westminster John Knox Press 2020) p. 202

had "turned the world upside down."[60] Jesus knew that intentional resistance (engaging in nonviolent, noncompliance whenever necessary) would carve out their distinctive identity. What we see in the book of Acts illustrates what *normal* Christ-followers should look like!

As the *ekklesia* of Christ today we are walking through life between the initial announcement of the gospel and the final victory it guarantees.[61] Our Key Scripture succinctly instructs us how we should live in this in-between moment in history. There is a sense in which every single member of the *ekklesia* is to look identical. If you were to hold up a mirror before each one, the reflection of each and every disciple should be Christ Himself. They were called "Christians" at Antioch meaning "little Christs."[62] The distinctiveness of their identity was founded in their call to be counter-cultural in thought and action. Their very life would bear witness to the reality of God's Kingdom – a Kingdom whose values were remarkably different from the dominant culture of the day.[63] What is vitally important to understand is that when we lose the unique identity that distinguishes us from the dominant culture we not only lose our witness, we lose our hope! When we are no different than the culture around us and no longer displaying God's Kingdom by our lifestyle, we remove ourselves from God's *Hope Waiting Room*. At that point, we disqualify ourselves from receiving God's promises – the very basis of hope!

"Having the hope and purifying yourself go together. They depend on each other."[64] It is our identity *in Christ* that gives us the privilege of being confident in God's faithfulness and fidelity to keep His promises. Because that is true, maintenance of our

---

60 Acts 17:6 ESV
61 Wright, N. T., *Simply Jesus: A New Vision of Who He Was, What He Did, and Why He Matters* (HarperOne 2011) p. 116
62 Acts 11:26
63 Brueggemann, Walter, *Truth & Hope: Essays For a Perilous Age* (Westminster John Knox Press 2020) p. 198
64 Gundry, Robert H., *Commentary on the New Testament* (Hendrickson Publishers 2010) 1 John 1:2-3, p. 975

peculiar identity in Him is inseparably intertwined with our hope. "Lack of self-purification kills the hope. Lack of the hope kills self-purification."[65] In other words, lose the identity – lose the hope! It's as simple as that.

Every Christ-follower needs to personally answer the question, "How am *I* doing with *my* assignment to live a purified life in the dominant culture I presently live in?" Was my salvation experience an "event" or did it launch an entirely new lifestyle? As we have been learning, our hope depends on our answer!

Hear What The Spirit is Saying to the Church: *I am calling my people to come out. Come out and be truly set apart from the world around you. Be willing to be distinct and set apart. Then you will inherit all that I have promised you.*

---

65 Gundry, Robert H., *Commentary on the New Testament* (Hendrickson Publishers 2010) 1 John 1:2-3, p. 975

Lesson 12:

The Powerful Hope of God's New Creation

"Then I saw a new heaven and a new earth …. And I saw the holy city, new Jerusalem, coming down out of heaven from God, prepared as a bride adorned for her husband…. And I heard a loud voice from the throne, saying, '… [God] will wipe away every tear from their eyes; and there will no longer be *any* death; there will no longer be *any* mourning, or crying, or pain; the first things have passed away.'" Revelation 21:1-4, italics in original

HISTORY REVEALS THAT the followers of Christ who "did the most for the present world are … the ones that thought the most of the next."[1] Our Key Scripture for this lesson is penned by the aging Apostle John who was privileged by Christ to see the beauty and perfection of the "new" heaven and earth God had promised. It is everything prophesied and everything hoped for.

Beginning with Abraham, God's design has been to have a "called out people." His desire is for a covenant community, a family who would respond to the truth of who He is and be holy unto Himself. They would be ones who would not be absorbed or integrated into the dominant culture that surrounds them even though they are faced with never-ending pressure to conform! To those facing that pressure, Jeremiah's instruction lived out by Jesus and repeated by Peter to the first-century *talmidim* can be sim-

---

1 Kendall, R.T., *We've Never Been This Way Before: Trusting God in Unprecedented Times* (Charisma House 2020) p. 72, quoting C. S. Lewis

ply stated. It is the way of love – the type of love that accurately RE•presents Christ and in so doing benefits others without regard to their race, nationality or political views. At the cross, God took all the evil of the world unto Himself and gave back love![2] Those of us who have chosen to follow Him have been entrusted with that love. It is a love motivated by what He has done for us and therefore uniquely "wills the good of all and never wills harm or evil to any."[3] As His disciples we are now compelled to engage our culture in the distinctive manner and power of that same type of love. We don't turn a blind eye to social issues and concerns; however, it is vitally important we recognize in the biblical model *love* does the heavy lifting.

The book of Revelation actually provides us with an amazing road map to follow as we live out life amid a dominant culture that is increasingly hostile to the God we worship and serve. In Lesson 9 we learned how adversity strengthens hope. Then in Lessons 10 and 11 we considered the reality that identity is best formed in the crucible of struggle. In this lesson we will see how Christ Himself addressed His *ekklesia* struggling to find their way amid increasing threat of persecution.[4] To that end we'll turn to the messages He

---

[2] Oswalt, John N., *Isaiah, A Video Study: Session 12, Isaiah 9:1-7*, MasterLectures, Zondervanacademic.com. Retrieved from https://masterlectures.zondervanacademic.com/isaiah-john-n-oswalt/videos/isaiah-a-video-study-session-12-isaiah-9-1-7?code=newyear&utm_source=zaoc_newsletter&utm_medium=email&utm_campaign=christmas2021 (last accessed December 25, 2021)

[3] Tozer, A. W., *The Knowledge of the Holy* (HarperSanFranciso 1961) p. 98

[4] The honor of a number of these communities who followed Christ was apparently challenged. For example, the letters to Smyrna and Philadelphia both speak of slander directed at those communities. Christ-followers in Smyrna seem to be threatened with affliction and possible imprisonment which is likely an attempt by dominant culture to shame their deviant behavior. Martyrdom has already happened in Pergamum. Pressure is being applied in Asia Minor to disassociate with the *ekklesia* to regain honor as defined by the dominant culture. "John envisions such pressure growing in the future, so that in Antipas the martyr one might see the shape of things to come." deSilva, David A., *Hope of*

The Power of Hope

asked John to deliver to seven churches in Asia Minor (Revelation 2-3).[5]

We will begin our discussion by considering the historical backdrop to these messages. Scholars believe it is likely that they were given to John by the resurrected Christ in the later part of the first century. In that case John received them when the Roman Empire was ruled by Domitian. Nero's[6] persecution of Christ-followers was primarily contained to Rome. On the other hand, Domitian[7] adopted an empire-wide policy of persecution and that would of course reach all the way to Asia Minor.[8] In fact, it is thought that John was on the Isle of Patmos[9] because he was banished there by Domitian.[10] Keep in mind the hostility these Christ-followers

---

Glory: Honor Discourse and New Testament Interpretation (Wipf & Stock 1999) p. 180

5 Revelation belongs to a type of ancient Jewish and Christian literature which modern scholars call "apocalypses." Most were written at a time of crisis, danger and distress when it was difficult to stand firm in trust. They use symbolic imagery to communicate hope (in the ultimate triumph of God) to those in the midst of persecution. The purpose is to comfort God's people by providing a uniquely heavenly perspective on events of the past, present and future. The message of an apocalypse typically anticipates that evil and political oppression will cease. Blackwell, Goodrich, and Maston, editors, *Reading Romans in Context: Paul and Second Temple Judaism* (Zondervan 2015) Forward, p. 26

6 Nero ruled as Roman Emperor between 54 and 68 A.D.

7 Domitian reigned as Emperor over the Roman Empire between 81 and 96 A.D.

8 Under the reign of Domitian Christ-followers, whether Jew or Gentile, could be persecuted for two offenses: failure to pay the *fiscus Judaicus* tax (because Gentiles Christ-followers "lived as Jews" they were subject to the tax) and for converting pagans in the Roman Empire to Christian beliefs. Both offenses were punishable by death. Heemstra, Marius, *Dissertation: How Rome's Administration of the Fiscus Judaicus Accelerated the Parting of the Ways between Judaism and Christianity*, Hoogeveen, The Netherlands, July 2009. Retrieved from http://dissertations.ub.rug.nl/FILES/faculties/theology/2009/m.heemstra/thesis.pdf (last accessed March 13, 2010)

9 Revelation 1:9

10 Patmos was likely the site of a Roman penal colony. *NIV Study Bible* (Zondervan Publishing 1995) Revelation Introduction under *Occasion*, p. 1922

would have been facing when Christ told John to tell them He *knew* what they were going through. And yet for the majority of those churches Christ pointed out matters that were keeping them from His full commendation. In other words, Jesus did not excuse away actions that did not honor Him even though to obey what He had commanded may have been costly to them. From those seven messages to the churches in Asia Minor we are able to see what is important to Christ even when consistently living an obedient life-style was anything but easy. In spite of the hostile political climate, the disciples of Christ were called to be vessels of love who were "convinced that people need to be saved [and] that the Gospel is the only hope."[11] No doubt it loomed large in the minds of John's audience that they could be put to death if they were found guilty of converting a pagan in the Roman Empire to a gospel-believing *talmid*.[12] However, even under those threatening circumstances Jesus said:

- endurance and vigilance matters
- holding on to the Name of Christ matters
- continually growing in love as evidenced by deeds that benefit others matters
- keeping His word (obeying His commands) matters
- not denying His Name matters
- holding fast to the truth matters

---

11 Kendall, R.T., *We've Never Been This Way Before: Trusting God in Unprecedented Times* (Charisma House 2020) p. 105. The people who will have the greatest Kingdom impact in our lifetime will be people who know how to forgive, "who are unashamed of the Gospel and ... filled with love for people, no matter their race or political views; they will have a genuine love for the Gospel and whoever needs to be saved." Ibid. pp. 105-106,114

12 The ultimate message of the New Testament however is that such death is a "mark of honor within the [*ekklesia*] and before the court of God. When dying is a sign of being held in esteem by God and favored what pressures can the outside world bring to bear on one's commitment?" deSilva, David A., *Hope of Glory: Honor Discourse and New Testament Interpretation* (Wipf & Stock 1999) p. 194

- not tolerating false teachers matters
- not compromising with the world's culture matters
- spiritual discernment matters

As God's new creation we have work to do in this lifetime.[13] Under the rule of a civil government that did not honor God and in an environment that was increasingly hostile to His disciples, Jesus' message to His followers was, "Don't stop. Keep going! Keep doing what I called you to do." Continuing the work of discipling the nations in the midst of persecution and spiritual apathy was not new instruction. Jesus had warned His disciples before of their need to endure to the end in spite of such hostility.[14]

This is a good place to introduce a biblical truth found in the Old Testament, although one that may not be widely recognized. In Judges 2:22 God acknowledged that He did not drive out the evil nations that remained after Joshua's death so He could test (*nāsâ*) Israel and see whether they would walk in His ways.[15] Judges 3:1,4 restates that purpose and then enumerates the nations God left in the land to test Israel – the Canaanites, Hittites, Amorites, Perizzites, Hivites and Jebusites. In other words, God intentionally allowed evil empires to live alongside Israel in the Promised Land so that Israel could be tested! In God's Kingdom, His faithfulness is visibly demonstrated in the way in which He is steadfastly loyal to the covenant promises He makes. Similarly, His *talmidim* visibly demonstrate their loyalty to Him through their actions – actions that must be steadfast enough to stand the test of trial and suffering.[16] Throughout her history, Israel has been expected to demonstrate that she would follow God's commands

---

13 Ephesians 2:10
14 See for example: Matthew 24:9-14
15 Divine testing brings "someone into a critical situation in order to observe reaction and behavior" to see whether it aligns with God's expectations. Nelson, Richard D., *Deuteronomy*, The Old Testament Library (Westminster John Knox Press 2002) Deuteronomy 8:2-6, p. 111
16 Sarna, Nahum M., *Understanding Genesis Through Rabbinic Tradition and Modern Scholarship* (The Jewish Theological Seminary 2015) p. 163

and not succumb to the temptation to do evil in His sight through compromise with the surrounding culture.

Could it be that God's pattern has never changed? Could it be that for the *talmidim* in John's day the Roman Empire was in essence the first-century replacement for the Canaanites, Hittites, Amorites, Perizzites, Hivites and Jebusites? In other words, God was using the hostile Roman Empire so that His *talmidim* could be tested! Jesus did not refocus His disciples and give them a new assignment. He did not change the rules of discipleship. His message was simple, straightforward and clear. "Stay the course. Don't get sidetracked. Do what I created you to do. Fulfill your destiny. Let your hope carry you across the finish line as you complete the work I have prepared in advance for you to do." That *work* is aptly summarized by the command Jesus gave His disciples before He ascended. "Go make disciples!"[17] And that is best done when His disciples are walking billboards who put Him on display.

Let's go back one more time to the message Jeremiah gave Israel for life in Babylon. Jeremiah knew the ways of God and trusted Him. He knew there would be a day when God would restore Israel to their own land and punish Babylon for her wickedness against Israel. The counsel he gave Israel in her captivity was essentially twofold. First, they should concern themselves with the things that bring God glory in the midst of their captivity. Things like building houses, planting gardens, getting married, raising their family and seeking the welfare of those who rule over them. In these daily activities they would be testifying to the goodness of God and to the reality of who He is.[18] By their proper focus they would replace anxiety with trust, fear with love and short-term vision with hope. Second, implicit in what God told them to

---

17 Matthew 28:19
18 Activity like constructing houses and planting vineyards are concrete symbols of security. Block, Daniel I., *The Book of Ezekiel: Chapters 25-48*, The New International Commentary on the Old Testament (Eerdmans 1998) Ezekiel 28:26, p. 127. One who was living in the midst of captivity could undertake these types of activities only because they had placed their trust in Yahweh who had given them the instruction.

focus on was what *not* to focus on. They were not to spend their time and energy complaining about their captivity. They were not to waste life longing for changed circumstances. Even though they were living in a hostile culture, they were to let God alone be concerned with when and how to alter their circumstances. Their longing should be that God be glorified in them and through them for His name's sake in their present circumstances. This was the message walked out by Jesus during His earthly ministry, it was His message in Revelation to those facing increased persecution in Asia Minor and it is His message to us today.

We have already learned that the culture of the Bible was largely driven by what was honorable behavior and what was shameful (or disgraceful) behavior. Down through the ages the question of "who" decides what is honorable has been at stake. On every level the Bible makes clear that God alone has the right to define honorable behavior. Revelation draws very clear boundaries between what *God* considers honorable and what *He* considers to be shameful. The visions recorded in Revelation present Christ-followers with "models of praise-worthy action for emulation and anti-models of those whose actions are censurable and lead to disgrace …."[19] For those who continue to align their conduct with what the world says is honorable, the visions given to John are "a wake-up call to see that one's easy alliance with society is a partnership with the Whore of Babylon."[20] The warning is that those actions will be subject to God's judgment. On the other hand, those Christ-followers who have chosen well are encouraged to stay the course because the path they have chosen "will lead them to true and lasting honor."[21]

God can work with us in whatever shape we're in, but He needs the desires of our hearts to be the desires of His heart. From the message He sent to the Laodiceans, we learn He refuses to work

---

19   deSilva, David A., *Hope of Glory: Honor Discourse and New Testament Interpretation* (Wipf & Stock 1999) p. 178
20   deSilva, David A., *Hope of Glory: Honor Discourse and New Testament Interpretation* (Wipf & Stock 1999) p. 179
21   deSilva, David A., *Hope of Glory: Honor Discourse and New Testament Interpretation* (Wipf & Stock 1999) p. 182

with lukewarm Christianity (Revelation 3:15-16).[22] There is, in fact, a biblical example of this truth that precedes that first century warning to the *ekklesia* at Laodicea. It is found in the story of Esau selling his birthright to Jacob for some stew.[23] Esau was being tested by God. When God tests someone, it is to prompt "a decision that proves [the person's] character and faith."[24] The quality of character that exists only as a *potential* before the test must be put into practice to pass the test.[25] Esau, as the first-born son of Isaac, was in line to receive the covenant blessing given to his grandfather Abraham and his father Isaac. God wanted that covenant blessing to mean something to Esau – something strong enough to warrant sacrifice and suffering. Would he be willing to go hungry in order to hold on to his birthright, the right to the covenant blessing? Jacob was desperate enough for that blessing that he was willing to act deceptively to get it. God saw the heart in Jacob and permitted the blessing to flow to him from his father Isaac. God later dealt with Jacob and changed his character over the years till finally he was no longer called Jacob (meaning deceiver, supplanter). God renamed him Israel, which can mean "[The God] El Rules" or "Prince with God."[26] That name change "signifies a final purging of the unsavory character traits" which had long identified Jacob.[27]

---

22 Lesson 11 introduced the term "nominal Christians." It is an appropriate term for the *ekklesia* at Laodicea.
23 See Genesis 25:29-34
24 Nelson, Richard D., *Deuteronomy*, The Old Testament Library (Westminster John Knox Press 2002) Deuteronomy 8:2-6, p. 111
25 Sarna, Nahum M., *The JPS Torah Commentary: Genesis*, The Traditional Hebrew Text with the New JPS Translation Commentary (The Jewish Publication Society 1989) Genesis 22:12 under *for now I know*, p. 153
26 Berlin and Brettler, editors, *The Jewish Study Bible: Featuring The Jewish Publication Society Tanakh Translation* (Oxford University Press 2004) study note Genesis 32:29, p. 68; *Spirit Filled Life Bible* (Thomas Nelson 1991) study note Genesis 32:28, p. 54
27 Sarna, Nahum M., *The JPS Torah Commentary: Genesis*, The Traditional Hebrew Text with the New JPS Translation Commentary (The Jewish Publication Society 1989) Genesis 32:28-29, p. 227

Notice God was willing to work with flawed character. What He was not willing to work with was apathy towards the covenant – apathy that led to placing physical need above spiritual blessing. In this way, Esau was a type of lukewarm church, like the church at Laodicea.[28] Jesus had a strong word for the Laodiceans. He was ready to vomit them out of His mouth. That warning suggests it is prudent for us to look a little more carefully at the risk associated with being lukewarm. To help with this subject I'd like to return to the thoughts of Old Testament scholar Walter Brueggemann.

In his book *Truth & Hope: Essays For a Perilous Age*, Brueggemann surprisingly points out a successful scheme of dominant culture. Generally, they are able to bank on the fact that over time resistance to their ideology will succumb to "passivity and acquiescence."[29] As in the first-century Roman Empire of John's day, when the dominant political culture is based on humanism it seeks to force its beliefs, perceptions and cultural norms on *everyone*. In that way control is maintained of the masses, ideology is instilled and a new order is established. That dominant political system will work overtime to convince the people under its rule that there are no alternatives available to them – that choices have already been made for them. Their mantra is that the cultural war is already won and the matter is now beyond change.[30] The intended outcome is what Brueggemann labels "*passivity* and *acquiescence*."[31] In other words, the recurring claims of the dominant culture that *their* worldview *is assured* victory in the culture war is carefully

---

28 I credit Paul Keith Davis for this teaching. Davis, **Paul Keith**, *An Open Heaven Impartation: Receiving the El Shaddai Blessing!* Video released by Glory of Zion on Pentecost 2022. Retrieved from https://tv.gloryofzion.org/free-replays/season:1/videos/paul-keith-davis-an-open-heaven-impartation-receiving-the-el-shaddai-blessing (last accessed June 6, 2022)
29 Brueggemann, Walter, *Truth & Hope: Essays For a Perilous Age* (Westminster John Knox Press 2020) pp. 130-131, italics in original
30 Brueggemann, Walter, *Truth & Hope: Essays For a Perilous Age* (Westminster John Knox Press 2020) p. 131
31 Brueggemann, Walter, *Truth & Hope: Essays For a Perilous Age* (Westminster John Knox Press 2020) pp. 130-131, italics in original

calculated to lead to tolerant submission to their ideology. Passivity and acquiescence flow naturally from hopeless despair. Unless challenged, the usual consequence is:

> ... *abdication [resignation]*, a refusal to engage issues, an inability to think or act outside the box of dominant power arrangements .... [Notably] [t]**he [dominant] empire does not require agreement or need approval. It requires only passive conformity among those who believe that there is no [viable] alternative.**[32]

Before I state the obvious counterpoint, it is important to take seriously the warning contained in this quote. From the standpoint of the dominant ideology, passivity and acquiescence are perfectly acceptable results because they will inevitably lead to hopeless resignation. It's a waiting game! The dominant culture simply waits for the opposition (that means Christ-followers) to lay down their hope, to stop lovingly engaging the issues and to surrender the fight. Did you notice in this warning that Christ-followers do ***not*** need to either approve of or agree with the opposing worldview? The world wins the culture war when we become passively compliant, no longer believing there is any other viable option. As we've said before, loss of identity results in loss of hope. The enemy of our souls (the one who is truly behind the anti-God narrative) wins by default. Being lukewarm is not an acceptable option for Christ-followers!

Now let's return to the messages John received for the seven churches of Asia Minor. Christ personally knows the condition of each and every part of His *ekklesia* and it matters! He knew these trial-weary disciples were at risk of substituting their own expectations for His promises. Christ not only promised sufficient sustaining and overcoming power, He restated His promises to refresh hope.

---

32 Brueggemann, Walter, *Truth & Hope: Essays For a Perilous Age* (Westminster John Knox Press 2020) pp. 130-131, italics in original, bold added

The Power of Hope

- To the church at Ephesus He promised the right to eat from the tree of Life
- To the church at Smyrna He promised the second death would not harm them
- To the church at Pergamum He promised hidden manna and a new name
- To the church at Thyatira He promised to give authority over the nations
- To the church at Sardis He promised they would be acknowledged before His Father
- To the church at Philadelphia He promised they would become a pillar in His temple
- To the church at Laodicea He promised the right to sit with Him on His throne

By now you should be able to recognize that Jesus was adjusting the hope magnifying glass held in the hands of His *talmidim*. He was redirecting them from focusing on the pain and suffering of the present to the promised glory of the future. Jesus knew hope is uniquely designed to be a catalyst for endurance when facing faith-testing trials.

> Sustaining a vision, even an inspired vision, that runs counter to the status quo is no small feat. It demands quiet commitment for the long haul (Isa. 42:2). It entails daily discipline and receptiveness to God's alternative vision for the world (50:5-6). It requires the ability to look beyond the cusp of the near future ....[33]

Jesus knew that evil can win by default when we lay down our hope, so He gave John a clear message of hope. Our Key Scripture for this Lesson records the highlight of the revelation John received on Patmos. John was given a glimpse of the glory of the new heaven and new earth. Then Jesus told him, "Go tell the people to hang in

---

33 Levison, Jack, *A Boundless God: The Spirit according to the Old Testament* (Baker Academic 2020) p. 68

there – tell them the things that you've seen. Tell them that what I've promised will become a reality. Tell them not to give up." "Hope is what you get when you suddenly realize that a different worldview is possible, a worldview in which the rich, the powerful and the unscrupulous do not after all have the last word."[34] Hope knows with certainty that God alone has the last word!

Because God's new world has already begun in the present, every *talmid* participates in a new quality of life now which will be consummated when Jesus, the focal point of our hope, returns.[35] However, as we acknowledged in Lesson 9, our new life, even though part of God's new creation, "does not yet remove us from the old life of the fallen world; rather, it places us at the center of the battle between the [new and the old]."[36] What we need is active hope that strengthens us in between "what God has already done and what God has yet to do, between 'the already' and 'the not yet.'"[37] That's the exact realm in which hope is so perfectly designed to work. Let me explain with an example.

In 2019 my husband and I found ourselves in a season of life in which God had instructed us to move to a different part of Florida. We were at that time living in the place He had moved us to five years earlier. It was a place where we had found great contentment because of the church family, neighbors and Kingdom assignments God had blessed us with. As we anticipated a move we would have readily chosen *not* to make, we were discussing the promise God had given us of great future blessing in the new place He was calling us to. We believed God for that *future* blessing,

---

34 Wright, Tom, *Surprised by HOPE* (Society for Promoting Christian Knowledge 2007, reissued 2011) p. 87
35 *God's Word of Hope*, Precept Austin. Retrieved from https://www.preceptaustin.org/gods_word_of_hope (last accessed August 8, 2021)
36 Beale and Carson, editors, *Commentary on the New Testament Use of the Old Testament* (Baker Academic 2007) The Love of God In Christ And Hope In Tribulation ([Romans] 5:1-8:39), p. 628
37 Keck, Leander E., *Romans*, Abingdon New Testament Commentaries (Abingdon Press 2005) Beyond Rectification: Rescued and Reconciled ([Romans] 5:1-11), p. 134

however, my husband nailed it when he remarked, "but we aren't there yet." What he meant was that we were still in the hard season of transition and not yet walking in that blessing which God had promised. *That* is when I truly understood biblical hope for the first time. Hope allows that which is "not yet" to remain in clear view. Biblical hope is the **confident expectation** that God *will* be faithful to do what He said He would do **and** then **choosing to live today** as if He had already fulfilled that promise. That means we reach forward into the future, grab hold of *that* joy of blessing and pull it towards us so that we rejoice in *that* joy today! The actual fulfillment of God's promise does not come sooner – but we choose to *act* as if it did because of the certainty that God *will* fulfill all He has promised. In essence, we borrow against future joy, but with the certainty that what we are borrowing *will* become reality.

Every couple who plans a wedding knows how this works. An engaged couple may set a date for a wedding that will take place twelve months from now, but they begin to anticipate that wedding *today*! They begin to plan for it *today*. They can experience joy and excitement *today* even though they need to wait twelve months for the actual date of fulfillment. *That* is how biblical hope works. Hope compels you to reach into the future and pull that joy *back towards you* and when you do you can walk in that joy in the present.[38] In other words, your future experience of joy is actualized through hope so that it can be experienced today!

Studies have shown that the power of life itself is contained in the seed of hope! Dr. Harold Wolff of Cornell University Medical School completed an investigation involving 25,000 American soldiers imprisoned during WWII. Many died and almost all became sick. Dr. Wolff conducted interviews with those former POWs who had shown the least physical problems. His interviews confirmed that these men had no inherent physical superiority, but what they did have was a far-above-average ability to *hope*! Dr. Wolff took notice that to simply hope in thought alone was not enough. The men who showed only slight physical problems not only *thought*

---

38 Personal Journal October 18, 2019

hopefully, their hope motivated some type of *action*. For example, some of these men drew pictures of future things they hoped for like the women they intended to marry or the future homes they hoped to have. Others planned and organized business seminars they expected to conduct someday. From his investigation, Dr. Wolff found there was a direct correlation between exercised hope and physical stamina. He concluded it was their *hope* that had kept these men alive![39] Similarly, an Austrian psychiatrist observed that a prisoner did not continue to live very long after he lost hope. On the other hand, the slightest ray of hope, even something as simple as the rumor of better food or a whisper about an escape, helped others continue to live under the most appalling of conditions.[40]

The *apparent* absence of viable alternatives amid a dominant humanistic ideology/political governance breeds hopelessness which inevitably leads to despair. Despair is what happens when we have emotionally spiraled downward through disappointment and discouragement without seeing any light at the end of the tunnel. It is that feeling of being permanently trapped in the lie, "This is all there is, so pull yourself up by your bootstraps and prepare to make the best of it." Left unchecked, despair will inevitably lead to disillusionment, which is in essence the result of laying down our expectation for something different. In other words, the outcome of disillusionment is forfeited hope!

Renewed expectation in the form of biblical hope is the antidote for despair. The psalmist who poured out his heart to God

---

39 Wagner, Keith, *A Living Hope*, citing the conclusions of Dr. Victor Frankl. Retrieved from https://sermonwriter.com/sermons/new-testament-1-peter-13-9-living-hope-wagner (last accessed August 8, 2021); Peale, Norman Vincent, *Light Your New Year with Hope*, posted on December 3, 2010. Retrieved from https://www.guideposts.org/faith-and-prayer/bible-resources/light-your-new-year-with-hope (last accessed August 8, 2021)

40 *God's Word of Hope*, Precept Austin, citing *Man's Search for Meaning*, George Sweeting. Retrieved from https://www.preceptaustin.org /gods_word_of_hope (last accessed August 8, 2021)

in Psalm 42 understood the powerful truth that hope can dislodge despair.

> Why are you in despair, O my soul? And why have you become restless *and* disturbed within me? Hope in God *and* wait expectantly for Him, for I shall again praise Him For the help of His presence. Psalm 42:5 AMP, italics in original

> Why are you in despair, O my soul? Why have you become restless *and* disquieted within me? Hope in God *and* wait expectantly for Him, for I shall yet praise Him, The help of my countenance and my God. Psalm 42:11 AMP, italics in original

Knowing that God is the source of all true hope (remember we learned in Lesson 8 that it is a grace gift He pours into our prepared heart)[41] the psalmist was acknowledging to the Lord the despair which had filled his heart because of his present circumstances. Recognizing (and perhaps being alarmed at) that despair, he chose to turn his magnifying glass toward God. When that magnifying glass was firmly focused on God, rather than on his circumstances, the psalmist could choose to wait expectantly in God's *Hope Waiting Room.* He could choose to wait on God for what only He could do. The psalmist had a renewed sense of patient, expectant, waiting confidence once again. He stood firm in his trust that waiting on the Lord is not *wasted* time, it is *invested* time! With a heart full of hope the psalmist could begin to praise God in the present and wait expectantly for the fulfillment of the promises of deliverance contained in God's word. Hope not only replaced his despair, it actively *displaced* it.

---

41 Scholar Bruce Waltke points out that, "Faith in God's promises and renouncing confidence in oneself are unnatural and gifts of God …." Waltke, Bruce K., *The Book of Proverbs: Chapters 1-15*, The New International Commentary on the Old Testament (Eerdmans 2004) Proverbs 3:5-6, p. 243, Scripture references omitted

No matter how dark the world around us seems, we are *not* left to despair, we are *not* without viable alternatives. Like the hope-filled prophetic voices of the Old Testament, the good news of the gospel is that hope *is* possible. There is no need to despair because the truth of the gospel tells us that the way of the dominant evil culture is *not* the only way.[42] God spoke to His prophets in ages past so they would refrain from conforming to the beliefs of the prevailing culture which were not aligned with Him![43] What the prophets did in the Old Testament, indeed what John did in the New Testament, was create the opportunity for hope. The prophets saw what God saw. As a result, they were able to look the dominant anti-God culture squarely in the eye and boldly declare that acquiescence is *not* the only choice. As a matter of fact, intentionally choosing the alternative offered by God is the *required choice* for every Christ-follower. Such choice is solidly grounded in the truth. The biblical promises have been given to us by a loving God who faithfully fulfills *every* promise. The truth is that the unrelenting narrative of the dominant culture that seeks to suppress an alternative Godly choice is a lie!

The developing church in the first-century Roman Empire was not interested in blending in with a pluralistic community that thought their growth and long-term survival depended on accommodating many different gods.[44] If that were the case, persecution would not have broken out against the early church! The goal of the early church, empowered by Holy Spirit, was to form a unique community of radically obedient Christ-followers.[45] Ac-

---

42 Brueggemann, Walter, *Truth & Hope: Essays For a Perilous Age* (Westminster John Knox Press 2020) p. 134
43 "For this is what the Lord said to me [Isaiah] with great power, to keep me from going the way of this people." Isaiah 8:11 HCSB
44 Bracamonte, Daniel, *Acts and Mission in the 21st Century*, ApostolicReview, September 30, 2019. Retrieved from https://apostolicreview.com/2019/09/30/acts-and-mission-in-the-21st-century/ (last accessed August 8, 2021)
45 Bracamonte, Daniel, *Acts and Mission in the 21st Century*, ApostolicReview, September 30, 2019. Retrieved from https://apostolicreview.com

cording to scholar Craig Keener, the *ekklesia* was called to be a different kind of multicultural worshipping community – one that surpassed normal human boundaries and crossed over barriers created by culture.[46] The separation of these Christ-followers is "not self-appointed exclusivism but (like all true biblical separation) obedience to the word of God."[47] The New Testament does not call the *ekklesia* to standoffishness from the world, escape from the world, or detachment from the world.   Rather Christ-followers are called to take:

> … a radical new stance toward the world, predicated on the saving event of Christ that has marked off our existence in a totally new way…. [It is a stance of being] totally free from [the world's] control…. The Christian is marked by eternity, therefore, he or she is not under the dominating power of those things that dictate the existence of others.[48]

A choice *is* available as long as we have breath in our lungs! And choose we must! The darker the culture gets the more attractive the alternative choice of Light offered by the *ekklesia* becomes. A significant portion of the church in America today wrongly assumes that to grow (maybe even in fact to survive) it *must* compromise and accommodate culture. However, the very opposite has proven to be true. In fact, research shows that the higher the tension

/2019/09/30/acts-and-mission-in-the-21st-century/ (last accessed August 8, 2021)

46   Keener, Craig S. *Power of Pentecost: Luke's Missiology in Acts 1-2*, Asian Journal of Pentecostal Studies, Vol. 12:1 (January 2009) pp. 47–73, at p. 72. Retrieved from https://learn.schoolofleadership.co.za/wp-content/uploads/2020/01/Power-of-Pentecost-Lukes-Missiology-in-Acts-1-2-1.pdf (last accessed January 25, 2022)

47   Motyer, J. Alec, *The Prophecy of Isaiah: An Introduction & Commentary* (InterVarsity Press 1993) Isaiah 8:11, p. 94

48   Fee, Gordon D., *The First Epistle To The Corinthians*, The New International Commentary on the New Testament (Eerdmans 1987) 1 Corinthians 7:29b-31a, p. 340, citing D. J. Doughty, *The Presence and Future of Salvation in Corinth*, ZNW 66 (1975) pp. 61-90

between mainstream society and the church, the higher the rate of true church growth!⁴⁹

Let me say that again another way, the more distinct the church in America is from the prevailing dominant culture the more attractive the church becomes! That makes perfect sense when we think about it. If I'm flowing along with the mainstream anti-God culture and suddenly come to my senses (like the prodigal son) realizing life doesn't work out so well under the world's philosophies, I will naturally begin to look around for another alternative. If the *ekklesia* looks just like that worldly culture, it ceases to provide an alternate option. On the other hand, when the *ekklesia* is obedient to her calling, the difference she presents is contagiously attractive to the person who is searching for another viable option.

Throughout the New Testament, and perhaps especially in Revelation, we see the attempt of first-century Christ-followers to find a happy medium – a middle of the road position. Scripture never condones this approach. Let's look at one example from Revelation. The letters to both Pergamum and Thyatira assert Christ's displeasure at what appears to be teaching that leads to cultural compromise within those churches. We have previously pointed out that failure to participate in honoring the pagan gods through sacrifice, festival and other worship activities was considered shameful conduct in the Roman Empire. As a result of cultural pressure, there was a persistent temptation to engage in those activities at the same time as confessing Christ as Lord and Savior. Scholar David deSilva summarizes the issue well:⁵⁰

> There are obvious advantages for doing so; it eliminates all the tension between Church and society if one

---

49 Pearcey, R. Nancy, *Total Truth: Liberating Christianity from Its Cultural Captivity* (Crossway Books 2005) p. 261 as quoted in Bracamonte, Daniel, *Acts and Mission in the 21st Century*, ApostolicReview, September 30, 2019. Retrieved from https://apostolicreview.com /2019/09/30/acts-and-mission-in-the-21st-century/ (last accessed August 8, 2021)
50 deSilva, David A., *Hope of Glory: Honor Discourse and New Testament Interpretation* (Wipf & Stock 1999) p. 181

can again go out in public and show oneself pious and reliable through participation in the cults of the traditional gods and emperors. [After all] if it could be shown that "an idol is nothing" and that these empty rituals could not offend God why should the Christians suffer society's hostility unnecessarily?

God's answer in Revelation, indeed consistently in the New Testament as well as the Old, is that sacrificing to pagan gods is idol worship and it does not honor Him. In fact, He repeatedly condemns it as spiritual adultery. *Talmidim* are called to live with a non-negotiable determination to obey God's teaching no matter the social cost.[51]

It is the obedient *ekklesia*, not the world, nor the dominant culture of any anti-God society, which gives birth to needed spiritual tension between the true church and the *rest of the world.* Did you get that? It is the church herself that is the cause of the spiritual tension. That means when the church creates spiritual tension she is fulfilling her God-given role in the world! This type of dynamic tension is necessary because it alone distinguishes the culture of God's Kingdom from the predominant culture of the world. "Any endeavor to remove or reimagine this tension will subsequently remove the distinction that is vitally necessary for the church to remain a counter-cultural bastion of hope and truth."[52]

According to Nancy Pearcy, an American evangelical author on the Christian worldview, unless the *ekklesia* maintains this dynamic tension with the prevailing ways of the world it is guaranteed to

---

51 Keener, Craig, S., *Spirit Hermeneutics: Reading Scripture in the Light of Pentecost* (Eerdmans Publishing 2016) p. 46 as quoted in Bracamonte, Daniel, *Acts and Mission in the 21st Century*, ApostolicReview, September 30, 2019. Retrieved from https://apostolicreview.com /2019/09/30/acts-and-mission-in-the-21st-century/ (last accessed August 8, 2021)

52 Bracamonte, Daniel, *Acts and Mission in the 21st Century*, ApostolicReview, September 30, 2019. Retrieved from https://apostolicreview.com /2019/09/30/acts-and-mission-in-the-21st-century/ (last accessed August 8, 2021)

fail.⁵³ In fact, a July 2012 *New York Times* article concluded that virtually every denomination whether Methodist, Lutheran, or Presbyterian that decided to adapt itself in order to accommodate contemporary liberal values has seen a "plunge" in church attendance.⁵⁴ This type of compromising modification of their God-given mission resulted in a 23% average decline in attendance over the ten years between 2007 and 2017.⁵⁵ The cause of this dramatic drop in attendance was attributed to the reality that they have become *irrelevant* in their desire to become *progressive*. Although their goal was presumably to attract younger, more open-minded individuals, the death of the Church proceeded swiftly.⁵⁶ Plain and simple, when the church begins to look like the world her death

---

53 Pearcey, R. Nancy, *Total Truth: Liberating Christianity from Its Cultural Captivity* (Crossway Books 2005) p. 261 as quoted in Bracamonte, Daniel, *Acts and Mission in the 21st Century*, ApostolicReview, September 30, 2019. Retrieved from https://apostolicreview.com /2019/09/30/acts-and-mission-in-the-21st-century/ (last accessed August 8, 2021)

54 Douthat, Ross, *Can Liberal Christianity be Saved?* New York Times, Opinion, July 14, 2012. A version of this article appears in print on July 15, 2012, Section SR, Page 11 of the New York edition with the headline: *Can Liberal Christianity Be Saved?* Retrieved from https://www.nytimes.com/2012/07/15/opinion/sunday/douthat-can-liberal-christianity-be-saved.html (last accessed January 25, 2022)

55 Bracamonte, Daniel, *Acts and Mission in the 21st Century*, ApostolicReview, September 30, 2019, citing *The Episcopal Church*. "*Membership and Average Sunday Attendance: Parochial Report*" Research and Statistics, 2017. Daniel Bracamonte cites the retrieval source for his information as https://www.episcopalchurch.org/files/3._average_sunday_attendance_ by_province_and_diocese_2007-2017.pdf (accessed by Bracamonte March 2, 2019). Bracamonte article retrieved https://apostolicreview.com /2019/09/30/acts-and-mission-in-the-21st-century/ (last accessed August 8, 2021)

56 Douthat, Ross, *Can Liberal Christianity be Saved?* New York Times, Opinion, July 14, 2012. A version of this article appears in print on July 15, 2012, Section SR, Page 11 of the New York edition with the headline: *Can Liberal Christianity Be Saved?* Retrieved from https://www.nytimes.com/2012/07/15/opinion/sunday/douthat-can-liberal-christianity-be-saved.html (last accessed January 25, 2022)

The Power of Hope

is imminent. That is perhaps one of the most central messages of the book of Revelation!

On the other hand, those who believe in the resurrection and believe, as the early church did, that turning the world upside down is, in reality, turning it right side up "are *unstoppably motivated* to work for that new world in the present."[57] That will make them compellingly attractive to every person who wakes up to the reality that any lifestyle that does not honor God is incapable of satisfactorily sustaining life.

> In the biblical horizon, the world of power and control does not know the mystery that makes life possible. It is this mystery that has been entrusted to the unassimilated people of God [the ones not absorbed or integrated into a wider society or culture]. In Christian confession, that mystery is this: Christ has died. Christ is risen. Christ will come again.[58]

Christ-followers have been set apart by God who saved us so that we may do His will. We do not have to go with the flow of a prevailing anti-God culture. God designed the *ekklesia* to present the world with a choice! When we read the book of Acts we read the unfolding story of a Holy Spirit empowered *ekklesia* energetically spreading the gospel of the resurrected Christ. They were allowing His love to change hardened hearts. As we noted in our last lesson, they were so faithful to their God-given assignment that they were accused of turning the world upside down (Acts 17:6). This is not a description of a *let's all get along* mindset. The truth is that Acts 17:6 describes the perception of those who disagreed with the gospel message. In their mind's eye, those who were spreading the gospel were stirring up a rebellious political in-

---

57 Wright, Tom, *Surprised by HOPE* (Society for Promoting Christian Knowledge 2007, reissued 2011) p. 226, italics added
58 Brueggemann, Walter, *Truth & Hope Essays: For a Perilous Age* (Westminster John Knox Press 2020) p. 10

surrection against the Roman Empire.[59] Those who were preaching the good news of God's Kingdom were considered to be outcasts from the norms of society.[60] But those who were spreading the gospel in the first century understood that what the world viewed as being turned upside down was in reality God turning the inhabited world right side up![61]

The truth is, "an obedient people are magnetic to the watching world."[62] The biblical model of evangelism is that other people groups are reached not so much by organized "outreach efforts" as by God's redeemed people becoming walking billboards that put His true nature and character on display through their obedient lifestyle. The way they live life attracts others to God's growing Kingdom. In other words, God's Kingdom on earth simply cannot grow without our obedience. Unless we live an obedient lifestyle (which *will* put us at odds with a dominant anti-God culture), a lost and dying world cannot come to know the true nature of God! Said more bluntly, our disobedience – our blending in with the world – cheats the world out of coming in contact with God's true character.

As I was close to finishing this study my attention was drawn to a decorative pillow in a local store. It has become popular

---

59 The Greek noun *anastatoo* {an-as-tat-o'-o} refers not only to an "unsettling" or "disturbance" but sometimes a "destruction." The idea of destruction is found in the Septuagint's use of *anastatoo* in Daniel 7:23. The fourth beast in Daniel's dream was interpreted as a fourth kingdom that will "trample (*anastatōsei*) the earth and destroy it." *Acts 17 Commentary*, Precept Austin, citing Gilbrant, *Complete Biblical Library Greek-English Dictionary*. Retrieved from https://www.preceptaustin.org/acts-17-commentary (last accessed August 8, 2021)

60 Spence-Jones and Exell, general editors, *The Pulpit Commentary*, Acts 17:6. Retrieved from Hill, Gary, *The Discovery Bible*, HELPS Ministries, Inc.

61 *Acts 17 Commentary*, Precept Austin, citing Gilbrant, *Complete Biblical Library Greek-English Dictionary*. Retrieved from https://www.preceptaustin.org/acts-17-commentary (last accessed August 8, 2021)

62 Motyer, J. Alec, *The Prophecy of Isaiah: An Introduction & Commentary* (InterVarsity Press 1993) Isaiah 2:5, p. 55

to decorate our homes with *words* and *sayings* that have meaning to us – words that reflect something about who we are and what we believe. So, I find this decorative pillow particularly interesting in light of our study.⁶³ It pro-vides a good, albeit tragic, definition of the world's type of *hope*.

The world's hope is woefully misplaced on self-reliance! Remember in Lesson 2 we said that biblical hope inherently envisions a sense of well-being and security that results from placing confidence *in God*. God knows full well that hope tethers us to Him as nothing else will. And being tethered to a trustworthy and faithful God makes all the difference in the world! Our end is secure, our hope is certain! "Having expectancy that we will make it through these perilous times will keep one with a level head."⁶⁴

In its early years the church advanced forcefully, not with the aid of secular power, but with the power of belief.⁶⁵ As followers of Christ, we are called in the present "to share in the surprising hope of God's [already, but not yet] whole new creation."⁶⁶ Hope reaches

---

63 Photo taken with my cell phone
64 Kendall, R.T., *We've Never Been This Way Before: Trusting God in Unprecedented Times* (Charisma House 2020) p. 64
65 In the words of Thomas Aquinas, "the most efficacious argument" for Christ's divinity is that "without the support of the secular power he has changed the whole world." Quoted by Ross Douthat, Opinion Columnist, New York Times, Opinion, *Can Politics Save Christianity?* The New York Times (nytimes.com). A version of this article appears in print on Dec. 19, 2021, Section SR, Page 9 of the New York edition with the headline: *Can Politics Save Christianity?* Retrieved from https://www.nytimes.com/2021/12/18/opinion/christianity-politics.html (last accessed January 25, 2022)
66 Wright, Tom, *Surprised by HOPE* (Society for Promoting Christian Knowledge 2007, reissued 2011) p. 220

beyond this present life, it is "faith in future tense."[67] "The [very essence and] nature of hope is to expect that which faith believes."[68]

When we hope, we are attaching "our trust to God's eternal blessings."[69] That long-term mindset will then impact our short-term decisions.[70] We have a message to tell the world – a message of undeniable hope that will explode with power when it is lived out in day-to-day life.

> For we through the Spirit, by faith [*pistis*], are waiting for the hope [*elpis*] of righteousness. Galatians 5:5

Hear What The Spirit is Saying to the Church: *Indeed do you now understand hope – begin to practice hope. Children do this all the time – they do it with birthday celebrations and Christmas. Become like a child and experience the hope of what I have planned for you.*

---

67 Rogers, Adrian, *How to Have a Rock-Solid Faith*, LoveWorthFinding. Retrieved from https://www.lwf.org/sermons/audio/how-to-have-a-rock-solid-faith-2054#:~:text=%E2%80%9CNow%20hope%20does%20not%20disappoint%2C%20because%20the%20love,for%20the%20future.%E2%80%9D%20Apply%20it%20to%20your%20life (last accessed August 8, 2021)
68 *God's Word of Hope*, Precept Austin, citing Richard Sibbes. Retrieved from https://www.preceptaustin.org/gods_word_of_hope (last accessed August 8, 2021)
69 Spoelstra, Melissa, *Isaiah: Striving Less And Trusting More* (Lifeway Press 2022) p. 61
70 Spoelstra, Melissa, *Isaiah: Striving Less And Trusting More* (Lifeway Press 2022) p. 52

Appendix

How to do basic WORD STUDIES when you don't read Hebrew or Greek

To understand why Word Studies are important refer to "Preface: About Word Studies."

Begin with prayer

The best counsel I have seen from anyone about how to do Word Studies on the internet comes from the Precept Austin website, "And so as you begin your word study, remember to begin with prayer beseeching our Father to grant that our Teacher, the Holy Spirit might guide us into all truth (Jn 16:13), for spiritual truth is spiritually revealed by the Spirit."[1]

There are multiple ways to do word searches using internet reference tools. As you become proficient at using these tools you will develop your favorites and find shortcuts to locating the information you are seeking. I am providing a basic starting point here for those just beginning.

As an initial matter, don't forget to check the English Dictionary for how your word of interest is defined in the English language. You may not be aware of all the nuances of a given English word. As a result, sometimes that research alone provides greater clarity to a word's usage.

Next, read your targeted Scripture in multiple Bible translations. Reading your passage in several translations may provide you with all the information you need.

---

1   *How to Perform a Greek Word Study*, Precept Austin. Retrieved from https://www.preceptaustin.org/greek_word_study#web (last accessed January 24, 2022). Note, as with the other materials on this website, this is an overall helpful article regarding Word Studies.

As a general rule of thumb, I "over research" my word of interest to be as assured of accuracy as I can possibly be. When I am in doubt I check with someone more knowledgeable than I am.

Strong's Numbers are the Starting Point for Your Research

When you've decided to proceed with an internet search the Strong's number associated with your word of interest is a must! A Strong's Number is the unique number that has been assigned to a word used in the Bible.[2] For example: the Hebrew word יָשַׁע *yasha*` {yaw-shah'} has been assigned the number: 03467. The Greek word δοῦλος *doulos* {doo'-los} has been assigned the number: 1401. Each number links the root meaning of the word back to the original meanings in the Hebrew and Greek manuscripts from which they were translated. *NOTE: When you use this number in internet searches you will generally need to add a "H" before the number for a Hebrew word or a "G" before the number for a Greek word.*

Caveat: Strong's concordance, keyed to numbers for roots in the original languages, is a valuable resource. Users need to be aware of some issues: 1) Strong's is old enough to almost be outdated. Because it is keyed to the language of the KJV it is advisable to check your results against more modern commentaries and other Bible translations. 2) Strong's provides glosses (words or phrases proposed as possible translations of a particular Greek or Hebrew word) rather than definitions.[3] That's because those Greek and Hebrew words have many potential meanings in different contexts. It

---

[2] Strong's Numbers originate from a reference book known as *Strong's Exhaustive Concordance of the Bible*.

[3] When a Greek student is taught that *"pistis"* means "faith" what he is learning is a "gloss." Contrast that with the following from the *Greek-English Lexicon of the New Testament Based on Semantic Domains*: "that which is completely believable—'what can be fully believed, that which is worthy of belief, believable evidence, proof'" [Louw, J. P., & Nida, E. A. (1996, c1989). *Greek-English lexicon of the New Testament: Based on semantic domains* (electronic ed. of the 2nd edition.) (Vol. 1, p. 370). New York: United Bible societies)].

The Power of Hope 247

is imperative that you check carefully which word definition works best for the passage you are studying.

HOW TO LOCATE A STRONG'S NUMBER ON THE INTERNET USING FREE RESOURCES:

1. Go to https://biblehub.com.

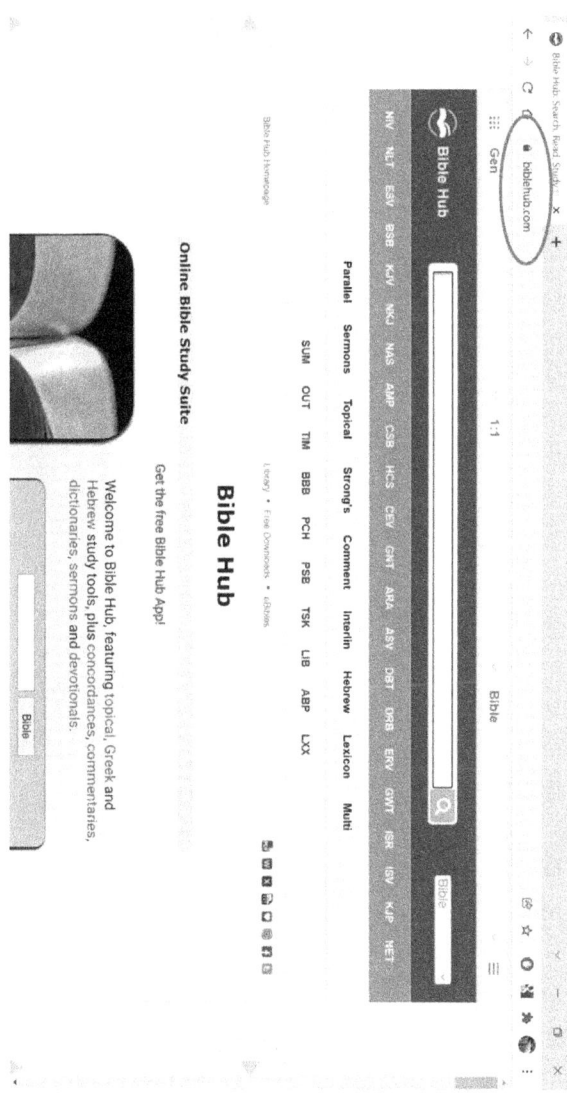

248   *How to do basic WORD STUDIES when you don't read Hebrew or Greek*

2. Across the tool bar find the header for "Interlin."

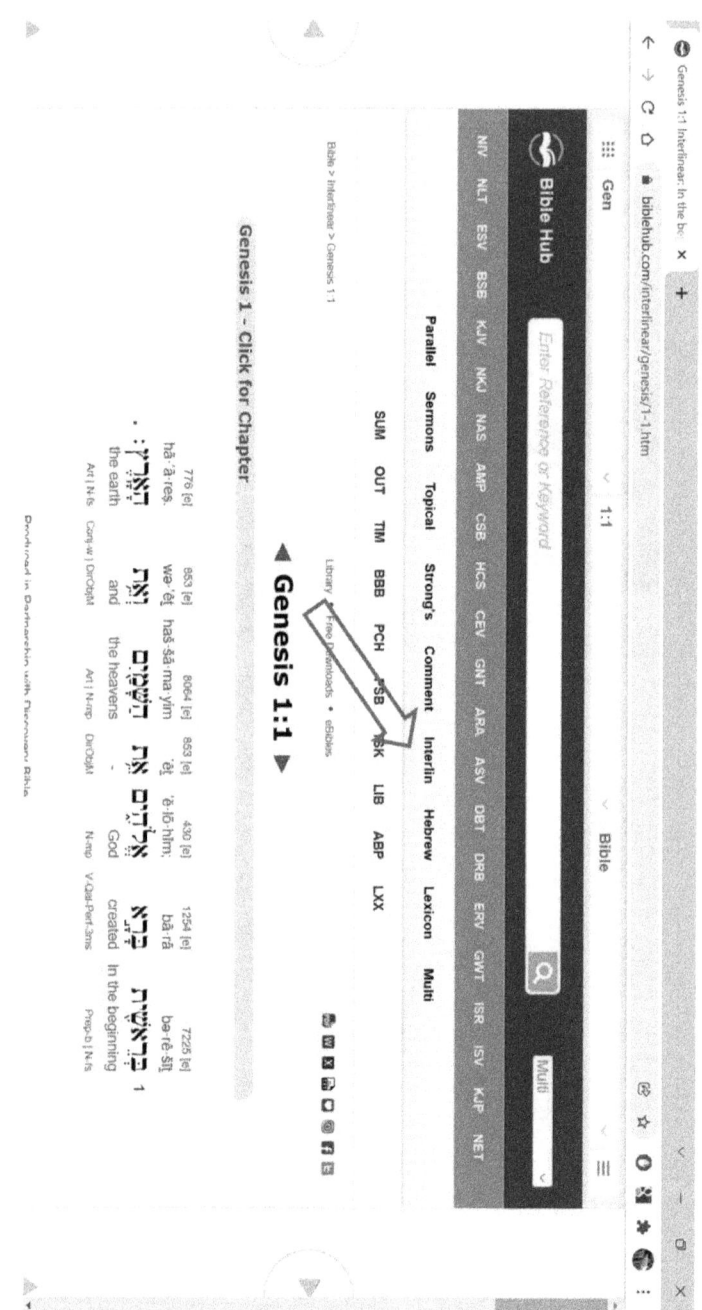

The Power of Hope 249

3. When you click that header, it will take you to the Interlinear page for Genesis 1:1. Find the search box at the top of the page and enter the verse address containing your word of interest. The search engine will take you directly to the Interlinear entry (either Hebrew or Greek) for that verse.

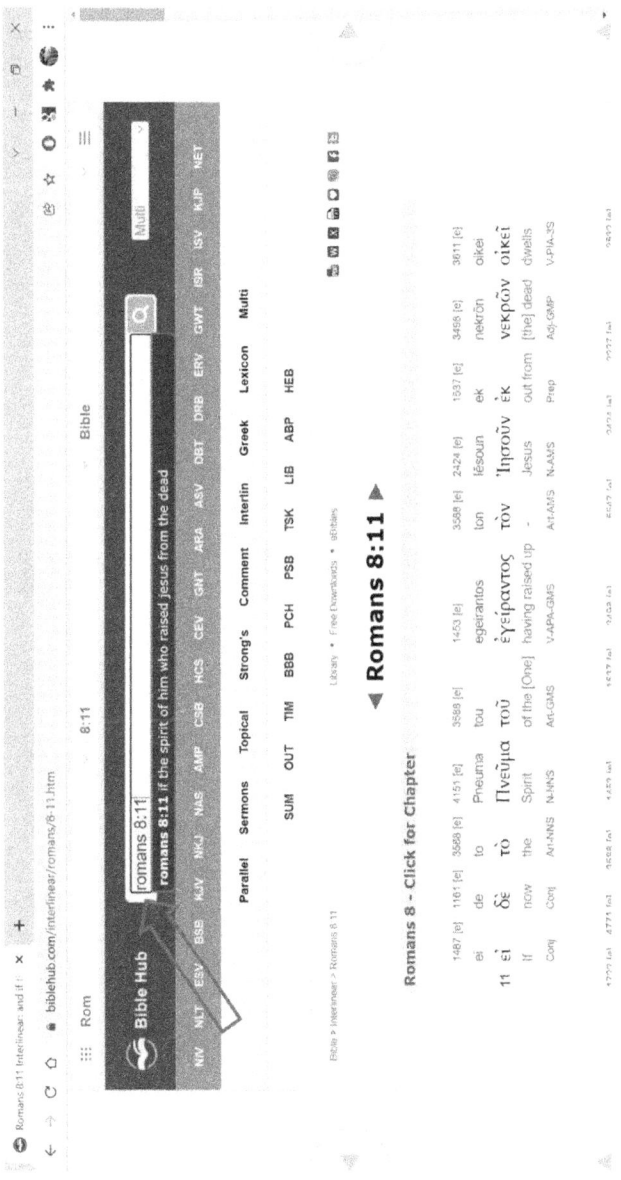

250   How to do basic WORD STUDIES when you don't read Hebrew or Greek

4. The numbers in blue across the top of each word is the Strong's number. You can click on that blue number and it will take you to a page with the Strong's Concordance information and other Bible Dictionary entries for that word. However, once you have the Strong's # you can research in a wide variety of other reference sources as well.

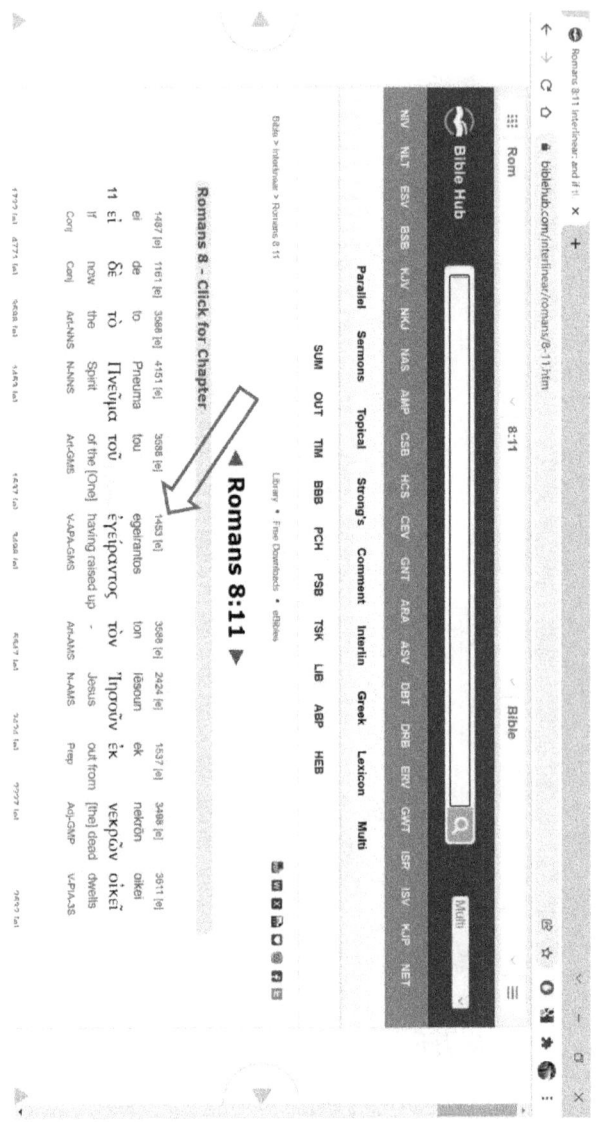

COMMENTARIES CAN BE A GREAT SOURCE OF INFORMATION IN UNDERSTANDING HOW A WORD IS USED

Often the Commentary will define the word itself, but even if no definition is provided checking a variety of Commentaries for that particular verse/section of Scripture is a good way to gain additional understanding regarding the context surrounding your word of interest.

Bible Dictionaries and Bible Encyclopedias are another free resource worth searching to view any entries that might be available for the word you are studying.

Caveat: As you consider broadening your internet search a quote from Yale University Library helps us place the usefulness of internet resources in their proper context.[4]

> 1. Searching on the Internet. Care must be taken in searching for information on the Internet .... [F]reely available Internet resources have not necessarily been published by reputable academic publishers nor have they been selected by librarians with expertise in their subject area. Nearly anything can be posted on a website, and just because it is available online does not mean it is valid or authoritative. **However, this does not mean that you cannot find good resources on the Internet; the key to doing so is to carefully evaluate what you find on the web.** If you use web resources, be sure to ask these questions:
>
> - Who is the author of the website? Are the author's credentials listed?
> - What institution or organization is behind the website?

---

4   Yale University Library, *Biblical Studies Guide: Websites*, Yale University Library Research Guides at Yale University, bold added. Retrieved from https://guides.library.yale.edu/c.php?g=295834&p=1972575 (site last updated Apr 30, 2021 1:08 PM) (last accessed January 24, 2022)

- When was the website created or last updated?
- Who is the intended audience for the website?
- Is the information provided objective or biased?
- How does information provided by the site compare to other works, including print works?

There are times when a website you are viewing provides you with the opportunity to view the beliefs and doctrines behind those who post articles on that particular site. Taking the time to read that information can provide valuable insight about the biases the author(s) may have about biblical points of view. Understanding the framework (lens) though which the author is operating may explain cases where their viewpoint is radically different than others you have read in your research efforts. It helps you evaluate the weight you may want to give to their characterization of your word of interest or its biblical context.

A Caution Regarding Commentaries: The advice provided by the Yale University Library quote above concerning internet searches is equally wise counsel when using Commentaries.

A Few Remaining Observations

Words can have multiple meanings. As an example, the word "dig" has a wide range of meanings in the English language. It can refer to excavation (for archaeological or other purposes); an insult, taunt or sarcastic remark; a jab or nudge; to tunnel, to burrow or mine; or to plow a field. Dig can imply using large commercial equipment, a simple hand trowel or shovel; or it can refer to words that come out of your mouth. The same is true in Greek and Hebrew. However, generally speaking a word only carries one specific meaning at a time.

Caveat: Without getting too complicated, let me add one quick caveat to my last statement. The Apostle John is well known for using a word to mean two things at once (known as double entendre).[5]

The goal in a Word Study is to determine the author's originally intended meaning. It is a fundamental principle for Word Studies that the author's usage determines the word's meaning. In other words, the author's original intent, as determined by context, must be the guide you use to choose the most applicable meaning from the range of possible word meanings. The goal of your research is to find a working definition that fits precisely in the specific context. As my Publisher warns, "Most errors in interpretation come from focusing too narrowly on a single verse or even phrase. If you come up with an understanding of the meaning of a particular word that contradicts the teaching of that author in the rest of his writings, you might want to reconsider. Who is more likely to have made a mistake?"

A research technique I often use in Word Studies is to locate the first use of that word in the Bible. Let me first explain why I do that and then I'll provide an easy way to locate that first biblical usage for your word of interest.

---

[5] Keener, Craig S., *The Gospel Of John: A Commentary*, Volume Two (Hendrickson Publishers 2003) John 19:30b, p. 1148; Levison, Jack, *Filled with the Spirit* (Eerdmans 2009) p. 245. "One of the unique devices used by the author of the Fourth Gospel is that of double meaning. The author uses two meanings of a word, both of which are distinct enough that they could not convey one aspect of thought. He probably did not intend to present an either/or situation wherein a Christian must make a choice of meaning. More likely he was following a pattern of usage found in Qumran and the Old Testament wherein two meanings were intended to be conveyed through one expression." Wead, David W., *The Johannine Double Meaning*, Restoration Quarterly, 13 no 2 1970, pp. 106-120. Language: English; Publication Type: Article; (AN ATLA0001588405), citing 1. S. Cohen, "The Political Background of the Words of Amos," Hebrew Union College Annual 36 (1965) pp. 153-160

REASON FIRST OCCURRENCE CAN BE IMPORTANT

The first time a key word or concept is mentioned in the Bible "gives us important details or facts regarding the subject, which will, of course, help us understand the person or thing introduced."[6] It is notable that "ancient Jewish commentators call special attention to [first mentions in Scripture], and lay great stress upon them as always having some significance. They generally help us in fixing the meaning of a word or point us to some lesson in connection with it."[7]

AN EASY WAY TO LOCATE FIRST USAGE

Using https://www.blueletterbible.org/lexicon/index.cfm enter the Strong's number for your word of interest, remember to use the "H" before the number for Hebrew words or the "G" before the number for Greek words. The search will take you to the Lexicon entry for that word. Scroll down past the definitions and reference section to the header: Concordance Results Shown Using the KJV. The first text box under this heading will show you how many times that particular word was used in WLC (Westminister Leningrad Codex) Hebrew. Following that entry will be a list of the verses where that word is used. You will be able to identify your word of interest by the superscript Strong's number next to the word. The first verse listed is the first instance of that word's biblical use.

---

6   Sheets, Dutch, *A Serpent In The Garden*, GiveHim15, February 20, 2021. Retrieved from http://gh15database.com/2021/02/february-20-2021/

7   Bullinger, E. W., *Number in Scripture: Its Supernatural Design and Spiritual Significance*, 4th Ed. (Eyre & Spottiswoode (Bible Warehouse) Ltd. 1921) Part II Its Spiritual Significance, One under *First Occurrences of Words*. Retrieved from https://www.levendwater.org/books/numbers/number_in_scripture_bullinger.pdf (last accessed January 25, 2022)

SOME ONLINE SOURCES OF COMMENTARIES (AND OTHER VALUABLE RESEARCH RESOURCES) ARE:

Biblehub.com Retrieved from https://biblehub.com/ (last accessed January 24, 2022). From the Home Page, find the tool bar that lists resources. Select the header for "Comment" which will open a page containing Commentaries for Genesis 1:1. You can enter your verse in the search box on that page and it will take you to the available Commentaries for that verse.

BibleStudyTools.com Bible Versions and Translations Online (biblestudytools.com). Retrieved from https://www.biblestudytools.com/bible-versions/ (last accessed January 24, 2022). From Home Page, locate study menu, drop down menu lists available resources such as: Commentaries, Concordances, Dictionaries, Encyclopedias, and others.

BlueLetterBible.org Bible Search and Study Tools - Blue Letter Bible. Retrieved from https://www.blueletterbible.org/study.cfm (last accessed January 24, 2022). This page lists Bible Commentaries, Bible References, Topical Indexes, among other resources. Blue Letter Bible also permits you to research a specific Hebrew or Greek word if you know the Strong's "G" or "H" number. By the way, this site provides you with the opportunity to hear how the word is pronounced. It's a great tool if you are planning to teach and need to say the Greek or Hebrew word.

NetBible.org Net Bible Translation with Notes. Retrieved from https://netbible.org/ (last accessed January 24, 2022). The NET Bible is a Bible translation containing almost 61,000 translators' notes from over 25 scholars. The translator's notes (identified with a number followed by the letters "tn" like this, [175]**tn**) document the decisions and choices they made for how/why they translated the original text. The notes make the original languages accessible to the reader who does not know Greek and Hebrew. Study notes (identified with a number followed by the letters "sn" like this, [2]**sn**) are often added to the notes section providing an additional layer of helpful information.

PreceptAustin.org Retrieved from https://www.preceptaustin.org/ (last accessed January 24, 2022). Home Page tool bar contains drop down menus for Commentaries, Verse By Verse (Commentaries), Study Tools with options for Greek or Hebrew Word Studies, among other resources. On the Home Page there is a search box that allows you to search for a particular Hebrew or Greek word using the common form transliteration (without markings) and/or search for a particular Bible verse. When you locate the verse you are studying, it will often have word study links to a particular Greek or Hebrew word used in that Scripture. You will also find a treasure trove of quotes from various Bible Dictionaries and Commentaries related to that verse.

Note: A transliteration is the form of a Greek or Hebrew word translated into letters in the English language making the word readable to one who does not read Hebrew or Greek. When you locate the Strong's number you will see your word of interest in its original language form and you will also see the common form transliteration for that word. It is important to point out that occasionally a given word has more than one acceptable transliteration. In those cases, you may need to research the alternate forms of transliteration. To be clear, let's use the examples I used above.

Hebrew word יָשַׁע *yasha`* {yaw-shah'} has been assigned the Strong's number: 03467. In this case "*yasha`*" is the transliteration; while {yaw-shah'} provides the reader with a key to pronunciation.

Greek word δοῦλος *doulos* {doo'-los} has been assigned the number: 1401. In this case "*doulos*" is the transliteration; while {doo'-los} provides the reader with a key to pronunciation.

StudyLight.org Retrieved from https://studylight.org/ (last accessed January 24, 2022). From Home page, the tool bar contains an option for "Bible Study Tools" that will take you to a list of available Bible Commentaries, Concordances, Dictionaries and Encyclopedias.

If you plan to do word studies often and have the ability to invest in a few published resources my recommendation for Greek words: Geoffrey W. Bromiley, *Theological Dictionary of the New Testament*, Abridged in One Volume (Eerdmans 1985)[8] and Hebrew words: Harris, Archer, and Waltke, editors, *Theological Wordbook of the Old Testament* (Moody Press 1999).[9] Additional valuable resources for your personal library include: Baker and Carpenter, *The Complete WordStudy Dictionary of the Old Testament* (AMG Publishers 2003) and Spiros Zodhiates, *The Complete Word Study Dictionary: New Testament* (AMG Publishers 1992) – both are keyed off of the Strong's Number. Suggestion: Search Amazon or eBay for used copies in very good / good condition to purchase these materials at a lower cost.

---

[8] When you know the Strong's word number you can enter it in the search box on BlueLetter Bible website. You will have to inform the search as to whether you are looking for a Hebrew Strong's number or a Greek Strong's number. To locate a Greek # place a "G" in front of the number with no spaces. The TDNT Reference (if applicable) will be provided under the header "Dictionary Aids." For example, G42 will be listed as: TDNT Reference 1:114,14. In this case, you would go to page 14 of the Abridged Volume to find the TDNT entry for your word. Note: the first part of the TDNT Reference [1:114] is given for the unabridged volumes of *The Theological Dictionary of the New Testament*.

[9] When you know the Strong's word number you can enter it in the search box on BlueLetter Bible website. You will have to inform the search as to whether you are looking for a Hebrew Strong's number or a Greek Strong's number. To locate a Hebrew # place a "H" in front of the number with no spaces. The "TWOT" (*Theological Wordbook of the Old Testament*) Reference (if applicable) is listed under the header "Dictionary Aids." For example, H3467 is listed as: TWOT Reference:929. In this case, you turn to word #929 on page 414 of *The Theological Wordbook of the Old Testament*.

Index to the Word Studies

Note: Words are alphabetized according to their transliterations under the English alphabet.

Greek

agapao 144
agape 144
dechomai 86
ekdechomai 88
elegchos 43
elpis 23
hypomone 80
makrothymia 82
pisteuo 15
pistis 36
prosdechomai 91
thlipsis 160

Hebrew

'aman 8
batach 26
batah 26
chalaph 107
hesed 51
koach 108
koah 108
kowach 108
masak 98
mashak 98
qavah 28
shalom 183
tiqvah 29
yachal 27

Meet the Author: Deborah L. Roeger

I confessed Christ as my Lord and Savior in 1962 when I was 9 years old. I was baptized the same day and I can still visualize that experience clearly in my memory. When God knit me together He did so in a way that blessed me with a deep love for research. It is one of the reasons I excelled in academic study resulting in a Bachelor's degree in Business Administration, Master's in Human Resources Management and Juris Doctor – all with highest honors. All glory belongs to God that my research skills and giftedness as a quick learner brought me out on top in every academic environment and led to an extremely successful professional career.

In the months leading up to February, 1999 God was drawing me closer and closer to Him through worship and His Word. That season culminated in an earnest prayer to *know* Him more. On my knees I offered to *go wherever* He sent me or *do whatever* He asked me to do that I might truly *know* Him. God answered that prayer in a most unanticipated way. Seven months later He shockingly led me to resign from my job with a large wireless phone carrier. At that time, I was employed as a regional Senior Counsel, overseeing the company's legal resources for the Eastern region of the United States. Little did I know that at only 46 years old I had just *retired* from the professional work world. Before a full year elapsed God had unexpectedly reconnected my heart to something He had buried deep within me when I had visited a men's medium security prison as a young college student. He then divinely arranged an invitation from the Christian Warden of that same prison to serve there as a volunteer working with both inmates and staff.[1] Nine years later God called me to lay down the prison ministry work which had by that time expanded into other men's prisons, the women's prison and Ohio's juvenile correctional facilities. His astonishing instruction was that I begin teaching Bible studies in our local church. It was an extremely challenging transition for me to make. However, looking back I see that my love for learning, commitment to advance on my knees in prayer and my well-developed research skills gave me a jump start on lesson preparation.

I cut my teeth on facilitating DVD-driven Bible studies others had written, supplementing those lessons with historical and cultural background information. From there God began to give me assignments to teach various books of the Bible verse by verse. The next step was to instruct me to begin writing Bible studies I would then teach. Eventually teaching assignments grew to include an international teaching ministry. From the rearview mirror, I can see that the progression was a natural one. Each step along the way was undertaken cautiously and prayerfully – undergirded by my own prayers, times of prayer with my husband and the prayer covering of our faithful prayer partners.

At the Lord's direction, my husband and I co-founded Hope of the Nations International Ministry, Inc. a nonprofit ministry with a goal to disciple others. Our earnest desire is to see the body of Christ mature by growing up in the grace, knowledge and love of God through the study and application of His Word. Every Bible Study I've written is well researched and profits from the fact that I whole heartedly embrace the goal of being a life-long

---

[1] In my first meeting with the Warden she asked me if I knew anything about mediation. I was in fact an experienced mediator and was presently mediating disputes for the Equal Employment Opportunity Commission. That began our working relationship which blossomed into a wide variety of ways in which God enabled me to serve both inmates and staff.

learner who seeks to apply the truth I teach others. I love drawing fellow Christ-followers into the biblical text for the purpose of life transformation.

My husband and I presently reside in Florida. We have celebrated 48 years of marriage and are blessed with two married children, Jeremy and Kimberly, daughter-in-law Jennifer, son-in-law Nathan and six amazing grandchildren: Jordan, Jackson, Hannah, Caleb, Jacob and Abigail.

www.ingramcontent.com/pod-product-compliance
Lightning Source LLC
Chambersburg PA
CBHW032036150426
43194CB00006B/307